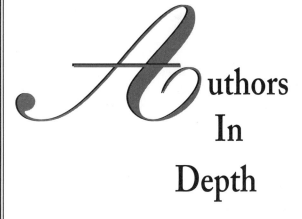uthors
In
Depth

. . . .

COPPER LEVEL

PRENTICE HALL
Upper Saddle River, New Jersey
Glenview, Illinois
Needham, Massachusetts

ISBN 0-13-052383-6

6 7 8 9 10   04

PRENTICE HALL

Acknowledgments

Grateful acknowledgment is made to the following for copyrighted material:

Curtis Brown Ltd (NY)

"Names" by Jane Yolen from *PASSAGER: THE YOUNG MERLIN TRILOGY, BOOK ONE.* Copyright © 1996 by Jane Yolen. "The Golden Stair" by Jane Yolen from *THE FAERY FLAG.* Text copyright © 1989, 1988, 1987, 1986, 1985, 1984, 1978 by Jane Yolen. "David and Leilah and D. Dog" from *The Wizard of Washington Square* by Jane Yolen.Text copyright © 1969 by Jane Yolen. From *The Mermaid's Three Wisdoms* by Jane Yolen. Text copyright © 1978 by Jane Yolen. From "The Great Silkie" by Laurence Yep from *SWEETWATER.* Text copyright © 1973 by Laurence Yep. All rights reserved. From "The Pearl Apartments" by Laurence Yep from *THE LOST GARDEN.* Copyright © 1991 by Laurence Yep.

Farrar, Straus & Giroux

"The Parakeet Named Dreidel," "Utzel & His Daughter, Poverty," and "Shrewd Todie & Lyzer the Miser" by Isaac Bashevis Singer from *STORIES FOR CHILDREN.* Copyright © 1962, 1967, 1968, 1970, 1972, 1973, 1974, 1975, 1976, 1979, 1980, 1984, by Isaac Bashevis Singer.

Harcourt, Inc.

"Tortillas Like Africa" by Gary Soto from *CANTO FAMILIAR.* Copyright © 1995 by Gary Soto. "Ode To Mi Perrito" by Gary Soto from *NEIGHBORHOOD ODES.* Text copyright © 1992 by Gary Soto. "Mother and Daughter" and "Baseball in April" by Gary Soto from *BASEBALL IN APRIL AND OTHER STORIES.* Copyright © 1990 by Gary Soto.

HarperCollins Publishers

From *DRAGON'S GATE* by Laurence Yep. Copyright © 1993 by Laurence Yep. "Ibrahima" by Walter Dean Myers from *NOW IS YOUR TIME!* Copyright © 1991 by Walter Dean Myers. From *THE TARANTULA IN MY PURSE* by Jean Craighead George. Copyright © 1996 by Jean Craighead George. "The Old Jar" by Laurence Yep from *THE RAINBOW PEOPLE.* Copyright © 1989 by Laurence Yep. From *THE WILD, WILD COOKBOOK* by Jean Craighead George. Text copyright © 1982 by Jean Craighead George. All rights reserved. From *THE MOON OF THE MOUNTAIN LIONS* by Jean Craighead George. Copyright © 1969, 1991 by Jean Craighead George.

Acknowledgments continue on page 210.

ontents

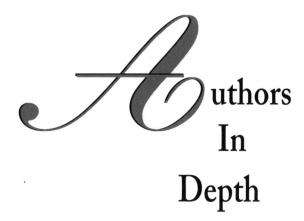

Authors In Depth

· · · ·

COPPER LEVEL

Walter Dean Myers In Depth

> "He is concerned with the development of youths, and his message is always the same: Young people must face the reality of growing up and must persevere, knowing that they can succeed despite any odds they face."
>
> —*Carmen Subryan*

WALTER DEAN MYERS has won numerous awards for his fiction, nonfiction, and poetry for young people. He is best known for his gritty, realistic stories about African American young people growing up in urban environments.

In addition to his realistic novels about inner-city life, Myers has also written fairy tales, ghost stories, science fiction, and adventure stories. A common theme runs through Myers's work. He believes in "the need to find strength within oneself and the possibility of finding strength within the group, whether the group is the family, the peer group, or the community."

Boyhood Days Walter Dean Myers was born in Martinsburg, West Virginia, in 1937. Before he was three years old, his mother died. His family was very poor, so young Walter and two of his sisters were sent to live with family friends, Herbert and Florence Dean. The new family moved to Harlem, a section of New York City.

The Deans were a loving couple who treated Myers kindly. His mother taught him to read, and his father enjoyed telling him stories. When he thinks back to his childhood in Harlem, Myers fondly remembers "the bright sun on Harlem streets, the easy rhythms of black and brown bodies, the sounds of children streaming in and out of red brick tenements."

However, Myers also faced some difficulties during this time. He suffered from a speech impediment, and found it especially trying to speak in front of his class at school. He discovered that writing was a way of communicating easily, and quickly grew to love it. He began filling notebooks with original stories, poetry, and journal entries. Myers also loved to read. He once said, "The George Bruce Branch of the public library was my most treasured place. I couldn't believe my luck in discovering that what I enjoyed most, reading, was free."

School and Work Myers's essays and poetry earned him many honors and awards. Despite this encouragement at school, though, Myers's family did not see writing as a part of his future. "I was from a family of laborers," he says, "and the idea of writing stories or essays was far removed from their experience."

When he was sixteen, Myers dropped out of high school. On his seventeenth birthday, he joined the Army. Though he continued to read and write, he regarded these activities as hobbies. After leaving the army at age twenty, Myers had trouble finding a good job. He began to wish he hadn't left school.

Myers decided to go to college. He began working toward a bachelor's degree, got married, and started a family. Myers supported his wife and children with a series of jobs, including working at the New York State Department of Labor and at the post office.

Myers continued to write in his spare time. By the late 1960's, he made up his mind to become a writer, and he began to work as an editor at a book publishing company. He would not be able to devote all his time to writing until 1977.

Making a Name for Himself In 1969, Myers published his first book, a children's book called *Where Does the Day Go?* It received an award from the Council on Interracial Books for Children. Myers was immediately seen as an author concerned with minority children, an author who could fill a void in American publishing.

Since then, Myers has written more than fifty books. He is best known for writing quality literature about African American young people. For example, the novel *Scorpions* is about a young black man who joins a gang. *The Glory Field* traces the story of an African American family from the period of slavery until today. Myers has won many prestigious awards, including the Coretta Scott King Award and a Newberry honor book citation.

◆ Harlem

Harlem, a section of New York City, provides the setting for many of Walter Dean Myers's books. It was established in 1658 by the Dutch, who named it after Haarlem in the Netherlands. In the eighteenth century, Harlem was a farming area. In the nineteenth century, it became a fashionable district with many summer vacation houses.

Around this time, many African Americans migrated from the South to big urban centers in the North. By 1910, Harlem had become one of the largest African American communities in the United States. During the 1920's and early 1930's, Harlem was the center of a black literary and intellectual movement known as the Harlem Renaissance. Among the writers associated with this period are Langston Hughes, Zora Neale Hurston, and W.E.B. DuBois.

The Harlem Renaissance faded with the Great Depression of the 1930's. By the end of World War II, housing and living conditions in the area deteriorated. Today, Harlem is developing renovated housing areas and a business district. African Americans constitute the majority of the population, and Hispanics are the second largest group.

◆ Literary Works

Fiction

- *Where Does the Day Go?* (1969)
- *Fast Sam, Cool Clyde, and Stuff* (1975)
- *Mojo and the Russians* (1977)
- *The Young Landlords* (1979)
- *Hoops* (1981)
- *Won't Know Till I Get There* (1982)
- *Motown and Didi: A Love Story* (1984)
- *Fallen Angels* (1988)
- *Me, Mop, and the Moondance Kid* (1988)
- *Scorpions* (1988)
- *The Mouse Rap* (1990)
- *Mop, Moondance, and the Nagasaki Knights* (1992)
- *Somewhere in the Darkness* (1992)
- *The Glory Field* (1994)
- *Darnell Rock Reporting* (1994)
- *Slam!* (1996)
- *The Journal of Joshua Loper, A Black Cowboy* (1999)
- *Monster* (1999)

Nonfiction

- *Now is Your Time! The African American Struggle for Freedom* (1992)
- *A Place Called Heartbreak: A Story of Vietnam* (1992)
- *Malcolm X: By Any Means Necessary* (1993)
- *One More River to Cross: An African American Photograph Album* (1995)
- *Amistad: A Long Road to Freedom* (1998)

Walter Dean Myers

Ibrahima
from Now Is Your Time!

Who were these Africans being brought to the New World?[1] What was their African world like? There is no single answer. The Africans came from many countries, and from many cultures. Like the Native Americans, they established their territories based on centuries of tradition. Most, but not all, of the Africans who were brought to the colonies came from central and west Africa. Among them was a man named Abd al-Rahman Ibrahima.

The European invaders, along with those Africans who cooperated with them, had made the times dangerous. African nations that had lived peacefully together for centuries now eyed each other warily.[2] Slight insults led to major battles. Bands of outlaws roamed the countryside attacking the small villages, kidnaping those unfortunate enough to have wandered from the protection of their people. The stories that came from the coast were frightening. Those kidnaped were taken to the sea and sold to whites, put on boats, and taken across the sea. No one knew what happened then.

Abd al-Rahman Ibrahima was born in 1762 in Fouta Djallon, a district of the present country of Guinea. It is a beautiful land of green mountains rising majestically from grassy plains, a land rich with minerals, especially bauxite.

Ibrahima was a member of the powerful and influential Fula people and a son of one of their chieftains. The religion of Islam had swept across Africa centuries before, and the young Ibrahima was raised in the tradition of the Moslems.

The Fula were taller and lighter in complexion than the other inhabitants of Africa's west coast; they had silky hair, which they often wore long. A pastoral[3] people, the Fula had a complex system of government, with the state divided into nine provinces and each province divided again into smaller districts. Each province had its chief and its subchiefs.

As the son of a chief Ibrahima was expected to assume a role of political leadership when he came of age. He would also be expected to set a moral example, and to be well versed in his religion. When he reached twelve he was sent to Timbuktu[4] to study.

---

1. **the New World:** Refers to the continents of North America and South America, which were new to the European explorers and settlers.
2. **warily:** In a careful manner; cautiously.
3. **pastoral:** Relating to a simple, peaceful country life.
4. **Timbuktu** (tim′ buk tōō′): A town in central Mali, Africa, that flourished as a center of trade and learning from the 1200's to the 1500's.

Under the Songhai dynasty leader Askia the Great, Timbuktu had become a center of learning and one of the largest cities in the Songhai Empire. The young Ibrahima knew he was privileged to attend the best-known school in west Africa. Large and sophisticated, with wide, tree-lined streets, the city attracted scholars from Africa, Europe, and Asia. Islamic law, medicine, and mathematics were taught to the young men destined to become the leaders of their nations. It was a good place for a young man to be. The city was well guarded, too. It had to be, to prevent the chaos that, more and more, dominated African life nearer the coast.

Ibrahima learned first to recite from the Koran, the Moslem holy book, and then to read it in Arabic. From the Koran, it was felt, came all other knowledge. After Ibrahima had finished his studies in Timbuktu, he returned to Fouta Djallon to continue to prepare himself to be a chief.

The Fula had little contact with whites, and what little contact they did have was filled with danger. So when, in 1781, a white man claiming to be a ship's surgeon stumbled into one of their villages, they were greatly surprised.

John Coates Cox hardly appeared to be a threat. A slight man, blind in one eye, he had been lost for days in the forested regions bordering the mountains. He had injured his leg, and it had become badly infected as he tried to find help. By the time he was found and brought to the Fula chiefs, he was more dead than alive.

Dr. Cox, an Irishman, told of being separated from a hunting party that had left from a ship on which he had sailed as ship's surgeon. The Fula chief decided that he would help Cox. He was taken into a hut, and a healer was assigned the task of curing his infected leg.

During the months Dr. Cox stayed with the Fula, he met Ibrahima, now a tall, brown-skinned youth who had reached manhood. His bearing reflected his status as the son of a major chief. Dr. Cox had learned some Fulani, the Fula language, and the two men spoke. Ibrahima was doubtless curious about the white man's world, and Dr. Cox was as impressed by Ibrahima's education as he had been by the kindness of his people.

When Dr. Cox was well enough to leave, he was provided with a guard; but before he left, he warned the Fula about the danger of venturing too near the ships that docked off the coast of Guinea. The white doctor knew that the ships were there to take captives.

Cox and Ibrahima embraced fondly and said their good-byes, thinking they would never meet again.

Ibrahima married and became the father of several children. He was in his mid-twenties when he found himself leading the Fula cavalry in their war with the Mandingo.

The first battles went well, with the enemy retreating before the advancing Fula. The foot warriors attacked first, breaking the enemy's ranks and making them easy prey for the well-trained Fula cavalry. With the enemy in full rout the infantry returned to their towns while the horsemen, led by Ibrahima, chased the remaining stragglers. The Fula fought their enemies with spears, bows, slings, swords, and courage.

The path of pursuit led along a path that narrowed sharply as the forests thickened. The fleeing warriors disappeared into the forest that covered a sharply rising mountain. Thinking the enemy had gone for good, Ibrahima felt it would be useless to chase them further.

"We could not see them," he would write later.

But against his better judgment, he decided to look for them. The horsemen dismounted at the foot of a hill and began the steep climb on foot. Halfway up the hill the Fula realized they had been lured into a trap! Ibrahima heard the rifles firing, saw the smoke from the powder and the men about him falling to the ground, screaming in agony. Some died instantly. Many horses, hit by the gunfire, thrashed about in pain and panic. The firing was coming from both sides, and Ibrahima ordered his men to the top of the hill, where they could, if time and Allah permitted it, try a charge using the speed and momentum of their remaining horses.

Ibrahima was among the first to mount, and urged his animal onward. The enemy warriors came out of the forests, some with bows and arrows, others with muskets that he knew they had obtained from the Europeans. The courage of the Fula could not match the fury of the guns. Ibrahima called out to his men to save themselves, to flee as they could. Many tried to escape, rushing madly past the guns. Few survived.

Those who did clustered about their young leader, determined to make one last, desperate stand. Ibrahima was hit in the back by an arrow, but the aim was not true and the arrow merely cut his broad shoulder. Then something smashed against his head from the rear.

The next thing Ibrahima knew was that he was choking. Then he felt himself being lifted from water. He tried to move his arms, but they had been fastened securely behind his back. He had been captured.

When he came to his full senses, he looked around him. Those of his noble cavalry who had not been captured were already dead. Ibrahima was unsteady on his legs as his clothes and sandals were stripped from him. The victorious Mandingo warriors now pushed him roughly into file with his men. They began the long trek that would lead them to the sea.

In Fouta Djallon being captured by the enemy meant being forced to do someone else's bidding, sometimes for years. If you could get a message to your people, you could, perhaps, buy your freedom. Otherwise, it was only if you were well liked, or if you married one of your captor's women, that you would be allowed to go free, or to live like a free person.

Ibrahima sensed that things would not go well for him.

The journey to the sea took weeks. Ibrahima was tied to other men, with ropes around their necks. Each day they walked from dawn to dusk. Those who were slow were knocked brutally to the ground. Some of those who could no longer walk were speared and left to die in agony. It was the lucky ones who were killed outright if they fell.

When they reached the sea, they remained bound hand and foot. There were men and women tied together. Small children clung to their mothers as they waited for the boats to come and the bargaining to begin.

Ibrahima, listening to the conversations of the men who held him captive, could understand those who spoke Arabic. These Africans were a low class of men, made powerful by the guns they had been given, made evil by the white man's goods. But it didn't matter who was evil and who was good. It only mattered who held the gun.

Ibrahima was inspected on the shore, then put into irons and herded into a small boat that took him out to a ship that was larger than any he had ever seen.

The ship onto which Ibrahima was taken was already crowded with black captives. Some shook in fear; others, still tied, fought by hurling their bodies at their captors. The beating and the killing continued until the ones who were left knew that their lot was hopeless.

On board the ship there were more whites with guns, who shoved them toward the open hatch. Some of the Africans hesitated at the hatch, and were clubbed down and pushed below-decks.

It was dark beneath the deck, and difficult to breathe. Bodies were pressed close against other bodies. In the section of the ship he was in, men prayed to various gods in various languages. It seemed that the whites would never stop pushing men into the already crowded space. Two sailors pushed the Africans into position so that each would lie in the smallest space possible. The sailors panted and sweated as they untied the men and then chained them to a railing that ran the length of the ship.

The ship rolled against its mooring as the anchor was lifted, and the journey began. The boards of the ship creaked and moaned as it lifted and fell in the sea. Some of the men got sick, vomiting upon themselves in the wretched darkness. They lay cramped, muscles aching, irons cutting into their legs and wrists, gasping for air.

Once a day they would be brought out on deck and made to jump about for exercise. They were each given a handful of either beans or rice cooked with yams and water from a cask. The white sailors looked hardly better than the Africans, but it was they who held the guns.

Illness and the stifling conditions on the ships caused many deaths. How many depended largely on how fast the ships could be loaded with Africans and how long the voyage from Africa took. It was not unusual for 10 percent of the Africans to die if the trip took longer than the usual twenty-five to thirty-five days.

Ibrahima, now twenty-six years old, reached Mississippi in 1788. As the ship approached land, the Africans were brought onto the deck and fed. Some had oil put on their skins so they would look better; their sores were treated or covered with pitch. Then they were given garments to wear in an obvious effort to improve their appearance.

Although Ibrahima could not speak English, he understood he was being bargained for. The white man who stood on the platform with him made him turn around, and several other white men neared him, touched his limbs, examined his teeth, looked into his eyes, and made him move about.

Thomas Foster, a tobacco grower and a hard-working man, had come from South Carolina with his family and had settled on the rich lands that took their minerals from the Mississippi River. He already held one captive, a young boy. In August 1788 he bought two more. One of them was named Sambo, which means "second son." The other was Ibrahima.

Foster agreed to pay $930 for the two Africans. He paid $150 down and signed an agreement to pay another $250 the following January and the remaining $530 in January of the following year.

When Ibrahima arrived at Foster's farm, he tried to find someone who could explain to the white man who he was—the son of a chief. He wanted to offer a ransom for his own release, but Foster wasn't interested. He understood, perhaps from the boy whom he had purchased previously, that this new African was claiming to be an important person. Foster had probably never heard of the Fula or their culture; he had paid good money for the African, and wasn't about to give him up. Foster gave Ibrahima a new name: He called him Prince.

For Ibrahima there was confusion and pain. What was he to do? A few months before, he had been a learned man and a leader among his people. Now he was a captive in a strange land where he neither spoke the language nor understood the customs. Was he never to see his family again? Were his sons forever lost to him?

As a Fula, Ibrahima wore his hair long; Foster insisted that it be cut. Ibrahima's clothing had been taken from him, and his sandals. Now the last remaining symbol of his people, his long hair, had been taken as well.

He was told to work in the fields. He refused, and he was tied and whipped. The sting of the whip across his naked flesh was terribly painful, but it was nothing like the pain he felt within. The whippings forced him to work.

For Ibrahima this was not life, but a mockery of life. There was the waking in the morning and the sleeping at night; he worked, he ate, but this was not life. What was more, he could not see an end to it. It was this feeling that made him attempt to escape.

Ibrahima escaped to the backwoods regions of Natchez. He hid there, eating wild berries and fruit, not daring to show his face to any man, white or black. There was no telling who could be trusted. Sometimes he saw men with dogs and knew they were searching for runaways, perhaps him.

Where was he to run? What was he to do? He didn't know the country, he didn't know how far it was from Fouta Djallon, or how to get back to his homeland. He could tell that this place was ruled by white men who held him in captivity. The other blacks he had seen were from all parts of Africa. Some he recognized by their tribal markings, some he did not. None were allowed to speak their native tongues around the white men. Some already knew nothing of the languages of their people.

As time passed Ibrahima's despair deepened. His choices were simple. He could stay in the woods and probably die, or he could submit his body back into bondage. There is no place in Islamic law for a man to take his own life. Ibrahima returned to Thomas Foster.

Foster still owed money to the man from whom he had purchased Ibrahima. The debt would remain whether he still possessed the African or not. Foster was undoubtedly glad to see that the African had returned. Thin, nearly starving, Ibrahima was put to work.

Ibrahima submitted himself to the will of Thomas Foster. He was a captive, held in bondage not only by Foster but by the society in which he found himself. Ibrahima maintained his beliefs in the religion of Islam and kept its rituals as best he could. He was determined to be the same person he had always been: Abd al-Rahman Ibrahima of Fouta Djallon and of the proud Fula people.

By 1807 the area had become the Mississippi Territory. Ibrahima was forty-five and had been in bondage for twenty years. During those years he met and married a woman whom Foster had purchased, and they began to raise a family. Fouta Djallon was more and more distant, and he had become resigned to the idea that he would never see it or his family again.

Thomas Foster had grown wealthy and had become an important man in the territory. At forty-five Ibrahima was considered old. He was less useful to Foster, who now let the tall African grow a few vegetables on a side plot and sell them in town, since there was nowhere in the territory that the black man could go where he would not be captured by some other white man and returned.

It was during one of these visits to town that Ibrahima saw a white man who looked familiar. The smallish man walked slowly and with a limp. Ibrahima cautiously approached the man and spoke to him. The man looked closely at Ibrahima, then spoke his name. It was Dr. Cox.

The two men shook hands and Dr. Cox, who now lived in the territory, took Ibrahima to his home. John Cox had not prospered over the years, but he was still hopeful. He listened carefully as Ibrahima told his story—the battle near Fouta Djallon, the defeat, the long journey across the Atlantic Ocean, and, finally, his sale to Thomas Foster and the years of labor.

Dr. Cox and Ibrahima went to the Foster plantation. Meeting with Foster, he explained how he had met the tall black man. Surely, he reasoned, knowing that Ibrahima was of royal blood, Foster would free him? The answer was a firm, but polite, no. No amount of pleading would make Foster change his mind. It didn't matter that Dr. Cox had supported what Ibrahima had told Foster so many years before, that he was a prince. To Foster the man was merely his property.

Dr. Cox had to leave the man whose people had saved his life, but he told Ibrahima that he would never stop working for his freedom.

Andrew Marschalk, the son of a Dutch baker, was a printer, a pioneer in his field, and a man of great curiosity. By the time Marschalk heard about it, Cox had told a great many people in the Natchez district the story of African royalty being held in slavery in America. Marschalk was fascinated. He suggested that Ibrahima write a letter to his people, telling them of his whereabouts and asking them to ransom him. But Ibrahima had not been to his homeland in twenty years. The people there were still being captured by slave traders. He would have to send a messenger who knew the countryside, and who knew the Fula. Where would he find such a man?

For a long time Ibrahima did nothing. Finally, some time after the death of Dr. Cox in 1816, Ibrahima wrote the letter that Marschalk suggested. He had little faith in the procedure but felt he had nothing to lose. Marschalk was surprised when Ibrahima appeared with the letter written neatly in Arabic. Since one place in Africa was the same as the next to Marschalk, he sent the letter not to Fouta Djallon but to Morocco.

The government of Morocco did not know Ibrahima but understood from his letter that he was a Moslem. Moroccan officials, in a letter to President James Monroe, pleaded for the release of Ibrahima. The letter reached Henry Clay, the American Secretary of State.

The United States had recently ended a bitter war with Tripoli in north Africa, and welcomed the idea of establishing good relations with Morocco, another north African country. Clay wrote to Foster about Ibrahima.

Foster resented the idea of releasing Ibrahima. The very idea that the government of Morocco had written to Clay and discussed a religion that Ibrahima shared with other Africans gave Ibrahima a past that Foster had long denied, a past as honorable as Foster's. This idea challenged a basic premise of slavery—a premise that Foster must have believed without reservation: that the Africans had been nothing but savages, with no humanity or human feelings, and therefore it was all right to enslave them. But after more letters and pressure from the State Department, Foster agreed to release Ibrahima if he could be assured that Ibrahima would leave the country and return to Fouta Djallon.

Many people who believed that slavery was wrong also believed that Africans could not live among white Americans. The American Colonization Society had been formed expressly to send freed Africans back to Africa. The society bought land, and a colony called Liberia was established on the west coast of Africa. Foster was assured that Ibrahima would be sent there.

By then Ibrahima's cause had been taken up by a number of abolitionist groups in the north as well as by many free Africans. They raised money to buy his wife's freedom as well.

On February 7, 1829, Ibrahima and his wife sailed on the ship *Harriet* for Africa. The ship reached Liberia, and Ibrahima now had to find a way to reach his people again. He never found that way. Abd al-Rahman Ibrahima died in Liberia in July 1829.

Who was Ibrahima? He was one of millions of Africans taken by force from their native lands. He was the son of a chief, a warrior, and a scholar. But to Ibrahima the only thing that mattered was that he had lost his freedom. If he had been a herder in Fouta Djallon, or an artist in Benin, or a farmer along the Gambia, it would have been the same. Ibrahima was an African who loved freedom no less than other beings on earth. And he was denied that freedom.

☑ **Check Your Comprehension**

1. How does Myers describe Ibrahima's social position among his people?
2. Explain how Ibrahima came to know Dr. John Coates Cox.
3. Describe the sequence of events leading to Ibrahima's capture by the slave traders.
4. According to the story, how was Ibrahima treated by Thomas Foster?
5. How did Dr. Cox try to help Ibrahima?
6. According to the story, how did the government of Morocco get involved in helping Ibrahima, and what was the outcome?

◆ **Critical Thinking**

INTERPRET

1. What evidence in the story suggests that the Fula were a highly civilized people? **[Support]**

2. After Dr. Cox's stay with the Fula people, what was his attitude toward them? **[Infer]**
3. What connection do you think the Mandingo people had with the slave traders? **[Draw Conclusions]**
4. Compare and contrast the treatment Ibrahima received from Thomas Foster with the treatment Dr. Cox received from the Fula people. **[Compare and Contrast]**

EVALUATE

5. Why do you think Thomas Foster insisted that Ibrahima leave the country as a condition of his release? **[Speculate]**

APPLY

6. In what way does the story of Ibrahima add to your understanding of slavery and the slave trade? **[Connect]**

*W*alter Dean Myers

from The Glory Field

The Glory Field *follows five generations of the Lewis family, beginning with the capture and enslavement of the first ancestor in West Africa in the 1700's. In the following excerpt, which takes place in New York City in the 1990's, Malcom Lewis tries to balance his desire to form a band with his family responsibilities.*

H*e was on the right side of the stage, just out of the circle of light that illuminated George and Deepak. Deepak rocked gently backward and forward as his fingers danced over his sitar.[1] Behind him George was setting a counter rhythm on the snare drums. There was something strange, almost otherworldly, about the sound they were creating. Malcolm took a deep breath as he silently fingered the keys of the alto flute he held in his hand. His sound would have to be full, he knew, and the tones round and lush enough to bring real warmth to the music. As he lifted the flute to his lips there was another sound. He listened for a moment and then lowered the flute. Offstage there was a telephone ringing. He thought of ignoring it as he lifted his flute again, but the telephone continued ringing. He turned toward the audience, then felt something over his face. . . .*

Malcolm Lewis pushed the pillow from his face and fought his way out of the sheets. He looked around frantically for the telephone, found it partway under the bed, and lifted the receiver.

"I'm leaving this afternoon for Curry," Luvenia Lewis spoke slowly, precisely. "I need to be at the airport at one-thirty, and I will be at your house at eleven-fifteen to talk to you. I won't be needing lunch."

"Yes, ma'am."

Malcolm repeated his "Yes, ma'am," once more, even though he had heard the telephone on the other end being hung up, then replaced his own receiver on its cradle. He shook his head twice, realized he was hanging off the low platform bed, and wriggled back onto the bed and into the comfortable nest he had made between the sheets.

It was too early to think. He would just lie in bed for an hour or so until his head cleared. Then he would plan his day. Maybe.

The light streamed through the windows of his room. He knew it was late, but all of him had not awakened yet. He took a deep

---

1. **sitar** (si tär´): A stringed instrument from India with a long neck and a rounded body.

breath, noted that his breath was terrible, and closed his eyes again. After a while he realized he had to go to the bathroom. He pushed the sheets away from his body, feeling how cool the room was, almost chilly. The cold air felt good against his skin. His parents and sister had already left for the family reunion on Curry so he didn't have to bother getting dressed. The bathroom light was still on from the night before. He looked at himself in the mirror. Not bad, he thought. A little too round in the chin area, which made him look younger than his fifteen years, but still he was looking pretty good.

He used the toilet and then started back to the bed. The digital clock on the end table read ten-oh-seven. He fell across the bed and rolled himself into a warm position. It was the first day in weeks that he hadn't been loading trucks at Mahogany Beauty Products, the cosmetics factory his great-aunt owned. He thought he would get up in an hour or so and then go downtown for a late lunch in one of those little restaurants near University Place.

Suddenly he sat straight up! What had Aunt Luvenia said? He shook his head, trying to jerk away the cobwebs from his mind. He went over the conservation again. She was going to be at the airport at one-thirty and at his house at eleven-fifteen.

He checked the time again. He was still cool. His room was a mess, but she wouldn't be coming into his room. Then he remembered what the living room looked like. His band, String Theory, had come over with some of their friends and had brought pizzas and sodas. George had made the popcorn, which had been used in the popcorn fight.

Malcolm got up, went back to the bathroom, and a moment later was in the shower. The shower was only warm, and he let it splash directly onto his face. The water felt good on his body, and he thought about splashing on some of his father's aftershave lotion even though he didn't shave.

Luvenia Lewis had never married, choosing instead to devote herself first to the beauty parlors she opened in Chicago and then to her nationwide beauty supply business. For years, she had dominated beauty supplies for the black and Hispanic market. It was only recently, when the white-owned cosmetics companies started marketing products for black women, that the business had experienced any difficulty. Now she was branching out into real estate and travel services. Malcolm had been glad when she offered him a summer job and had asked him about his grades. She had often told him that if he kept his grades up and worked hard, she would see to it that he went to college. He hadn't known that when the old woman said that he should work hard, she meant that she would personally see to it that his back would be broken.

Out of the shower, he took the large terry cloth towel to the hallway and dried himself while he surveyed the living room. There was popcorn all over the rug and on the seat cushions. The pizza boxes were on the floor under the coffee table, and soda cans were piled at the side of every chair. It looked bad, but he thought he could handle it. It was only twenty to eleven.

He put on his shorts and went into the kitchen for orange juice while planning his cleanup strategy. That was when he saw the note he had written to himself and put under the magnet on the refrigerator door.

Jenn Che Po—amplified cello, 11 A.M.

He remembered the phone call. He had had to get everyone to quiet down while he answered it. The caller was soft-spoken. She said that she had seen his notice on the bulletin board at La Guardia High School. Was he still looking for someone who played an amplified stringed instrument? And could she come the next day to audition?

She had asked what kind of music they played and was clearly disappointed when he had said it was kind of a new thing. Then he had said it was sort of like postmodern funk, and she had asked how old he was. She told him she was fifteen and had been playing since she was six. She said her name was Jenn Che Po. He had asked her to spell it twice before he was sure that he had it right.

He vacuumed up the popcorn first because that looked the worst. There was more of it on the floor than he had thought, and he wondered if anybody had eaten any of the stuff. It had been a good crowd of kids, most of them from his school, all of them into good jams and reasonably together. He had wondered if they would all come to Harlem for the party, but they did.

He brought out a big garbage pail and started stuffing boxes and cans into it. His aunt probably didn't expect him to be too neat, but he didn't know what to expect from the girl who had answered his ad for a string player. Actually, he didn't think she would want to play with his band. She sounded a little sophisticated to play for nothing in a band that was just starting to find its way.

The telephone rang and he rushed to it.

"Hello?"

"Did the cello player come over yet?" It was Deepak.

"No. She's due in a few minutes."

"What do you think she's going to be like?"

"I don't know, man," Malcolm answered. "And I gotta get this place cleaned up before she gets here. I'll call you later."

"Aww, man!"

Deepak was a little miffed at his ending the call so soon, but Malcolm knew he needed to get the place cleaned up. He had finished picking up the worst of the garbage and had just put the vacuum cleaner away when the buzzer for the downstairs door rang. Malcolm answered it. It was Jenn. He buzzed her in and looked around the room. Not too bad, he thought.

He went to close the door of his room, saw his jeans on the chair, and realized he still wasn't dressed. He rushed into the room, put on his jeans, grabbed a dress shirt from the closet, and buttoned it furiously as he went to answer the front doorbell.

Jenn Che Po was small, almost fragile. She wore shades, which she immediately took off for a better look at Malcolm.

"You're tall," she said. "How tall are you?"

"Six-one," Malcolm said, pleased that she had mentioned his height. "Come in."

She entered, carrying her cello directly into the center of the living room. She turned to him with the suggestion of a smile on her face, but her eyes looked cautiously around the room. "Can you tell me more about what kind of group you're trying to put together?" she asked.

"I'm trying to get a group that's not set in its ideas," Malcolm said. "I don't want it to be labeled this or that and then get stuck in that mode so we can't be creative. You know what I mean?"

"No," she said firmly.

"Well, if you're playing grunge, then you're playing grunge, and everybody expects the same kind of thing from you all the time. But I want people with ideas that can change and grow. I have a really cool Indian guy who plays guitar and sitar. I have a Native American who plays bass guitar. Me and the drummer are black, and I have this white piano player from Astoria who can play anything from an old-fashioned stride[2] to classical Coltrane and Mozart."

"What's race got to do with music?" she asked, glancing toward the door. "You want a band of different-*looking* people?"

"No. What I want to do is to be who I am and play from who I am," Malcolm said. "You know what I mean?"

"No."

"Well, I mean I want to play from a black point of view, but as an individual, not like I'm being forced into it. We on the same page yet?"

"That's cool," Jenn said as the doorbell rang again. "You have other people to try out?"

---

2. stride: A shortened version of *stride piano,* a style of jazz-piano playing in which the right hand plays the melody while the left hand plays either a single note or a higher chord.

"No, it's probably my aunt," Malcolm said. "I work for her, and she wants to go over some things with me."

He buzzed in his aunt.

"What do you play?" Jenn asked.

"Sax and flute," Malcolm said.

Jenn lifted her cello, and Malcolm thought she was about to leave when the doorbell rang and he went to answer it.

Luvenia Lewis was around eighty years old, but her posture was as good as it had ever been, and her step nearly as firm. She glanced at Jenn and nodded.

"She's here to audition for the band," Malcolm said.

"Oh, I would love to hear you play," Luvenia extended her hand. "I'm Malcolm's great-aunt. I heard his group play once, and it was . . . interesting. What kind of music do you play?"

"I've been playing European classical in school," Jenn said, glancing at Malcolm to see his reaction. "I think I want to try some other things, but I want to know what the other things are."

"I've got a tape you can take with you," Malcolm said.

"Put it on."

"I'm not sure how much time my aunt has—"

"Play the tape," the older woman said brusquely.[3]

Malcolm found the tape on the edge of the coffee table, picking up a kernel of popped corn with his other hand. He put the tape into the player, and pushed the play button.

The tape had been of one of the young group's best sessions. The music had been composed by Deepak and had a slightly bluesy tinge to it with a strong up-tempo beat. Jenn listened to it as she stood in the middle of the floor with her head down, not moving.

Malcolm had heard the tape many times, and he was constantly surprised that they had pulled it off. The music was fresh and interesting. He had thought about trying to beg out of the reunion so that he could practice with the group every day, but he knew how disappointed his parents would have been. For as long as he could remember, he had been told that the only real strength was in family, and this week the family was going to be on Curry.

The piece on tape was nearly seven minutes long and slowed in tempo as it neared the end, with instruments dropping off like voices leaving a party until only the sound of a small drum remained.

"Can you play it again?" Jenn asked.

Malcolm looked toward his aunt, who nodded. He rewound the tape, and pushed the play button again.

"This isn't the only thing we play," he said.

---

3. **brusquely** (brusk´ lē): In a blunt and abrupt manner.

Jenn listened for a while, then opened her cello case. She ran her fingers across the strings, adjusted two of them, and then picked up her bow and began playing with the tape.

She had heard the music once and not only knew it but could play with it!

When the tape had finished, she put the cello away. "When will you let me know if I've made the group?" she said.

"Uh." Malcolm rubbed the end of his nose. The young girl was good, and she knew it. "I have to go away for a week, but if you're interested, we're getting together on the second of September. A friend of mine is going to let us use his studio for rehearsals. If you leave your number."

"I'll send you a résumé," she said. She headed toward the door.

"Okay, well, it was nice meeting you," Malcolm said at the door.

"It was nice meeting you, too," she said. "The music's interesting."

When Jenn had left, Malcolm took a quick look around the room to see if there was anything he should censor before his aunt saw it.

"That was a very confident young woman," his aunt said. "Had you met her before?"

"No, ma'am." Malcolm sat on the couch. "But she can play."

"I have to be going soon," his aunt said. She was looking in the dark cloth pocketbook she carried. She pulled out an envelope and handed it to him. "Here's the money for tickets for you and your cousin Shep. I expect you to be on Curry by Monday evening, which gives you two and a half days. If what I hear about Shep's problems are true, then I think you need to be very careful. Young men who take to drink are never reliable."

"Yeah . . ." Malcolm looked away from his aunt. He turned the envelope over in his hand. "Look, I'm going to try to get him down there. I think I can pull it off."

☑ Check Your Comprehension

1. What is really happening when Malcolm is getting ready to play the flute on stage?
2. (a) Why does Aunt Luvenia come to Malcolm's house? (b) What must Malcolm do before she arrives?
3. What other appointment does Malcolm have?
4. Describe what happens when both visitors are at Malcolm's house.

◆ Critical Thinking

INTERPRET

1. (a) Describe Aunt Luvenia. (b) Describe Malcolm's relationship with Aunt Luvenia. Use details from the story to support your answers. **[Analyze]**
2. In your own words, describe the type of band that Malcolm is trying to form. **[Describe]**

3. Do you think Jenn Che Po will fit in well with Malcolm and his band? Support your opinion with details from the story. **[Speculate]**
4. What does Aunt Luvenia think of Jenn Che Po? Why does she think this? **[Infer]**

APPLY

5. Malcolm wants people from a variety of backgrounds to join his band. Think of a diverse group you've been a part of, and explain how this diversity added to the group. **[Relate]**

EVALUATE

6. (a) Would you describe Malcolm as a responsible person? (b) Based on your answer, predict what will happen next in the story. Will he arrive on time for the family reunion? Will he be able to form a band? **[Evaluate; Speculate]**

Walter Dean Myers
Comparing and Connecting the Author's Works

◆ Literary Focus: Social Commentary

Much of Walter Dean Myers's writing provides **social commentary,** or the writer's view about conditions in society. Writers who offer social commentary usually do so indirectly. In other words, they will not say directly what they think about a situation. Instead, they show, through the plot and characters, that certain conditions exist and may need improving.

For example, at the end of the chapter from *The Glory Field,* Myers hints that Shep has problems related to drinking. Myers does not directly state that he thinks the problem of teen alcoholism must be addressed. Instead, he lets Aunt Luvenia say it for him.

1. After reading "Ibrahima," what do you think Myers feels about slavery and the slave trade?
2. Myers does not directly state his opinion of slavery. Name two indirect ways in which he makes his opinion clear.
3. The chapter from *The Glory Field* gives social commentary in an indirect way. With the characters in mind, how would you describe Myers's opinion of what young people should and should not be doing?

◆ Drawing Conclusions About Myers's Work

In the *Dictionary of Literary Biography,* Carmen Subryan says this about Walter Dean Myers:

"Whether he is writing about the ghettoes of New York, the remote countries of Africa, or social institutions, Myers captures the essence of the developing experiences of youth."

Choose "Ibrahima" or the excerpt from *The Glory Field.* In a paragraph, explain how Myers captures a young person developing a new understanding of something. Before you write, organize your thoughts in a chart like the one below.

Character	Experience	What He or She Learns

◆ Idea Bank

Writing

1. **Change the Story** Imagine that Ibrahima is never captured by the slave traders. Write a story about how you think his life would have turned out.
2. **Continue the Story** What do you think will happen next in *The Glory Field?* Will Malcolm and Shep get to Curry on time? Will the band be successful? Write the next scene or chapter of the novel. Then, find *The Glory Field* in your library and read the next chapter. How does your version compare with Myers's?
3. **Interview** Imagine that you could speak to one of the characters described by Walter Dean Myers. Write five questions you would ask him or her. Then, write the answers you think the character would give. Set your work in the form of a dialogue, using the proper punctuation and starting a new paragraph every time the speaker changes.

Speaking and Listening

4. **Dramatic Presentation** With a partner or a small group, choose a scene from one of the stories to perform for your class. Divide the work of writing the script, acting in the performance, and directing. **[Performing Arts Link; Group Activity]**

5. **Social Commentary** With a small group, hold a panel discussion about an issue that currently affects your school. For example, you might focus on the need for more funding for computers, or students' anxieties about getting good grades. Make sure that both sides of the issue are well represented. **[Group Activity]**

Researching and Representing

6. **Oral Report** Many of Myers's stories are set in Harlem. With a small group, research the history of Harlem. Look for answers to these questions: What was Harlem like when it was first settled? What was Harlem like during the Harlem Renaissance? What is Harlem like today? Have each member of your group present a brief oral report answering one of these questions. **[Social Studies Link; Group Activity]**

7. **Learn About an Instrument** In the chapter from *The Glory Field,* Malcolm plays the flute and saxophone, Jenn plays the cello, and members of the band play bass guitar, drums, and sitar. Choose an instrument whose sound you find interesting, and research its history. Write a one-page summary of your findings. If possible, accompany your summary with a picture of the instrument and a recording of its sound. **[Music Link]**

◆ Further Reading, Listening, and Viewing

- Rudine Sims Bishop, *Presenting Walter Dean Myers* (1990).

- Denise M. Jordan, *Walter Dean Myers: Writer for Real Teens* (1999).

- *The Young Landlords,* a film adapted from a book by Walter Dean Myers, was produced by Topol Productions.

On the Web:

http://www.phschool.com/atschool/literature
Go to the student edition *Copper.* Proceed to Unit 1. Then, click Hot Links to find Web sites featuring Walter Dean Myers.

Isaac Bashevis Singer In Depth

"Literature stirs the mind: It makes you think about a million things, but it does not lead you. Whenever a writer tries to be more than a storyteller, he becomes less."

— *Isaac Bashevis Singer*

ISAAC BASHEVIS SINGER'S vibrant stories have made him immensely popular with audiences young and old. Much of his work evokes the small Polish village in which he was born. It describes the lives of Jews in Poland, many of whom were killed by the Nazis during World War II. "He'll turn wherever he is into the streets of Poland," Singer's friend Dorothea Straus said. "Consciously or unconsciously, he is interested in preserving the culture he left."

A Rabbi's Son Born in 1904 in the tiny Polish village of Radzymin, Singer was the son of a rabbi, a Jewish religious leader. When Singer was four, his family moved to Warsaw, the capital of Poland, where his father set up a rabbinical court in their run-down home. Singer described the many functions of the rabbinical court when he said, "My father's home on Krochmalna Street in Warsaw was a study house, a court of justice, a house of prayer, of storytelling, as well as a place for weddings and Hasidic banquets."

A rabbinical court is also a place where community members discuss their problems and ask the rabbi for advice. Young Isaac would listen, fascinated, to the people's stories. Later, he would use them as inspiration for his stories of his own.

A Traditional Education Singer received a traditional religious education. He studied the Torah, the Talmud, the Cabala, and other sacred Jewish books. He was born into a line of great rabbis so holy they were said to perform miracles, and he was expected to follow their lead. Instead, Singer followed the example of his older brother Israel Joseph, whom he called his mentor, and became a writer.

A New Life in America Like much of Eastern Europe during the rise of Hitler, Poland was a dangerous place for Jews. Alarmed by the possibility of a Nazi invasion, Singer fled Poland in 1935 and joined his beloved older brother in New York City. He began writing for *The Jewish Daily Forward,* a Yiddish-language newspaper. Shortly after that, Singer's old neighborhood in Warsaw was destroyed. In 1939, the Nazis killed his mother and one of his brothers in Poland. Devastated by these losses, Singer wrote nothing for seven years. He then became of the most prolific writers of his age, writing often about Polish Jews. In this way, he kept the ruined world of his childhood alive.

Writing Fiction Singer wrote almost exclusively in Yiddish, a language spoken by Eastern European Jews. Though he became fluent in English, Singer continued to write in his native language. He explained, "I always knew that a writer has to write in his own language or not at all."

Much of Singer's fiction takes place in the Yiddish-speaking Jewish ghettos of Poland. His stories are filled with Jewish folklore and legends. The struggles of Singer's characters display his understanding of the strengths and weaknesses of human nature.

Singer also wrote about Jews who fled Europe because of the Holocaust, and about Holocaust survivors in the New World. He believed that "the serious writer of our time must be deeply concerned about the problems of his generation." However, he also believed that the most important role of fiction is to entertain. He was a storyteller, a philosopher, and a preserver of the past.

The Nobel Prize Singer received the Nobel Prize for Literature in 1978, and was praised for his "impassioned narratives, which, with roots in a Polish-Jewish cultural tradition, bring universal human conditions to life." In his Nobel Prize Acceptance Speech, Singer noted that "the high honor bestowed upon me by the Swedish Academy is also a recognition of the Yiddish language." He spoke of the Jews who lived in European ghettos and said that we "can learn much from those Jews, their way of thinking, their way of bringing up children, their finding happiness where others see nothing but misery and humiliation."

After immigrating to the United States in 1935, Singer spent the rest of his life in New York and Florida. He became a familiar figure in his New York neighborhood, taking walks, feeding the pigeons, and eating vegetarian lunches in local cafeterias. In 1991, after several strokes, Singer died at the age of 87.

◆ Yiddish

Yiddish is the language of the Jews of Eastern and Central Europe. It is written in Hebrew, and it is based on a number of German dialects. Its vocabulary is mostly German, but it has been widely influenced by Hebrew, Slavic, English, and the Romance languages.

I. B. Singer called Yiddish "a language of exile, without a land, without frontiers, not supported by any government." Although it is not a national language, Yiddish has about four million speakers worldwide. Before the slaughter of six million Jews during the Holocaust in World War II, Yiddish was spoken by more than eleven million people.

While Hebrew was the language of scholars, Yiddish was the language of the street, spoken by ordinary people. For this reason, its vocabulary is weak in abstractions. It also has few words that describe nature, for the Jews of Eastern Europe lived in cities. However, it has a wealth of words and expressions that describe character and human relations. It has many terms of endearment and makes great use of proverbs and idioms. These qualities make Yiddish a warm, vibrant language.

◆ Literary Works

Novels
- *Satan in Goray* (1935, translated 1955)
- *The Family Moskat* (1950)
- *The Magician of Lublin* (1960)
- *The Slave* (1962)
- *Enemies: A Love Story* (1966, translated 1972)
- *Shosha* (1978)

Short Story Collections
- *Gimpel the Fool* (1957)
- *The Spinoza of Market Street* (1961)
- *Passions* (1975)
- *Old Love* (1979)
- *The Image* (1985)

Memoirs
- *In My Father's Court* (1956, translated 1966)
- *A Little Boy in Search of God* (1976)
- *A Young Man in Search of Love* (1978)
- *Lost in America* (1981)
- *The Golem* (1982)
- *The Penitent* (1983)
- *Love and Exile* (1984)

Children's Books
- *Mazel and Schlimazel* (1966)
- *The Fools of Chelm and Their History* (1973)
- *Stories for Children* (1984)

Isaac Bashevis Singer

Shrewd Todie & Lyzer the Miser

translated by the author and Elizabeth Shub

In a village somewhere in the Ukraine[1] there lived a poor man called Todie. Todie had a wife, Sheindel, and seven children, but he could never earn enough to feed them properly. He tried many trades, failing in all of them. It was said of Todie that if he decided to deal in candles the sun would never set. He was nicknamed Shrewd[2] Todie because whenever he managed to make some money, it was always by trickery.

This winter was an especially cold one. The snowfall was heavy and Todie had no money to buy wood for the stove. His seven children stayed in bed all day to keep warm. When the frost burns outside, hunger is stronger than ever, but Sheindel's larder[3] was empty. She reproached Todie bitterly, wailing, "If you can't feed your wife and children, I will go to the rabbi[4] and get a divorce."

"And what will you do with it, eat it?" Todie retorted.

In the same village there lived a rich man called Lyzer. Because of his stinginess he was known as Lyzer the miser.[5] He permitted his wife to bake bread only once in four weeks because he had discovered that fresh bread is eaten up more quickly than stale.

Todie had more than once gone to Lyzer for a loan of a few gulden, but Lyzer had always replied, "I sleep better when the money lies in my strongbox rather than in your pocket."

Lyzer had a goat, but he never fed her. The goat had learned to visit the houses of the neighbors, who pitied her and gave her potato peelings. Sometimes, when there were not enough peelings, she would gnaw on the old straw of the thatched roofs. She also had a liking for tree bark. Nevertheless, each year the goat gave birth to a kid. Lyzer milked her but, miser that he was, did not drink the milk himself. Instead, he sold it to others.

Todie decided that he would take revenge on Lyzer and at the same time make some much-needed money for himself.

One day, as Lyzer was sitting on a box eating borscht[6] and dry bread (he used his chairs only on holidays so that the upholstery would not wear out), the door opened and Todie came in.

---

1. **Ukraine** (yo͞o kran´ or yo͞o´ krän): A region between Poland and Russia, on the Black Sea.
2. **Shrewd:** Keen-witted, clever, or cunning in practical affairs.
3. **larder:** A place where food is stored; a pantry.
4. **rabbi** (rab´ ī): A Jewish religious leader.
5. **miser** (mī´ zər): A greedy, stingy person who holds on to money simply because of a love of money.
6. **borscht** (bôrsh): A soup made from beets, served hot or cold.

"Reb Lyzer," he said, "I would like to ask you a favor. My oldest daughter, Basha, is already fifteen and she's about to become engaged. A young man is coming from Janev to look her over. My cutlery is tin, and my wife is ashamed to ask the young man to eat soup with a tin spoon. Would you lend me one of your silver spoons? I give you my holy word that I will return it to you tomorrow."

Lyzer knew that Todie would not dare to break a holy oath and he lent him the spoon.

No young man came to see Basha that evening. As usual, the girl walked around barefoot and in rags, and the silver spoon lay hidden under Todie's shirt. In the early years of his marriage Todie had possessed a set of silver tableware himself. He had, however, long since sold it all, with the exception of three silver teaspoons that were used only on Passover.[7]

The following day, as Lyzer, his feet bare (in order to save his shoes), sat on his box eating borscht and dry bread, Todie returned.

"Here is the spoon I borrowed yesterday," he said, placing it on the table together with one of his own teaspoons.

"What is the teaspoon for?" Lyzer asked.

And Todie said, "Your tablespoon gave birth to a teaspoon. It is her child. Since I am an honest man, I'm returning both mother and child to you."

Lyzer looked at Todie in astonishment.[8] He had never heard of a silver spoon giving birth to another. Nevertheless, his greed overcame his doubt and he happily accepted both spoons. Such an unexpected piece of good fortune! He was overjoyed that he had loaned Todie the spoon.

A few days later, as Lyzer (without his coat, to save it) was again sitting on his box eating borscht with dry bread, the door opened and Todie appeared.

"The young man from Janev did not please Basha, because he had donkey ears, but this evening another young man is coming to look her over. Sheindel is cooking soup for him, but she's ashamed to serve him with a tin spoon. Would you lend me . . . "

Even before Todie could finish the sentence, Lyzer interrupted. "You want to borrow a silver spoon? Take it with pleasure."

The following day Todie once more returned the spoon and with it one of his own silver teaspoons. He again explained that during the night the large spoon had given birth to a small one and in all good conscience he was bringing back the mother and the newborn baby. As for the young man who had come to look

---

7. **Passover:** A Jewish holiday commemorating the deliverance of the ancient Hebrews from slavery in Egypt.
8. **astonishment:** Great surprise, amazement.

Basha over, she hadn't liked him either, because his nose was so long that it reached to his chin. Needless to say that Lyzer the miser was overjoyed.

Exactly the same thing happened a third time. Todie related that this time his daughter had rejected her suitor because he stammered. He also reported that Lyzer's silver spoon had again given birth to a baby spoon.

"Does it ever happen that a spoon has twins?" Lyzer inquired.

Todie thought it over for a moment. "Why not? I've even heard of a case where a spoon had triplets."

Almost a week passed by and Todie did not go to see Lyzer. But on Friday morning, as Lyzer (in his underdrawers, to save his pants) sat on his box eating borscht and dry bread, Todie came in and said, "Good day to you, Reb Lyzer."

"A good morning and many more to you," Lyzer replied in his friendliest manner. "What good fortune brings you here? Did you perhaps come to borrow a silver spoon? If so, help yourself."

"Today I have a very special favor to ask. This evening a young man from the big city of Lublin is coming to look Basha over. He is the son of a rich man, and I'm told he is clever and handsome as well. Not only do I need a silver spoon, but since he will remain with us over the Sabbath,[9] I need a pair of silver candlesticks, because mine are brass and my wife is ashamed to place them on the Sabbath table. Would you lend me your candlesticks? Immediately after the Sabbath, I will return them to you."

Silver candlesticks are of great value and Lyzer the miser hesitated, but only for a moment.

Remembering his good fortune with the spoons, he said, "I have eight silver candlesticks in my house. Take them all. I know you will return them to me just as you say. And if it should happen that any of them give birth, I have no doubt that you will be as honest as you have been in the past."

"Certainly," Todie said. "Let's hope for the best."

The silver spoon, Todie hid beneath his shirt as usual. But taking the candlesticks, he went directly to a merchant, sold them for a considerable sum, and brought the money to Sheindel. When Sheindel saw so much money, she demanded to know where he had gotten such a treasure.

"When I went out, a cow flew over our roof and dropped a dozen silver eggs," Todie replied. "I sold them and here is the money."

"I have never heard of a cow flying over a roof and laying silver eggs," Sheindel said doubtingly.

"There is always a first time," Todie answered. "If you don't want the money, give it back to me."

---

9. Sabbath: A day of the week set aside for rest and worship.

"There'll be no talk about giving it back," Sheindel said. She knew that her husband was full of cunning[10] and tricks—but when the children are hungry and the larder is empty, it is better not to ask too many questions. Sheindel went to the marketplace and bought meat, fish, white flour, and even some nuts and raisins for a pudding. And since a lot of money still remained, she bought shoes and clothes for the children.

It was a very gay Sabbath in Todie's house. The boys sang and the girls danced. When the children asked their father where he had gotten the money, he replied, "It is forbidden to mention money during the Sabbath."

Sunday, as Lyzer (barefoot and almost naked, to save his clothes) sat on his box finishing up a dry crust of bread with borscht, Todie arrived and, handing him his silver spoon, said, "It's too bad. This time your spoon did not give birth to a baby."

"What about the candlesticks?" Lyzer inquired anxiously.

Todie sighed deeply. "The candlesticks died."

Lyzer got up from his box so hastily that he overturned his plate of borscht.

"You fool! How can candlesticks die?" he screamed.

"If spoons can give birth, candlesticks can die."

Lyzer raised a great hue and cry and had Todie called before the rabbi. When the rabbi heard both sides of the story, he burst out laughing. "It serves you right," he said to Lyzer. "If you hadn't chosen to believe that spoons give birth, now you would not be forced to believe that your candlesticks died."

"But it's all nonsense," Lyzer objected.

"Did you not expect the candlesticks to give birth to other candlesticks?" the rabbi said admonishingly.[11] "If you accept nonsense when it brings you profit, you must also accept nonsense when it brings you loss." And he dismissed the case.

The following day, when Lyzer the miser's wife brought him his borscht and dry bread, Lyzer said to her, "I will eat only the bread. Borscht is too expensive a food, even without sour cream."

The story of the silver spoons that gave birth and the candlesticks that died spread quickly through the town. All the people enjoyed Todie's victory and Lyzer the miser's defeat. The shoemaker's and tailor's apprentices, as was their custom whenever there was an important happening, made up a song about it:

Lyzer, put your grief aside.
What if your candlesticks have died?
You're the richest man on earth
with silver spoons that can give birth

---

10. **cunning:** Slyness or cleverness.
11. **admonishingly:** In a way that warns or gives caution.

and silver eggs as living proof
of flying cows above your roof.
Don't sit there eating crusts of bread—
To silver grandsons look ahead.

However, time passed and Lyzer's silver spoons never gave birth again.

☑ **Check Your Comprehension**

I. What reason does Todie give Lyzer for wanting to borrow the silver spoons and, later, the candlesticks?

2. How does Todie explain the extra silver spoons?

3. How does Todie explain the missing candlesticks?

4. After Lyzer complains to the rabbi, what is the rabbi's decision?

5. What are the rabbi's reasons for making his decision?

◆ **Critical Thinking**

INTERPRET

I. Define the word *miser*. List two things that prove that Lyzer is a miser. **[Connect]**

2. Explain why Lyzer becomes more and more willing to lend valuable items to Todie. **[Analyze]**

3. Why doesn't Todie tell his wife the truth about the money? **[Speculate]**

4. Does Lyzer learn anything from the Rabbi's decision? Use details from the story to support your answer. **[Infer]**

EVALUATE

5. Do you think the rabbi's decision is fair? Why? **[Make a Judgment]**

APPLY

6. The shoemaker's and tailor's apprentices make up a song about the incident. What advice do they give Lyzer? Do you think he should follow the advice? Why? **[Make a Decision]**

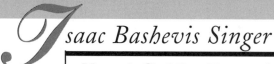

Isaac Bashevis Singer

Utzel & His Daughter, Poverty

translated by the author and Elizabeth Shub

Once there was a man named Utzel. He was very poor and even more lazy. Whenever anyone wanted to give him a job to do, his answer was always the same: "Not today."

"Why not today?" he was asked. And he always replied, "Why not tomorrow?"

Utzel lived in a cottage that had been built by his great-grandfather. The thatched roof needed mending, and although the holes let the rain in, they did not let the smoke from the stove out. Toadstools grew on the crooked walls and the floor had rotted away. There had been a time when mice lived there, but now there weren't any because there was nothing for them to eat. Utzel's wife had starved to death, but before she died she had given birth to a baby girl. The name Utzel gave his daughter was very fitting. He called her Poverty.

Utzel loved to sleep and each night he went to bed with the chickens. In the morning he would complain that he was tired from so much sleeping and so he went to sleep again. When he was not sleeping, he lay on his broken-down cot, yawning and complaining. He would say to his daughter, "Other people are lucky. They have money without working. I am cursed."

Utzel was a small man, but as his daughter, Poverty, grew, she spread out in all directions. She was tall, broad, and heavy. At fifteen she had to lower her head to get through the doorway. Her feet were the size of a man's and puffy with fat. The villagers maintained that the lazier Utzel got, the more Poverty grew.

Utzel loved nobody, was jealous of everybody. He even spoke with envy of cats, dogs, rabbits, and all creatures who didn't have to work for a living. Yes, Utzel hated everybody and everything, but he adored his daughter. He daydreamed that a rich young man would fall in love with her, marry her, and provide for his wife and his father-in-law. But not a young man in the village showed the slightest interest in Poverty. When her father reproached the girl for not making friends and not going out with young men, Poverty would say, "How can I go out in rags and bare feet?"

One day Utzel learned that a certain charitable society in the village loaned poor people money, which they could pay back in small sums over a long period. Lazy as he was, he made a great effort—got up, dressed, and went to the office of the society. "I would like to borrow five gulden," he said to the official in charge.

"What do you intend to do with the money?" he was asked. "We lend money only for useful purposes."

"I want to have a pair of shoes made for my daughter," Utzel explained. "If Poverty has shoes, she will go out with the young people of the village and some wealthy young man will surely fall in love with her. When they get married, I will be able to pay back the five gulden."

The official thought it over. The chances of anyone falling in love with Poverty were very small. Utzel, however, looked so miserable that the official decided to give him the loan. He asked Utzel to sign a promissory note[1] and gave him five gulden.

Utzel had tried to order a pair of shoes for his daughter a few months before. Sandler the shoemaker had gone so far as to take Poverty's measurements, but the shoemaker had wanted his money in advance. From the charitable society Utzel went directly to the shoemaker and asked whether he still had Poverty's measurements.

"And supposing I do?" Sandler replied. "My price is five gulden and I still want my money in advance."

Utzel took out the five gulden and handed them to Sandler. The shoemaker opened a drawer and after some searching brought out the order for Poverty's shoes. He promised to deliver the new shoes in a week, on Friday.

Utzel, who wanted to surprise his daughter, did not tell her about the shoes. The following Friday, as he lay on his cot yawning and complaining, there was a knock on the door and Sandler came in carrying the new shoes. When Poverty saw the shoemaker with a pair of shiny new shoes in his hand, she cried out in joy. The shoemaker handed her the shoes and told her to try them on. But, alas, she could not get them on her puffy feet. In the months since the measurements had been taken, Poverty's feet had become even larger than they were before. Now the girl cried out in grief.

Utzel looked on in consternation. "How is it possible?" he asked. "I thought her feet stopped growing long ago."

For a while Sandler, too, stood there puzzled. Then he inquired, "Tell me, Utzel, where did you get the five gulden?" Utzel explained that he had borrowed the money from the charitable loan society and had given them a promissory note in return.

"So now you have a debt," exclaimed Sandler. "That makes you even poorer than you were a few months ago. Then you had nothing, but today you have five gulden less than nothing. And since you have grown poorer, Poverty has grown bigger, and naturally her feet have grown with her. That is why the shoes don't fit. It is all clear to me now."

"What are we going to do?" Utzel asked in despair.

"There is only one way out for you," Sandler said. "Go to work. From borrowing one gets poorer and from work one gets richer.

---

1. promissory note: A written promise to pay a sum of money at a certain time or or on demand.

When you and your daughter work, she will have shoes that fit."

The idea of working did not appeal to either of them, but it was even worse to have new shoes and go around barefoot. Utzel and Poverty both decided that immediately after the Sabbath they would look for work.

Utzel got a job as a water carrier. Poverty became a maid. For the first time in their lives, they worked diligently. They were kept so busy that they did not even think of the new shoes, until one Sabbath morning Poverty decided she'd try them on again. Lo and behold, her feet slipped easily into them. The new shoes fit.

At last Utzel and Poverty understood that all a man possesses he gains through work, and not by lying in bed and being idle. Even animals were industrious. Bees make honey, spiders spin webs, birds build nests, moles dig holes in the earth, squirrels store food for the winter. Before long Utzel got a better job. He rebuilt his house and bought some furniture. Poverty lost more weight. She had new clothes made and dressed prettily like the other girls of the village. Her looks improved, too, and a young man began to court her. His name was Mahir and he was the son of a wealthy merchant. Utzel's dream of a rich son-in-law came true, but by then he no longer needed to be taken care of.

Love for his daughter had saved Utzel. In his later years he became so respected he was elected a warden of that same charitable loan society from which he had borrowed five gulden.

On the wall of his office there hung the string with which Sandler had once measured Poverty's feet, and above it the framed motto: *Whatever you can do today, don't put off till tomorrow.*

☑ Check Your Comprehension

1. Find at least two words that Singer uses to describe Utzel.
2. What is Utzel's dream for his daughter, Poverty?
3. Why does Utzel decide to ask for a loan from the charitable society?
4. What happens when the shoemaker brings the new shoes to Utzel's house?
5. When do Utzel's and Poverty's lives begin to improve?

◆ Critical Thinking

INTERPRET
1. Why is Utzel so poor? **[Analyze Cause and Effect]**

2. Does Utzel love his daughter? How can you tell? **[Infer]**
3. Why do you think the young men in the village show no interest in Poverty at the beginning of the story? **[Analyze]**
4. At the end of the story, what has changed in Poverty, besides her appearance, that makes her more attractive to others? **[Draw Conclusions]**

EVALUATE
5. What advice does the shoemaker give to Utzel? Do you think this is good advice? **[Make a Judgement]**

APPLY
6. What is the meaning of the motto that Utzel hangs on his wall? Do you think it is wise? Why? **[Assess]**

Isaac Bashevis Singer

The Parakeet Named Dreidel

It happened about ten years ago in Brooklyn, New York. All day long a heavy snow was falling. Toward evening the sky cleared and a few stars appeared. A frost set in. It was the eighth day of Hanukkah,[1] and my silver Hanukkah lamp stood on the windowsill with all candles burning. It was mirrored in the windowpane, and I imagined another lamp outside.

My wife, Esther, was frying potato pancakes. I sat with my son, David, at a table and played dreidel[2] with him. Suddenly David cried out, "Papa, look!" And he pointed to the window.

I looked up and saw something that seemed unbelievable. Outside on the windowsill stood a yellow-green bird watching the candles. In a moment I understood what had happened. A parakeet had escaped from its home somewhere, had flown out into the cold street and landed on my windowsill, perhaps attracted by the light.

A parakeet is native to a warm climate, and it cannot stand the cold and frost for very long. I immediately took steps to save the bird from freezing. First I carried away the Hanukkah lamp so that the bird would not burn itself when entering. Then I opened the window and with a quick wave of my hand shooed the parakeet inside. The whole thing took only a few seconds.

In the beginning the frightened bird flew from wall to wall. It hit itself against the ceiling and for a while hung from a crystal prism on the chandelier. David tried to calm it: "Don't be afraid, little bird, we are your friends." Presently the bird flew toward David and landed on his head, as though it had been trained and was accustomed to people. David began to dance and laugh with joy. My wife, in the kitchen, heard the noise and came out to see what had happened. When she saw the bird on David's head, she asked, "Where did you get a bird all of a sudden?"

"Mama, it just came to our window."

"To the window in the middle of winter?"

"Papa saved its life."

The bird was not afraid of us. David lifted his hand to his forehead and the bird settled on his finger. Esther placed a saucer of millet[3] and a dish of water on the table, and the parakeet ate and drank. It saw the dreidel and began to push it with its beak. David exclaimed, "Look, the bird plays dreidel."

---

1. Hanukkah (khä´ nōō kä): A Jewish festival that lasts eight days, in memory of the rededication of the Temple in Jerusalem in 165 B.C.
2. dreidel (drä´ d´l): A small top with Hebrew letters on each of four sides, spun in a game played by children, especially during Hanukkah.
3. millet: A cereal grass whose small grain is used for food in Asia and Europe.

David soon began to talk about buying a cage for the bird and also about giving it a name, but Esther and I reminded him that the bird was not ours. We would try to find the owners, who probably missed their pet and were worried about what had happened to it in the icy weather. David said, "Meanwhile, let's call it Dreidel."

That night Dreidel slept on a picture frame and woke us in the morning with its singing. The bird stood on the frame, its plumage brilliant in the purple light of the rising sun, shaking as in prayer, whistling, twittering, and talking all at the same time. The parakeet must have belonged to a house where Yiddish was spoken, because we heard it say *"Zeldele, geh schlofen"* (Zeldele, go to sleep), and these simple words uttered by the tiny creature filled us with wonder and delight.

The next day I posted a notice in the elevators of the neighborhood houses. It said that we had found a Yiddish-speaking parakeet. When a few days passed and no one called, I advertised in the newspaper for which I wrote, but a week went by and no one claimed the bird. Only then did Dreidel become ours. We bought a large cage with all the fittings and toys that a bird might want, but because Hanukkah is a festival of freedom, we resolved never to lock the cage. Dreidel was free to fly around the house whenever he pleased. (The man at the pet shop had told us that the bird was a male.)

Nine years passed and Dreidel remained with us. We became more attached to him from day to day. In our house Dreidel learned scores of Yiddish, English, and Hebrew words. David taught him to sing a Hanukkah song, and there was always a wooden dreidel in the cage for him to play with. When I wrote on my Yiddish typewriter, Dreidel would cling to the index finger of either my right or my left hand, jumping acrobatically with every letter I wrote. Esther often joked that Dreidel was helping me write and that he was entitled to half my earnings.

Our son, David, grew up and entered college. One winter night he went to a Hanukkah party. He told us that he would be home late, and Esther and I went to bed early. We had just fallen asleep when the telephone rang. It was David. As a rule he is a quiet and composed young man. This time he spoke so excitedly that we could barely understand what he was saying. It seemed that David had told the story of our parakeet to his fellow students at the party, and a girl named Zelda Rosen had exclaimed, "I am this Zeldele! We lost our parakeet nine years ago." Zelda and her parents lived not far from us, but they had never seen the notice in the newspaper or the ones posted in elevators. Zelda was now a student and a friend of David's. She had never visited us before, although our son often spoke about her to his mother.

We slept little that night. The next day Zelda and her parents came to see their long-lost pet. Zelda was a beautiful and gifted girl. David often took her to the theater and to museums. Not only did the Rosens recognize their bird, but the bird seemed to recognize his former owners. The Rosens used to call him Tsip-Tsip, and when the parakeet heard them say "Tsip-Tsip," he became flustered and started to fly from one member of the family to the other, screeching and flapping his wings. Both Zelda and her mother cried when they saw their beloved bird alive. The father stared silently. Then he said, "We have never forgotten our Tsip-Tsip."

I was ready to return the parakeet to his original owners, but Esther and David argued that they could never part with Dreidel. It was also not necessary, because that day David and Zelda decided to get married after their graduation from college. So Dreidel is still with us, always eager to learn new words and new games. When David and Zelda marry, they will take Dreidel to their new home. Zelda has often said, "Dreidel was our matchmaker."[4]

On Hanukkah he always gets a gift—a mirror, a ladder, a bathtub, a swing, or a jingle bell. He has even developed a taste for potato pancakes, as befits a parakeet named Dreidel.

---

4. **matchmaker:** A person who tries to arrange marriages.

☑ Check Your Comprehension

1. As the story opens, what unusual event happens?

2. In what two ways does David's father try to find the owner of the parakeet?

3. Name two ways in which the parakeet becomes a part of the narrator's family.

4. How does David eventually find the parakeet's original owners?

5. In the future, where will the parakeet live?

◆ Critical Thinking

INTERPRET

1. What characteristics of the parakeet reveal that it is someone's pet? **[Infer]**

2. How do you think Zelda feels when David tells the story of the parakeet at the party? **[Infer]**

3. What are two things this story teaches about the customs surrounding Hanukkah? **[Connect]**

EVALUATE

4. What does Zelda mean when she says, "Dreidel was our matchmaker"? **[Interpret]**

APPLY

5. Do you think the narrator's family should have returned the parakeet to Zelda's family? Why? **[Make a Decision]**

Isaac Bashevis Singer

Comparing and Connecting the Author's Works

◆ Literary Focus: Narration

Narration is writing that tells a story. The story that is told can be nonfiction (true) or fiction (made up). Narration is used in many genres, including poetry, short stories, novels, plays, and essays. All of the selections by Singer are examples of narratives because they tell stories.

The character who tells the story in a narrative is called the narrator. The narrator may be a main character in the story, a supporting character, or a speaker who is not involved in the story. A narrator may speak in the first person (using *I* and *me*) or the third person (using *he, she, it,* and *they*). In "The Parakeet Named Dreidel," for example, the narrator speaks in the first person. Because he participates in the action, he can tell only what he knows and sees. The reader sees the events and characters through his eyes.

1. Reread the first paragraphs of "Utzel & His Daughter, Poverty" and "Shrewd Todie & Lyzer the Miser." Are the stories told in the first or the third person?

2. How might "Utzel & His Daughter, Poverty" be different if it were told through the eyes of Utzel?

◆ Drawing Conclusions About Singer's Work

Singer once told a critic that "I prefer to write about the world which I knew, which I know, best."

This world, of course, is that of the Jews in Eastern Europe before World War II. The following diagram shows details from "Shrewd Todie & Lyzer the Miser" that give the reader insight into this world.

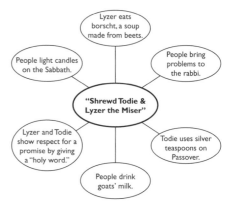

Create a similar diagram for "Utzel & His Daughter, Poverty." Try to find at least four details from Singer's "world." Then, write a paragraph explaining how this story can teach a reader about life in the Jewish ghettos of Eastern Europe.

◆ Idea Bank

Writing

1. **Diary Entry** The rabbi had quite a laugh after hearing Lyzer's story. Compose the diary entry he might have written after making his decision in Todie's favor.

2. **Poem** The shoemaker's and tailor's apprentices wrote a song for Lyzer. Following their example, write a short song or poem with advice for one of the characters in "Utzel & His Daughter, Poverty." **[Music Link]**

3. **Compare and Contrast** Write a one-page essay about the similarities and differences between Todie and Lyzer. Use examples from the story to support your ideas. Before you begin, organize your thoughts in a Venn diagram Like this one:

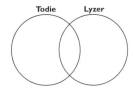
Todie   Lyzer

Speaking and Listening

4. **Make a Speech** Choose one of the characters from the stories by Singer, and put yourself in his or her place. Prepare and deliver a short speech explaining what you learned from your experiences. As you speak, keep "in character"—that is, speak in a way you think the character would speak. **[Performing Arts Link]**

5. **Skit** With a partner or a small group, act out an important scene from one of the stories. Before you begin, ask yourself these questions: What "body language" might the characters have used? What props might make the scene more interesting for the viewer? **[Performing Arts Link; Group Activity]**

Researching and Representing

6. **Multimedia Presentation** When Singer left Poland in 1935, the Nazis were gaining power. With a small group, research the effect of Hitler and the Nazis on Poland or another Eastern European country. In what ways did the country change? Present your findings to the class using photographs, maps, and charts. Include audio and video recordings, if possible. **[Media Link, Social Studies Link; Group Activity]**

7. **Singer and His Brother** Isaac Bashevis Singer called his older brother, Israel Joseph, his mentor. In your library or on the Internet, research the life and work of I. J. Singer. Write a one-page summary of your findings. If possible, read some of his work and compare it to that of his more famous brother.

◆ Further Reading, Listening, and Viewing

- I. B. Singer: *When Schlemiel Went to Warsaw and Other Stories* (1968).
- I. B. Singer: *The Fools of Chelm and their History* (1973).
- I. B. Singer: *Naftali the Storyteller and His Horse, Sus, and Other Stories* (1976).
- I. B. Singer: *A Day of Pleasure: Stories of a Boy Growing Up in Warsaw* (1969). This book contains wise and humorous autobiographical stories and a collection of photographs from Singer's life.
- Lester Goran: *The Bright Streets of Surfside: The Memoir of a Friendship With Isaac Bashevis Singer* (1994). Learn about Singer through the eyes of his close friend and translator.
- Grace Farrell, editor: *Isaac Bashevis Singer: Conversations* (1992). Read about Singer in his own words.
- Alida Allison: *Isaac Bashevis Singer: Children's Stories and Childhood Memoirs* (1996). This book presents critical essays on some of Singer's stories.
- *Yentl* (1983). This film (rated PG), directed by and starring Barbra Streisand, is based on a story by Singer about a woman who must disguise herself as a man to get an education.

On the Web:

http://www.phschool.com/atschool/literature
Go to the student edition *Copper*. Proceed to Unit 2. Then, click Hot Links to find Web sites featuring Isaac Bashevis Singer.

Rudyard Kipling In Depth

"His marvellous power of imagination enables him to give us not only copies from nature but also visions out of his own inner consciousness."

—**C. D. af Wirsén, Permanent Secretary of the Swedish Academy, announcing that Kipling had won the Nobel Prize for literature, 1907.**

RUDYARD KIPLING wrote short stories, novels, and poetry for both young people and adults. His writings ranged from stories about British schoolboys, to poems about life as a soldier, to tales of the Indian jungle. Kipling wrote most of his best-known pieces more than 100 years ago, and many of his works, such as the stories that make up *The Jungle Books* and his novels *Captains Courageous* and *Kim*, are still widely read today. One of his best-known poems, entitled "If—," ("If you can keep your head while others all about you/ Are losing theirs and blaming it on you . . .") continues to inspire many.

A Difficult Childhood Kipling was born in Bombay, India, in 1865. At that time India was ruled by Great Britain, and many British people and their families had gone to India as government workers, military personnel, or to fill various other jobs. Kipling's father, for example, worked in an Indian museum and was also an author who wrote about India.

When young Rudyard was about six, he was sent back to England and lived for five years in a foster home. These years were not happy, nor were the following ones, during which he attended a boarding school. At school, he was lonely and bullied by other boys, but when he wrote about English boarding schools in books such as *Stalky and Co.,* he presented life at such schools as important to the development of future citizens of the British empire.

Success in India In 1882 Kipling returned to India, where he remained for seven years. He took a job on the British-Indian newspaper *The Civil and Military Gazette* and later wrote for a paper called *The Pioneer.* He also composed stories and poetry on the side. His newspaper jobs gave him opportunities to travel around the country and to observe many aspects of Indian life, including the influence the British military had on how the land was governed. During his years in England, Kipling had always remained fascinated with the land of his birth, and his writings reflected his keen observations of India. Two of the books he published during this time, a collection of poems called *Departmental Ditties* and a short-story collection called *Plain Tales from the Hills,* helped to establish his literary reputation even in England. When Kipling returned there in 1889, he found that he had become a very popular writer. His 1892 collection of poems, *Barrack-Room Ballads,* further strengthened his reputation. Dealing with the lives of British soldiers, these poems were written in the down-to-earth dialect that soldiers actually spoke.

A Move to the United States Kipling moved to the United States with his American wife in 1892. The newlyweds settled in Vermont, where they remained for several years and had three children. It was during this that time Kipling wrote *The Jungle Book* and *The Second Jungle Book,* collections of stories about the Indian boy Mowgli and his friends in the jungle. In 1902 Kipling bought a house in Sussex, in southeast England, which would be his home for the rest of his life. Sussex also provided the background for many of the books that he wrote in his later years.

In 1907 Kipling was awarded the Nobel Prize for literature, the most prestigious award a writer can win. He was the first British citizen ever to receive this prize.

◆ The British Empire

When Kipling was young, Great Britain, as well as several other European countries, had colonies or possessions in various parts of the world. Britain, for example, controlled many countries in Africa and ruled Canada and Australia as well. It was said that, "The sun never sets on the British Empire," because British colonies lay in every part of the globe. This strong British influence is one reason that English is spoken in so many countries around the world.

Of the countries that made up the British Empire, India was one of the largest and most important. The British had taken almost complete control of the region by the mid-1700's, but they had begun doing business there as early as 1600, when the British East India Company was established and began trading in spices and cotton. By Kipling's time, British officials governed most

areas of India, and the Indian army was a mix of British and Indian soldiers.

British families that lived in India for more than one generation, as Kipling's did, were fairly common. Individuals might travel back to Britain for short and long stays, but many felt that India was as much their home as Britain. Many British citizens lived all or most of their lives in other countries.

◆ Literary Works
Fiction
* *The Light That Failed* (1890)
* *Captains Courageous* (1897)
* *Kim* (1901)

Story Collections
* *The Jungle Book* (1894)
* *The Second Jungle Book* (1895)
* *Just So Stories* (1902)

Poems
* "The Road to Mandalay"
* "If—"
* "Gunga Din"
* "Recessional"
* "Danny Deever"

Rudyard Kipling

from Captains Courageous

Harvey Cheyne, the spoiled son of a railroad millionaire, has been washed overboard from an ocean liner into the Atlantic Ocean. Rescued by the We're Here, *a New England fishing boat, Harvey begins to adjust to his new life. He will live and work on the boat while the crew makes its summerlong fishing run.*

It was the forty-fathom slumber that clears the soul and eye and heart, and sends you to breakfast ravening.[1] They emptied a big tin dish of juicy fragments of fish—the blood-ends the cook had collected overnight. They cleaned up the plates and pans of the elder mess, who were out fishing, sliced pork for the mid-day meal, swabbed down the foc'sle, filled the lamps, drew coal and water for the cook, and investigated the fore-hold, where the boat's stores were stacked. It was another perfect day—soft, mild, and clear; and Harvey breathed to the very bottom of his lungs.

More schooners had crept up in the night, and the long blue seas were full of sails and dories. Far away on the horizon, the smoke of some liner, her hull invisible, smudged the blue, and to eastward a big ship's top-gallant sails, just lifting, made a square nick in it. Disko Troop was smoking by the roof of the cabin—one eye on the craft around, and the other on the little fly at the mainmast-head.[2]

"When dad kerflummoxes that way," said Dan in a whisper, "he's doin' some high-line thinkin' fer all hands. I'll lay my wage an' share we'll make berth[3] soon. Dad he knows the cod, an' the fleet they know dad knows. See 'em comin' up one by one, lookin' fer nothin' in particular, o' course, but scrowgin' on us all the time? There's the 'Prince Leboo'; she's a Chatham boat. She's crep' up sence last night. An' see that big one with a patch in her fore-sail an' a new jib? She's the 'Carrie Pitman' from West Chatham. She won't keep her canvas long onless her luck's changed since last season. She don't do much 'cep' drift. There ain't an anchor made'll hold her. . . . When the smoke puffs up in little rings like that, dad's studyin' the fish. Ef we speak to him now, he'll git mad. Las' time I did, he jest took an' hove a boot at me."

---

1. **ravening** (rav′ ə ning): Greedily or wildly hungry.
2. **little fly at the mainmast head:** Small flag at the top of the largest mast, used to check which way the wind is blowing.
3. **I'll lay my wage and share we'll make berth soon:** I'll bet anything we'll stop to fish soon.

Disko Troop stared forward, the pipe between his teeth, with eyes that saw nothing. As his son said, he was studying the fish—pitting his knowledge and experience on the Banks against the roving cod in his own sea. He accepted the presence of the inquisitive schooners on the horizon as a compliment to his powers. But now that it was paid, he wished to draw away and make his berth alone, till it was time to go up to the Virgin and fish in the streets of that roaring town upon the waters.[4] So Disko Troop thought of recent weather, and gales, currents, food supplies, and other domestic arrangements, from the point of view of a twenty-pound cod; was, in fact, for an hour, a cod himself, and looked remarkably like one. Then he removed the pipe from his teeth.

"Dad," said Dan, "we've done our chores. Can't we go over-side a piece? It's good catchin' weather."

"Not in that cherry-coloured rig ner them ha'af-baked brown shoes. Give him suthin' fit to wear."

"Dad's pleased—that settles it," said Dan delightedly, dragging Harvey into the cabin, while Troop pitched a key down the steps. "Dad keeps my spare rig where he can overhaul it, 'cause ma sez I'm keerless." He rummaged through a locker, and in less than three minutes Harvey was adorned with fisherman's rubber boots that came half up his thigh, a heavy blue jersey well darned at the elbows, a pair of nippers, and a sou'wester.[5]

"Naow you look somethin' like," said Dan. "Hurry!"

"Keep nigh an' handy," said Troop, "an' don't go visitin' raound the fleet. Ef any one asks you what I'm cal'latin to do, speak the truth an' say ye don't know."

A little red dory, labelled 'Hattie S.', lay astern of the schooner. Dan hauled in the painter,[6] and dropped lightly on to the bottom boards, while Harvey tumbled clumsily after.

"That's no way o' gettin' into a boat," said Dan. "Ef there was any sea you'd go to the bottom, sure. You've got to learn to meet her."

Dan fitted the thole-pins, took the forward thwart, and watched Harvey's work. The boy had rowed, in a lady-like fashion, on the Adirondack ponds; but there is a difference between squeaking pins and well-balanced rullocks—light sculls and stubby, eight-foot sea-oars.[7] They stuck in the gentle swell, and Harvey grunted.

---

4. **the Virgin . . . that roaring town upon the waters:** Location where boats gathered to compare their catches at the end of the fishing season.
5. **a heavy blue jersey . . . , a pair of nippers, and a sou'wester:** A sweater or knitted jacket; thick, fingerless gloves to protect one's hands from heavy fishing line; and a rain hat.
6. **painter:** Rope attached to a boat, used to tie it.
7. **a difference between squeaking pins and . . . eight-foot sea-oars:** A comparison between the long, heavy oars on the fishing dory and the flimsy ones Harvey was used to on rowboats.

"Short! Row short!" said Dan. "Ef you cramp your oar in any kind o' sea you're liable to turn her over. Ain't she a daisy? Mine, too."

The little dory was specklessly clean. In her bows lay a tiny anchor, two jugs of water, and some seventy fathoms of thin brown dory-roding.[8] A tin dinner-horn rested in cleats just under Harvey's right hand, beside an ugly-looking maul, a short gaff,[9] and a shorter wooden stick. A couple of lines, with very heavy leads and double cod-hooks, all neatly coiled on square reels, were stuck in their place by the gunwale.

"Where's the sail and mast?" said Harvey, for his hands were beginning to blister.

Dan chuckled. "Ye don't sail fishin'-dories much. Ye pull; but ye needn't pull so hard. Don't you wish you owned her?"

"Well, I guess my father might give me one or two if I asked 'em," Harvey replied. He had been too busy to think much of his family till then.

"That's so. I forgot your dad's a millionaire. You don't act millionary any, naow. But a dory an' craft an' gear"—Dan spoke as though she were a whaleboat—"costs a heap. Think your dad 'ud give you one fer—fer a pet like?"

"Shouldn't wonder. It would be 'most the only thing I haven't stuck him for yet."

"Must be an expensive kinder kid to home. Don't slitheroo thet way, Harve. Short's the trick, because no sea's ever dead still, an' the swells 'll—"

Crack! The loom of the oar kicked Harvey under the chin and knocked him backwards.

"That was what I was goin' to say. I hed to learn too, but I wasn't more than eight years old when I got my schoolin'."

Harvey regained his seat with aching jaws and a frown.

"No good gettin' mad at things, dad says. It's our own fault ef we can't handle 'em, he says. Le's try here. Manuel 'll give us the water."

The 'Portugee' was rocking fully a mile away,[10] but when Dan up-ended an oar, he waved his left arm three times.

"Thirty fathom,[11]" said Dan, stringing a salt clam on to the hook. "Over with the doughboys. Bait same's I do, Harve, an' don't snarl your reel."

Dan's line was out long before Harvey had mastered the mystery of baiting and heaving out the leads. The dory drifted along

---

8. **dory-roding:** Thin cord attached to a dory's anchor.
9. **gaff:** A strong hook on a handle, used for bringing large fish out of the water.
10. **the "Portugee" was rocking fully a mile away:** Kipling refers to Manuel, the sailor who had earlier rescued Harvey and who is now fishing about a mile away.
11. **Thirty fathom:** 180 feet; a fathom is six feet.

easily. It was not worth while to anchor till they were sure of good ground.

"Here we come!" Dan shouted, and a shower of spray rattled on Harvey's shoulders as a big cod flapped and kicked alongside. "Muckle, Harvey, muckle! Under your hand! Quick!"

Evidently 'muckle' could not be the dinner-horn, so Harvey passed over the maul, and Dan scientifically stunned the fish before he pulled it inboard, and wrenched out the hook with the short wooden stick he called a 'gob-stick.' Then Harvey felt a tug, and pulled up zealously.

"Why, these are strawberries!" he shouted. "Look!"

The hook had fouled among a bunch of strawberries, red on one side and white on the other—perfect reproductions of the land fruit, except that there were no leaves, and the stem was all pipy and slimy.

"Don't tech' em! Slat 'em off. Don't—"

The warning came too late. Harvey had picked them from the hook, and was admiring them.

"Ouch!" he cried, for his fingers throbbed as though he had grasped many nettles.

"Naow ye know what strawberry-bottom means. Nothin' 'cep' fish should be teched with the naked fingers, dad says. Slat 'em off agin the gunnel, an' bait up, Harve. Lookin' won't help any. It's all in the wages."

Harvey smiled at the thought of his ten and a half dollars a month, and wondered what his mother would say if she could see him hanging over the edge of a fishing-dory in mid-ocean. She suffered agonies whenever he went out on Saranac Lake; and, by the way, Harvey remembered distinctly that he used to laugh at her anxieties. Suddenly the line flashed through his hand, stinging even through the 'nippers,' the woollen circlets supposed to protect it.

"He's a logy.[12] Give him room accordin' to his strength," cried Dan. "I'll help ye."

"No, you won't," Harvey snapped, as he hung on to the line. "It's my first fish. Is—is it a whale?"

"Halibut, mebbe." Dan peered down into the water alongside and flourished the big 'muckle,' ready for all chances. Something white and oval flickered and fluttered through the green. "I'll lay my wage an' share he's over a hundred. Are you so everlastin' anxious to land him alone?"

Harvey's knuckles were raw and bleeding where they had been banged against the gunwale; his face was purple-blue between excitement and exertion; he dripped with sweat, and was half-blinded from staring at the circling sunlit ripples about the

12. **logy:** A big fish

swiftly-moving line. The boys were tired long ere the halibut, who took charge of them and the dory for the next twenty minutes. But the big flat fish was gaffed and hauled in at last.

"Beginner's luck," said Dan, wiping his forehead. "He's all of a hundred."

Harvey looked at the huge gray-and-mottled creature with unspeakable pride. He had seen halibut many times on marble slabs ashore, but it had never occurred to him to ask how they came inland. Now he knew; and every inch of his body ached with fatigue.

☑ Check Your Comprehension

1. How are Disko Troop and Dan related to each other?

2. How does Disko Troop prepare himself for fishing?

3. Where do Dan and Harvey go when they take out the dory?

4. What mistake does Harvey make with the strawberries?

5. What does Harvey finally catch?

◆ Critical Thinking

INTERPRET

1. How does the reader know that Dan has more experience at sea than Harvey has? **[Analyze; Connect]**

2. How does Dan seem to feel about Harvey's lack of experience? Give examples from the story. **[Infer; Support]**

3. Why do you think Harvey wants to land his fish alone? **[Draw Conclusions]**

EVALUATE

4. What effect does Kipling create by having Dan speak in dialect? Why doesn't Harvey use this dialect? What effect does this difference have on the reader? **[Evaluate]**

APPLY

5. Describe a time when you did something difficult for the first time. Was your reaction similar to Harvey's? Explain. **[Relate]**

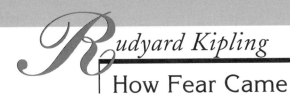

Rudyard Kipling

How Fear Came

The Law of the Jungle—which is by far the oldest law in the world—has arranged for almost every kind of accident that may befall the Jungle-People, till now its code is as perfect as time and custom can make it. If you have read the other stories about Mowgli, you will remember that he spent a great part of his life in the Seeonee Wolf Pack, learning the Law from Baloo the brown bear; and it was Baloo who told him, when the boy grew impatient at the constant orders, that the Law was like the giant creeper, because it dropped across everyone's back and no one could escape. "When thou hast lived as long as I have, Little Brother, thou wilt see how all the Jungle obeys at least one Law. And that will be no pleasant sight," said Baloo.

This talk went in at one ear and out at the other, for a boy who spends his life eating and sleeping does not worry about anything till it actually stares him in the face. But one year Baloo's words came true, and Mowgli saw all the jungle working under one Law.

It began when the winter rains failed almost entirely, and Sahi the Porcupine, meeting Mowgli in a bamboo thicket, told him that the wild yams were drying up. Now everybody knows that Sahi is ridiculously fastidious in his choice of food, and will eat nothing but the very best and ripest. So Mowgli laughed and said, "What is that to me?"

"Not much *now*," said Sahi, rattling his quills in a stiff, uncomfortable way, "but later we shall see. Is there any more diving into the deep rock pool below the Bee Rocks, Little Brother?"

"No. The foolish water is going all away, and I do not wish to break my head," said Mowgli, who was quite sure he knew as much as any five of the Jungle-People put together.

"That is thy loss. A small crack might let in some wisdom." Sahi ducked quickly to prevent Mowgli from pulling his nose bristles, and Mowgli told Baloo what Sahi had said. Baloo looked very grave, and mumbled half to himself: "If I were alone I would change my hunting grounds now, before the others began to think. And yet—hunting among strangers ends in fighting—and they might hurt my man-cub. We must wait and see how the *mohwa* blooms."

That spring the *mohwa* tree, that Baloo was so fond of, never flowered. The greeny, cream-colored, waxy blossoms were heat-killed before they were born, and only a few bad-smelling petals came down when he stood on his hind legs and shook the tree. Then, inch by inch, the untempered heat crept into the heart of the jungle, turning it yellow, brown, and at last black. The green growths in the sides of the ravines burned up to broken wires and curled films of dead stuff; the hidden pools sank down and caked over, keeping the last least footmark on their edges as if it had been cast in iron; the juicy-stemmed creepers fell away from the trees they clung to and died at their feet; the bamboos withered, clanking when the hot winds blew, and the moss peeled off the rocks deep in the jungle, till they were as bare and as hot as the quivering blue boulders in the bed of the stream.

The birds and the Monkey-People went north early in the year, for they knew what was coming; and the deer and the wild pig broke far away into the perished fields of the villages, dying sometimes before the eyes of men too weak to kill them. Chil the Kite stayed and grew fat, for there was a great deal of carrion, and evening after evening he brought the news to the beasts, too weak to force their way to fresh hunting grounds, that the sun was killing the jungle for three days' flight in every direction.

Mowgli, who had never known what real hunger meant, fell back on stale honey, three years old, scraped out of deserted rock hives—honey black as a sloe,[1] and dusty with dried sugar. He hunted, too, for deep-boring grubs under the bark of the trees, and robbed the wasps of their new broods. All the game in the jungle was no more than skin and bone, and Bagheera could kill thrice in a night and hardly get a full meal. But the want of water was the worst, for though the Jungle-People drink seldom they must drink deep.

And the heat went on and on, and sucked up all the moisture, till at last the main channel of the Wainganga was the only stream that carried a trickle of water between its dead banks; and when Hathi the Wild Elephant, who lives for a hundred years and more, saw a long, lean blue ridge of rock show dry in the very center of the stream, he knew that he was looking at the Peace Rock, and then and there he lifted up his trunk and proclaimed the Water Truce, as his father before him had proclaimed it fifty years ago. The deer, wild pig, and buffalo took up the cry hoarsely; and Chil the Kite flew in great circles far and wide, whistling and shrieking the warning.

By the Law of the Jungle it is death to kill at the drinking places when once the Water Truce has been declared. The reason for this is that drinking comes before eating. Everyone in the jungle can scramble along somehow when only game is scarce; but water is water, and when there is but one source of supply, all

---

1. **sloe:** The small, blue-black, plumlike fruit of the blackthorn.

hunting stops while the Jungle-People go there for their needs. In good seasons, when water was plentiful, those who came down to drink at the Wainganga—or anywhere else, for that matter—did so at the risk of their lives, and that risk made no small part of the fascination of the night's doings. To move down so cunningly that never a leaf stirred; to wade knee-deep in the roaring shallows that drown all noise from behind; to drink, looking backward over one shoulder, every muscle ready for the first desperate bound of keen terror; to roll on the sandy margin, and return, wet-muzzled and well plumped out, to the admiring herd, was a thing that all glossy-horned young bucks took a delight in, precisely because they knew that at any moment Bagheera or Shere Khan[2] might leap upon them and bear them down. But now that life-and-death fun was ended, and the Jungle-People came up, starved and weary, to the shrunken river—tiger, bear, deer, buffalo, and pig together—drank the fouled waters, and hung above them, too exhausted to move off.

The deer and pig had tramped all day in search of something better than dried bark and withered leaves. The buffaloes had found no wallows to be cool in, and no green crops to steal. The snakes had left the jungle and come down to the river in the hope of catching a stray frog. They curled round wet stones, and never offered to strike when the snout of a rooting pig dislodged them. The river turtles had long ago been killed by Bagheera, cleverest of hunters, and the fish had buried themselves deep in the cracked mud. Only the Peace Rock lay across the shallows like a long snake, and the little tired ripples hissed as they dried on its hot side.

It was here that Mowgli came nightly for the cool and the companionship. The most hungry of his enemies would hardly have cared for the boy then. His naked skin made him look more lean and wretched[3] than any of his fellows. His hair was bleached to tow color by the sun; his ribs stood out like the ribs of a basket, and the lumps on his knees and elbows, where he was used to track on all fours, gave his shrunken limbs the look of knotted grass stems. But his eye, under his matted forelock, was cool and quiet, for Bagheera, his adviser in this time of trouble, told him to move quietly, hunt slowly, and never, on any account, to lose his temper.

"It is an evil time," said the Black Panther, one furnace-hot evening, "but it will go if we can live till the end. Is thy stomach full, man-cub?"

"There is stuff in my stomach, but I get no good of it. Think you, Bagheera, the rains have forgotten us and will never come again?"

---

2. **Bagheera or Shere Khan:** A black panther and a tiger.
3. **wretched:** Miserable; distressed.

"Not I. We shall see the *mohwa* in blossom yet, and the little fawns all fat with new grass. Come down to the Peace Rock and hear the news. On my back, Little Brother."

"This is no time to carry weight. I can still stand alone, but—indeed we be no fatted bullocks, we two."

Bagheera looked along his ragged, dusty flank and whispered: "Last night I killed a bullock under the yoke. So low was I brought that I think I should not have dared to spring if he had been loose. *Wou!*"

Mowgli laughed. "Yes, we are great hunters now," said he. "I am very bold—to eat grubs," and the two came down together through the crackling undergrowth to the riverbank and the lace-work of shoals that ran out from it in every direction.

"The water cannot live long," said Baloo, joining them. "Look across! Yonder are trails like the roads of Man."

On the level plain of the farther bank the stiff jungle grass had died standing, and, dying, had mummied. The beaten tracks of the deer and the pig, all heading towards the river, had striped that colorless plain with dusty gullies driven through the ten-foot grass, and, early as it was, each long avenue was full of firstcomers hastening to the water. You could hear the does and fawns coughing in the snufflike dust.

Upstream, at the bend of the sluggish pool round the Peace Rock, and Warden of the Water Truce, stood Hathi the Wild Elephant with his sons, gaunt and gray in the moonlight, rocking to and fro—always rocking. Below him a little were the vanguard of the deer; below these, again, the pig and the wild buffalo; and on the opposite bank, where the tall trees came down to the water's edge, was the place set apart for the eaters of flesh—the tiger, the wolves, the panther, the bear, and the others.

"We be under one Law, indeed," said Bagheera, wading into the water and looking across at the lines of clicking horns and starting eyes where the deer and the pig pushed each other to and fro. "Good hunting, all of you of my blood," he added, lying down at full length, one flank thrust out of the shallows; and then, between his teeth, "But for that which is the Law it would be *very* good hunting."

The quick-spread ears of the deer caught the last sentence, and a frightened whisper ran along the ranks. "The Truce! Remember the Truce!"

"Peace there, peace!" gurgled Hathi the Wild Elephant. "The Truce holds, Bagheera. This is no time to talk of hunting."

"Who should know better than I?" Bagheera answered, rolling his yellow eyes upstream. "I am an eater of turtle—a fisher of frogs. *Ngaayah!* Would I could get good from chewing branches!"

"*We* wish so, very greatly," bleated a young fawn, who had only been born that spring, and did not at all like it. Wretched as the Jungle-People were, even Hathi could not help chuckling; while Mowgli, lying on his elbows in the warm water, laughed aloud, and beat up the foam with his feet.

"Well spoken, little bud-horn," Bagheera purred. "When the Truce ends that shall be remembered in thy favor," and he looked keenly through the darkness to make sure of recognizing the fawn again.

Gradually the talk spread up and down the drinking places. you could hear the scuffling, snorting pig asking for more room; the buffaloes grunting among themselves as they lurched out across the sandbars, and the deer telling pitiful stories of their long footsore searches in quest of food. Now and again they asked some question of the eaters of flesh across the river, but all the news was bad, and the roaring hot wind of the jungle came and went, between the rocks and the rattling branches, and scattered twigs and dust on the water.

"The menfolk too, they die beside their plows," said a young sambur. "I passed three between sunset and night. They lay still, and their bullocks with them. We also shall lie still in a little."

"The river has fallen since last night," said Baloo. "O Hathi, hast thou ever seen the like of this drought?"

"It will pass, it will pass," said Hathi, squirting water along his back and sides.

"We have one here that cannot endure long," said Baloo; and he looked towards the boy he loved.

"I?" said Mowgli indignantly, sitting up in the water. "I have no long fur to cover my bones, but—but if thy hide were pulled off, Baloo—"

Hathi shook all over at the idea, and Baloo said severely:

"Man-cub, that is not seemly to tell a Teacher of the Law. Never have I been seen without my hide."

"Nay, I meant no harm, Baloo; but only that thou art, as it were, like the coconut in the husk, and I am the same coconut all naked. Now that brown husk of thine—" Mowgli was sitting cross-legged, and explaining things with his forefinger in his usual way, when Bagheera put out a paddy paw and pulled him over backwards into the water.

"Worse and worse," said the Black Panther, as the boy rose spluttering. "First, Baloo is to be skinned and now he is a coconut. Be careful that he does not do what the ripe coconuts do."

"And what is that?" said Mowgli, off his guard for the minute, though that is one of the oldest catches in the jungle.

"Break thy head," said Bagheera quietly, pulling him under again.

"It is not good to make a jest of thy teacher," said the Bear, when Mowgli had been ducked for the third time.

"Not good! What would ye have? That naked thing running to and fro makes a monkey-jest of those who have once been good hunters, and pulls the best of us by the whiskers for sport." This was Shere Khan the Lame Tiger, limping down to the water. He waited a little to enjoy the sensation he made among the deer on the opposite bank; then he dropped his square, frilled head and began to lap, growling: "The jungle has become a whelping ground for naked cubs now. Look at me, man-cub!"

Mowgli looked—stared, rather—as insolently as he knew how, and in a minute Shere Khan turned away uneasily. "Man-cub this, and man-cub that," he rumbled, going on with his drink. "The cub is neither man nor cub, or he would have been afraid. Next season I shall have to get his leave for a drink. *Aurgh!*"

"That may come, too," said Bagheera, looking him steadily between the eyes. "That may come, too. . . . Faugh, Shere Khan! What new shame hast thou brought here?"

The Lame Tiger had dipped his chin and jowl in the water, and dark oily streaks were floating from it downstream.

"Man!" said Shere Khan coolly. "I killed an hour since." He went on purring and growling to himself.

The line of beasts shook and wavered to and fro, and a whisper went up that grew to a cry: "Man! Man! He has killed Man!" Then all looked towards Hathi the Wild Elephant, but he seemed not to hear. Hathi never does anything till the time comes, and that is one of the reasons why he lives so long.

"At such a season as this to kill Man! Was there no other game afoot?" said Bagheera scornfully, drawing himself out of the tainted water, and shaking each paw, cat-fashion, as he did so.

"I killed for choice—not for food." The horrified whisper began again, and Hathi's watchful little white eye cocked itself in Shere Khan's direction. "For choice," Shere Khan drawled. "Now come I to drink and make me clean again. Is there any to forbid?"

Bagheera's back began to curve like a bamboo in a high wind, but Hathi lifted up his trunk and spoke quietly.

"Thy kill was from choice?" he asked; and when Hathi asks a question it is best to answer.

"Even so. It was my right and my Night. Thou knowest, O Hathi" Shere Khan spoke almost courteously.

"Yea, I know," Hathi answered; and, after a little silence, "Hast thou drunk thy fill?"

"For tonight, yes."

"Go, then. The river is to drink, and not to defile. None but the Lame Tiger would have boasted of his right at this season when—when we suffer together—Man and Jungle-People alike. Clean or unclean, get to thy lair, Shere Khan!"

The last words rang out like silver trumpets, and Hathi's three sons rolled forward half a pace, though there was no need. Shere Khan slunk away, not daring to growl, for he knew—what everyone else knows—that when the last comes to the last Hathi is the Master of the Jungle.

"What is this right Shere Khan speaks of?" Mowgli whispered in Bagheera's ear. "To kill Man is *always* shameful. The Law says so.[4] And yet Hathi says—"

"Ask him. I do not know, Little Brother. Right or no right, if Hathi had not spoken I would have taught that lame butcher his lesson. To come to the Peace Rock fresh from a kill of Man—and to boast of it—is a jackal's trick. Besides, he tainted the good water."

Mowgli waited for a minute to pick up his courage, because no one cared to address Hathi directly, and then he cried: "What is Shere Khan's right, O Hathi?" Both banks echoed his words, for all the People of the Jungle are intensely curious, and they had just seen something that no one, except Baloo, who looked very thoughtful, seemed to understand.

"It is an old tale," said Hathi, "a tale older than the Jungle. Keep silence along the banks, and I will tell that tale."

There was a minute or two of pushing and shouldering among the pigs and the buffalo, and then the leaders of the herds grunted, one after another, "We wait," and Hathi strode forward till he was almost knee-deep in the pool by the Peace Rock. Lean and wrinkled and yellow-tusked though he was, he looked what the jungle held him to be—their master.

"Ye know, children," he began, "that of all things ye most fear Man." There was a mutter of agreement.

"This tale touches thee, Little Brother," said Bagheera to Mowgli.

"I? I am of the pack—a hunter of the Free People," Mowgli answered. "What have I to do with Man?"

"And ye do not know why ye fear Man?" Hathi went on. "This is the reason. In the beginning of the jungle, and none know when that was, we of the jungle walked together, having no fear of one another. In those days there was no drought, and leaves and flowers and fruit grew on the same tree, and we ate nothing at all except leaves and flowers and grass and fruit and bark."

---

4. To kill Man is always shameful. The Law says so.: The killing of human beings is shameful and forbidden because it brings men with guns into the jungle in revenge.

"I am glad I was not born in those days," said Bagheera. "Bark is only good to sharpen claws."

"And the Lord of the Jungle was Tha the First of the Elephants. He drew the jungle out of deep waters with his trunk, and where he made furrows in the ground with his tusks, there the rivers ran, and where he struck with his foot, there rose ponds of good water, and when he blew through his trunk— thus—the trees fell. That was the manner in which the jungle was made by Tha; and so the tale was told to me."

"It has not lost fat in the telling," Bagheera whispered, and Mowgli laughed behind his hand.

"In those days there was no corn or melons or pepper or sugarcane, nor were there any little huts such as ye have all seen; and the Jungle-People knew nothing of Man, but lived in the jungle together, making one people. But presently they began to dispute over their food, though there was grazing enough for all. They were lazy. Each wished to eat where he lay, as sometimes we may do now when the spring rains are good. Tha the First of the Elephants was busy making new jungles and leading the rivers in their beds. He could not walk everywhere, so he made the First of the Tigers the master and the judge of the jungle, to whom the Jungle-People should bring their disputes. In those days the First of the Tigers ate fruit and grass with the others. He was as large as I am, and he was very beautiful, in color all over like the blossom of the yellow creeper. There was never stripe nor bar upon his hide in those good days when the jungle was new. All the Jungle-People came before him without fear, and his word was the Law of the Jungle. We were then, remember ye, one people. Yet, upon a night, there was a dispute between two bucks—a grazing quarrel such as ye now try out with the head and the forefeet—and it is said that as the two spoke together before the First of the Tigers lying among the flowers, a buck pushed him with his horns, and the First of the Tigers forgot that he was the master and judge of the jungle, and, leaping upon that buck, broke his neck.

"Till that night never one of us had died, and the First of the Tigers, seeing what he had done, and being made foolish by the scent of the blood, ran away into the marshes of the north, and we of the jungle, left without a judge, fell to fighting among ourselves. Tha heard the noise of it and came back; and some of us said this and some of us said that, but he saw the dead buck among the flowers, and asked who had killed, and we of the jungle would not tell because the smell of the blood made us foolish, even as that same smell makes us foolish today. We ran to and fro in circles, capering and crying out and shaking our heads. So therefore Tha gave an order to the trees that hang low, and to the trailing creepers of the jungle, that they should mark the killer of the buck that he should know him again; and Tha said, 'Who will now be Master of the Jungle-People?' Then up leaped the Gray Ape who lives in the branches, and said, 'I will now be Master of the Jungle.' At this Tha laughed, and said, 'So be it,' and went away very angry.

"Children, ye know the Gray Ape. He was then as he is now. At the first he made a wise face for himself, but in a little while he began to scratch and to leap up and down, and when Tha returned he found the Gray Ape hanging, head down, from a bough, mocking those who stood below; and they mocked him again. And so there was no Law in the Jungle—only foolish talk and senseless words.

"Then Tha called us all together, and said: 'The first of your masters has brought Death into the Jungle, and the second Shame. Now it is time there was a Law, and a Law that ye may not break. Now ye shall know Fear, and when ye have found him ye shall know that he is your master, and the rest shall follow.' Then we of the jungle said, 'What is Fear?' And Tha said, 'Seek till ye find.' So we went up and down the jungle seeking for Fear, and presently the buffaloes—"

"Ugh!" said Mysa, the leader of the buffaloes, from their sand-bank.

"Yes, Mysa, it was the buffaloes. They came back with the news that in a cave in the jungle sat Fear, and that he had no hair, and went upon his hind legs. Then we of the jungle followed the herd till we came to that cave, and Fear stood at the mouth of it, and he was, as the buffaloes had said, hairless, and he walked upon his hind legs. When he saw us he cried out, and his voice filled us with the fear that we have now, and we ran away, tramping upon and tearing each other because we were afraid. That night, it was told to me, we of the jungle did not lie down together as used to be our custom, but each tribe drew off by itself—the pig with the pig, the deer with the deer; horn to horn, hoof to hoof—like keeping to like, and so lay shaking in the jungle.

"Only the First of the Tigers was not with us, for he was still hidden in the marshes of the North, and when word was brought to him of the Thing we had seen in the cave, he said: 'I will go to this Thing and break his neck.' So he ran all the night till he came to the cave, but the trees and the creepers on his path, remembering the order Tha had given, let down their branches and marked him as he ran, drawing their fingers across his back, his flank, his forehead, and his jowl. Wherever they touched him there was a mark and a stripe upon his yellow hide. *And those stripes do his children wear to this day!* When he came to the cave, Fear the Hairless One put out his hand and called him 'The Striped One that comes by night,' and the First of the Tigers was afraid of the Hairless One, and ran back to the swamps howling."

Mowgli chuckled quietly here, his chin in the water.

"So loud did he howl that Tha heard him and said, 'What is the sorrow?' And the First of the Tigers, lifting up his muzzle to the new-made sky, which is now so old, said: 'Give me back my power, O Tha. I am made ashamed before all the jungle, and I have run away from a Hairless One, and he has called me a shameful name.' 'And why?' said Tha. 'Because I am smeared with the mud of the marshes,' said the First of the Tigers. 'Swim, then, and roll on the wet grass, and if it be mud it will surely wash away,' said Tha; and the First of the Tigers swam, and rolled, and rolled, till the jungle ran round and round before his eyes, but not one little bar upon his hide was changed, and Tha, watching him, laughed. Then the First of the Tigers said, 'What have I done that this comes to me?' Tha said, 'Thou hast killed the buck, and thou hast let Death loose in the jungle, and with Death has come Fear, so that the People of the Jungle are afraid one of the other as thou art afraid of the Hairless One.' The First of the Tigers said, 'They will never fear me, for I knew them since the beginning.' Tha said, 'Go and see.' And the First of the Tigers ran to and fro, calling aloud to the deer and the pig and the sambur and the porcupine and all the Jungle-Peoples; but they all ran away from him who had been their Judge, because they were afraid.

"Then the First of the Tigers came back, his pride was broken in him, and, beating his head upon the ground, he tore up the earth with all his feet and said: 'Remember that I was once the Master of the Jungle! Do not forget me, O Tha. Let my children remember that I was once without shame or fear!" And Tha said: 'This much will I do, because thou and I together saw the jungle made. For one night of each year it shall be as it was before the buck was killed—for thee and for thy children. In that one night, if ye meet the Hairless One—and his name is Man—ye shall not be afraid of him, but he shall be afraid of you as though ye were judges of the jungle and masters of all things. Show him mercy in that night of his fear; for thou hast known what Fear is.'

"Then the First of the Tigers answered, 'I am content'; but when next he drank he saw the black stripes upon his flank and his side, and he remembered the name that the Hairless One had given him, and he was angry. For a year he lived in the marshes, waiting till Tha should keep his promise. And upon a night when the Jackal of the Moon (the Evening Star) stood clear of the jungle, he felt that his Night was upon him, and he went to that cave to meet the Hairless One. Then it happened as Tha promised, for the Hairless One fell down before him and lay along the ground, and the First of the Tigers struck him and broke his back, for he thought that there was but one such a Thing in the Jungle, and that he had killed Fear. Then, nosing above the kill, he heard Tha coming down from the woods of the North, and presently the voice of the First of the Elephants, which is the voice that we hear now—"

The thunder was rolling up and down the dry, scarred hills, but it brought no rain—only heat lightning that flickered behind the ridges—and Hathi went on: "*That* was the voice he heard, and it said: 'Is this thy mercy?' The First of the Tigers licked his lips and said: 'What matter? I have killed Fear.' And Tha said: 'O blind and foolish! Thou hast untied the feet of Death, and he will follow thy trail till thou diest. Thou hast taught Man to kill!'

"The First of the Tigers, standing stiffly to his kill, said 'He is as the buck was. There is no Fear. Now I will judge the Jungle-Peoples once more.'

"And Tha said: 'Never again shall the Jungle-Peoples come to thee. They shall never cross thy trail, nor sleep near thee, nor follow after thee, nor browse by thy lair. Only Fear shall follow thee, and with a blow that thou canst not see shall bid thee wait his pleasure. He shall make the ground to open under thy feet, and the creeper to twist about thy neck, and the tree trunks to grow together about thee higher than thou canst leap, and at the last he shall take thy hide to wrap his cubs when they are cold. Thou hast shown him no mercy, and none will he show thee.'

"The First of the Tigers was very bold, for his Night was still on him, and he said: 'The Promise of Tha is the Promise of Tha. He will not take away my Night?' And Tha said: 'Thy one Night is thine, as I have said, but there is a price to pay. Thou hast taught Man to kill, and he is no slow learner.'

"The First of the Tigers said: 'He is here under my foot. where his back is broken. Let the jungle know that I have killed Fear.'

"Then Tha laughed and said: 'Thou hast killed one of many, but thou thyself shalt tell the jungle—for thy Night is ended!'

"So the day came; and from the mouth of the cave went out another Hairless One, and he saw the kill in the path, and the First of the Tigers above it, and he took a pointed stick—"

"They throw a thing that cuts now," said Sahi, rustling down the bank; for Sahi was considered uncommonly good eating by the Gonds—they called him Ho-Igoo—and he knew something of the wicked little Gondee ax that whirls across a clearing like a dragonfly.

"It was a pointed stick, such as they set in the foot of a pit trap," said Hathi. "And throwing it, he struck the First of the Tigers deep in the flank. Thus it happened as Tha said, for the

First of the Tigers ran howling up and down the jungle till he tore out the stick, and all the jungle knew that the Hairless One could strike from far off, and they feared more than before. So it came about that the First of the Tigers taught the Hairless One to kill—and ye know what harm that has since done to all our peoples—through the noose, and the pitfall, and the hidden trap, and the flying stick, and the stinging fly that comes out of white smoke (Hathi meant the rifle), and the Red Flower that drives us into the open. Yet for one night in the year the Hairless One fears the Tiger, as Tha promised, and never has the Tiger given him cause to be less afraid. Where he finds him, there he kills him, remembering how the First of the Tigers was made ashamed. For the rest, Fear walks up and down the jungle by day and by night."

"Ahi! Aoo!" said the deer, thinking of what it all meant to them.

"And only when there is one great Fear over all, as there is now, can we of the jungle lay aside our little fears, and meet together in one place as we do now."

"For one night only does Man fear the Tiger?" said Mowgli.

"For one night only," said Hathi.

"But I—but we—but all the jungle knows that Shere Khan kills Man twice and thrice in a moon."

"Even so. *Then* he springs from behind and turns his head aside as he strikes, for he is full of fear. If Man looked at him he would run. But on his Night he goes openly down to the village. He walks between the houses and thrusts his head into the doorway, and the men fall on their faces, and there he does his kill. One kill in that Night."

"Oh!" said Mowgli to himself, rolling over in the water. *"Now* I see why Shere Khan bade me look at him. He got no good of it, for he could not hold his eyes steady, and—and I certainly did not fall down at his feet. But then I am not a man, being of the Free People."[5]

"Umm!" said Bagheera deep in his furry throat. "Does the Tiger know his Night?"

"Never till the Jackal of the Moon stands clear of the evening mist. Sometimes it falls in the dry summer and sometimes in the wet rains—this one Night of the Tiger. But for the First of the Tigers this would never have been, nor would any of us have known fear."

The deer grunted sorrowfully, and Bagheera's lips curled in a wicked smile. "Do men know this—tale?" said he.

"None know it except the tigers, and we, the elephants—the Children of Tha. Now ye by the pools have heard it, and I have spoken."

---

5. **The Free People:** The wolves of the Seeonee wolf pack.

Hathi dipped his trunk into the water as a sign that he did not wish to talk.

"But—but—but," said Mowgli, turning to Baloo, "why did not the First of the Tigers continue to eat grass and leaves and trees? He did but break the buck's neck. He did not *eat*. What led him to the hot meat?"

"The trees and the creepers marked him, Little Brother, and made him the striped thing that we see. Never again would he eat their fruit; but from that day he revenged himself upon the deer, and the others, the eaters of grass," said Baloo.

"Then *thou* knowest the tale. Heh? Why have I never heard?"

"Because the jungle is full of such tales. If I made a beginning there would never be an end to them. Let go my ear, Little Brother."

☑ Check Your Comprehension

1. What are the early signs in the story that a drought is coming?
2. What are the terms of the Water Truce? Who puts the truce into effect?
3. What shameful thing does Shere Khan the Lame Tiger do? Why does Hathi the Elephant say it is particularly shameful at this time?
4. Who are the three masters that Tha the First of the Elephants gives to the jungle?
5. What begins to happen after the First of the Tigers kills a human being?

◆ Critical Thinking

INTERPRET

1. Who is the leader of the jungle animals? Why do you think the author made this animal the leader? **[Draw Conclusions]**
2. What does the way the animals group themselves at the Peace Rock tell you about them? **[Infer]**
3. How does the Law of the Jungle organize and protect the animals? Give several examples. **[Analyze; Classify]**

EXTEND

4. All societies—small groups as well as large countries—have laws that keep things running smoothly. Think of a small group you belong to, such as your school community or your family. Explain several of its laws and how they help the group. **[Relate]**

Rudyard Kipling
Comparing and Connecting the Author's Works

◆ Literary Focus: Imagery

Both of the selections by Kipling that you have read are set in places that were probably unfamiliar to you. To make these locales come to life for readers who most likely knew little about them, Kipling frequently uses **imagery,** descriptive language that creates vivid word pictures.

Imagery is based on details that appeal to the various senses, such as sight, touch, and taste. When Kipling describes, at the beginning of *Captains Courageous,* the "big tin dish of juicy fragments of fish" that Harvey and Dan ate, he is appealing to the reader's senses of sight and taste (and maybe even smell). Often the words Kipling uses in creating an image are what make the image memorable. For example, when he says that the smoke of an ocean liner "smudged the blue [sky]," the word *smudged* creates a much stronger picture than *appeared in* or *darkened.*

Kipling uses a great deal of imagery in describing the drought in "How Fear Came." For example, in telling about the condition of the *mohwa* tree, he mentions how the "greeny, cream-colored, waxy blossoms" died on the tree, with only "a few bad-smelling petals" remaining. Kipling describes how, in the ravines, the "green growths . . . burned up to broken wires and curled films of dead stuff," and how "the bamboos withered, clanking when the hot winds blew." Imaginative readers can almost place themselves in the middle of this setting, experiencing the sights, smells, and sounds of the drought-stricken jungle firsthand.

1. Find the place in *Captains Courageous* where Kipling describes Harvey's struggle to catch the fish. List at least five vivid verbs that help bring this description to life.
2. Find five vivid adjectives in "How Fear Came" that describe how characters act and speak. Write a paragraph telling how these words affect the reader.

◆ Drawing Conclusions About Kipling's Work

One of the strengths of Kipling's work is his careful attention to detail. This quality can be seen in his descriptions, and it is also present in his character development. One critic has stated that "In sketching a personality he makes clear, almost in his first words, the peculiar traits of that person's character and temper." Another critic points out that this is true even of his animal characters, such as those in "How Fear Came." These characters are portrayed with "simplicity, humor, and dignity," and are given personalities that are "remarkably fitting."

Choose three characters from "How Fear Came." Examine how Kipling portrays them by completing the chart.

Character	Character Trait	Example From the Story
1.		
2.		
3.		

◆ Idea Bank

Writing

1. **Letter** Imagine that you are Harvey Cheyne in *Captains Courageous*. Write a letter describing how you caught the fish. Include details that tell what you did and how you felt.

2. **Description** Choose one of the animals from Hathi's story about how Fear came to the jungle. Write a description of the animal, using appropriate imagery to create a vivid word picture of it.

3. **News Article** Write a news article entitled "Severe Drought Hits Jungle." Begin by telling what happened, and where and when and how. (You may make up some of these details.) Complete the rest of the article using details from "How Fear Came." Don't forget to quote some of the characters in the story. **[Career Link]**

Speaking and Listening

4. **Dialogue** Suppose that Mowgli and Shere Khan meet alone in the forest. What would they say to each other? With a partner, write a dialogue and perform it for the class. Your dialogue should be at least one minute long. **[Performing Arts Link]**

Researching and Representing

5. **Diagram** Do library research on, and draw a diagram of, a fishing boat such as the *We're Here.* Label all important parts of the boat. **[Art Link]**

6. **Drought Conditions** How are drought conditions defined? Where is drought most likely to happen? What severe droughts have made an impact on the United States? Research these and other questions about drought and write a short report on the topic. **[Science Link, Social Studies Link]**

◆ Further Reading, Listening, and Viewing

- *Captains Courageous* (1897). A pampered young millionaire, rescued by a fishing boat crew after he has fallen overboard from an ocean liner, learns the value of hard work and self-discipline.

- *The Jungle Book* (1894). Raised by wolves, the young Indian boy Mowgli learns wisdom from such jungle animals as Bagheera the panther and Baloo the bear.

- Gloria Kamen: *Kipling: Storyteller of East and West* (1985). This easy-to-read biography covers many aspects of Kipling's life and writing.

- *The Jungle Book* (1994). Audiocassette. Hear more stories of Mowgli and his friends on this unabridged tape of Kipling's famous work.

- *Captains Courageous* (1937). Videocassette. This is the first film made from Kipling's novel; Spencer Tracy won an Oscar playing Harvey's rescuer Manuel.

- *Captains Courageous* (1996). Videocassette. This made-for-television version of the novel stars Robert Urich, Kenny Vadas, and Robert Wisden.

- *The Jungle Book.* DVD (1999), Videocassette (1991). This is an animated version of Kipling's story.

On the Web:

http://www.phschool.com/atschool/literature
Go to the student edition *Copper.* Proceed to Unit 3. Then, click Hot Links to find Web sites featuring Rudyard Kipling.

J ane Yolen In Depth

> "Folklore is the perfect second skin. From under its hide, we can see all the shimmering, shadowy uncertainties of the world."
>
> *—Jane Yolen*

JANE YOLEN has written more than two hundred books for children, young adults, and adults, as well as hundreds of short stories and poems. Her many fairy tales have earned her the title of "the Hans Christian Andersen of America," and she has been called "a modern equivalent of Aesop" for her fable-like stories. She moves easily from poetry, folk tales, and songs to fantasy and science fiction. Her books have been translated into fourteen languages, including Japanese, French, Spanish, Chinese, German, Swedish, Norwegian, Danish, Afrikaans, Xhosa, Portuguese, and Braille.

A House Full of Writers Yolen was born in 1939 in New York City, the daughter of writers. Her father wrote for newspapers. Her mother wrote short stories and created crossword puzzles and acrostics (a type of word puzzle) for magazines and newspapers. Many of her parents' friends were authors. Yolen says she "just assumed all grownups were writers," and she always knew that was what she would do.

School Days Yolen started writing at a very young age, producing poems and songs before she started going to school. "My first big success as a writer was in first grade where I wrote the class musical. It was all about vegetables and I played the chief carrot. We all ended up in a salad together!"

In junior high, she once wrote an essay about New York State manufacturing entirely in verse. Later, at Smith College, she wrote her final exam in American Intellectual History in rhyme. Her "very surprised" teacher gave her an A+.

A Professional Writer Yolen sold her first book the day she turned twenty-one; *Pirates in Petticoats* is a history book about women who were pirates. After that, she says, she was a book writer for good. She has since written over two hundred books and is usually working on several projects (up to ten) at a time.

In addition to being a writer, Yolen has been an editor, a teacher, a storyteller, a critic, and a songwriter, and she is active in several professional organizations. She has been on the Board of Directors of the Society of Children's Book Writers and Illustrators for more than twenty-five years. She was president of the Science Fiction Writers of America from 1986 to 1988. For twenty years, she ran a monthly writer's workshop for new authors of children's books.

Yolen writes every day and says, "Like an athlete or a dancer, I am uncomfortable—and even damaged—by a day away from my work."

To would-be authors, Yolen says, "I have three pieces of advice for young writers. One: read, read, read! You must read every day and try to read a wide range of books. Two: write, write, write! Keep a journal, write letters, anything to keep the 'writing muscles' in shape. Three: don't let anyone stop you from writing. Be persistent no matter what 'naysayers' or critical editors have to say about your writing."

Family Life Yolen has been married to Dr. David Stemple, a university professor, since 1962. Even though her husband is the chairman of a university computer science department, Yolen has been using a computer for her writing only since 1997. Before that, she wrote everything on a typewriter, revising and retyping frequently to polish her work.

Yolen and her husband have three grown children and three granddaughters. Most of her stories are written for children, and some of them are dedicated to family members. She gets some of her story ideas from her family members, but she says that ideas come from many sources, such as paintings, other books, eavesdropping on conversations, dreams, newspaper articles, song lyrics, and folk culture. She says that every time she gets an idea, she writes it down and files it in her Idea File. "There is no organization to it; all the ideas are jumbled together."

◆ Legends About Mermaids

In *The Mermaid's Three Wisdoms,* Melusina is very much like a human girl, right down to making a careless mistake. Mermaids in more traditional tales seem less like humans. Such legends and folklore about mermaids abound.

In these tales, mermaids (and mermen) are legendary creatures of the sea with the head and upper body of a human being and the tail of a fish. In European folklore, mermaids were sometimes called sirens. The seafolk in these tales were beings who, like fairies, could perform magic and reveal the future. They loved music and sang hauntingly. According to the stories, they lived long lives, but were quite inhuman.

Many folk tales tell about mermaids who could take on human form and marry human beings. In many of these stories, a man takes something belonging to the mermaid, such as a cap, belt, comb, or mirror. As long as the objects remain hidden, the mermaid stays with her human husband, but as soon as she finds the hidden object, she returns to the sea.

In some stories, a mermaid passing as a human will stay with her husband only as long as he promises to abide by certain conditions. If he breaks his promise, she leaves. In one story, once a month a mer-bride in disguise insists on being left alone the whole night through. After a few years, her husband's curiosity gets the best of him and he hides himself to spy on his wife. He is shocked to see her in her true form, lying in a tub of water with her fish tail hanging over the side. When she senses him watching her, she plunges into the sea, never to return.

In some stories, mermaids and mermen are dangerous to humans. If sailors see a mermaid on a voyage, it means that they will have a shipwreck. Sometimes mermaids in these tales lure humans to their death by drowning or hypnotizing them into living with them under the sea.

◆ Literary Works

Middle Grade Novels
- *The Transfigured Hart* (1975)
- *The Mermaid's Three Wisdoms* (1978)
- *Uncle Lemon's Spring* (1981)
- *Wizard's Hall* (1991)
- *Passager* (1996)
- *Merlin* (1997)

Young Adult Novels
- *The Gift of Sarah Barker* (1981)
- *Children of the Wolf* (1984)
- *The Dragon's Boy* (1990)

Short Stories
- *Milk and Honey* (1996)
- *Twelve Impossible Things Before Breakfast* (1997)
- *The Fairies' Ring* (1999)

Nonfiction
- *House/House* (1998)
- *The Mary Celeste: An Unsolved Mystery* (1999)

ane Yolen

from The Mermaid's Three Wisdoms

1. Have patience, like the sea.
2. Move with the rhythm of life around you.
3. Know that all things touch all others, as all life touches the sea.

"It is dolphin weather," thought the mermaid. "It is for chasing whales and telling tales and exploring far beneath the sea."

She touched the old tortoise on the shell. His shell was hard and crisscrossed with scars, and her touch as light as a droplet. Though the tortoise looked too ponderous for games, he loved to play. He had been waiting for her to beckon,[1] so he knew when her webbed fingers brushed his husk.

He followed her lead then. She swam with arms by her side, her tail making scant murmurs in the waves. He was close behind, graceful despite his bulk and age. He loved her as only a tortoise can, with patient distance, like a fond grandfather.

They were scarcely beyond the nearest reef when they were joined by a school of pout, then by a jetting squid.[2] The procession was solemn at first, one after another. But the pout could not be restrained, and soon it was a full game of tag.

The mermaid Melusina leaped high into the air, laughing soundlessly at the squid who remained water-bound. She arched her back, flipped over, and landed with a splash not a yard off the port bow of a blue-and-white dinghy.[3]

As she plunged downward, she realized with horror that she had been *seen*. There, in the dinghy, was a landgirl with hair caught up in two fat yellow braids. The girl was smiling.

Melusina hurried underwater to the water-carved grotto where she lived with her clan. She knew she must never be seen close up in the daylight by landfolk, but she had acted without thinking. It was her worst fault. Now, as each flash of her tail drove her deeper below the waves, she had only one hope. She swam frantically as if by putting the dinghy behind her, she could put the *seeing* behind her as well. She could feel her heart throbbing wildly in her breast and the pressure building up in her ears. She felt that she must hide away and forget what had been, make it exist no more.

---

1. beckon: Call or summon by silent gesture.
2. a school of pout . . . a jetting squid: Pout are a species of fish; squid swim by propelling themselves with jets of water.
3. dinghy (din´ gē): A small boat.

But she was too late. The tattletale pout had gone ahead to tell the news to the merfolk. By the time Melusina reached her home, most of the clan had already gathered. They swayed by the side of the reef and spoke with their hands. Ripples formed soundlessly at their fingertips and spread their agitation to the top of the sea. But not before Melusina had understood.

There was anger there—and fear. Anger at her playful, unthinking violation of the laws; fear of what that violation might mean for them all.

"She has done it. This time she has really done it." The speaker was a merrowman named Dylan. His squinty, little pigeyes narrowed to slits and his hands worked furiously. Anger was always communicated with the hands. The gentler emotions—shyness, happiness, and love—were usually formed in bubbles.

"The other things were annoyances. Hanging an anchor with a chain of pearls. Leaving a barnacled portrait on a boat's bottom. Mere pranks. Pranks that might have been done by the landfolk themselves—if they had the imagination. But this. *This!*"

His hands wrangled with one another in fury. Melusina was angry in return. Dylan, after all, was only newly come to their clan, having swum on a turbulent sea from Ireland in the last century. And everyone knew about the merrow and their tricks. What right had he to scold?

But Dylan's words were quickly picked up by the others. What could be worse than being sighted close up in this age of land-science when landfolk in shiny, black water clothes with rubber webbing on their feet and death sticks sometimes came hunting deep down in the sea, forcing the merfolk to seek refuge in the bottomless trenches and fault lines of the coast. In the old days, to be *seen* was a game played on unsuspecting sailors. But now all was changed. To be *unseen* was safe. To be *seen* was the deadliest threat to them all.

Hands moved ceaselessly: fear-waves rippled to the top with such vehemence, it surprised even the minnows. Never had such a commotion come from the merfolk within memory.

Melusina shivered as if caught in a sudden icy stream. What would they do to her? She had heard all their lectures before. The Three Wisdoms had been drummed into her since she was a tad:[4] have patience; move with life's rhythm; know that all lives touch. It was difficult enough to remain still and listen while each adult member of the clan in turn gave essentially the same scolding. That was the punishment she hated. Not the lectures; she could always fog her eyes and not see them. But the immobility. To have to remain quiet, hands at her side, resting on her stilled tail, while the current pulled and called its siren song.

---

4. tad: A young child, a tot, a tyke.

"It will be another boring lecture about the wisdoms and the rules," she said to her mother as she was led from the clan. She sighed. "That's it, isn't it?"

Her mother was silent, swimming by her side. "Melusina," she began suddenly, awkwardly turning to Melusina and stroking her daughter's hair, signing the name into the black strands. Then she fell silent again.

Melusina stood upright edgily on her wavering tail. Her mother, one of the gayest, most bubbling of the mermaids, was unusually still.

"Melusina," she began again, her fingers now on Melusina's arm, light filtering through the webbing that was already thickening with age. She stopped and turned away.

Melusina swam after, dove under, and came up before her mother. Then she began to reach out to touch her and stopped. Her mother was crying. Melusina knew about the tears of merfolk from the tales they told, but she had never actually seen any of them cry.

At the corner of her mother's eye a crystal formed and then dropped slowly, turning over and over in the lazy current, burying itself at last in the sand.

"Mother," Melusina said, her fingers hard on her mother's shoulder, bubbles and hand sign merging in one desperate cry. "Mother, why are you crying? What is going to happen to me?"

☑ Check Your Comprehension

1. With what friends is Melusina playing as the story begins?
2. Who sees Melusina at play, and how?
3. Why is Melusina's behavior dangerous to the merfolk?
4. How do the merfolk discover what Melusina has done?
5. How does Melusina respond to the merfolks' anger? How does her mother respond?

◆ Critical Thinking

INTERPRET

1. Do you think the landgirl in the dinghy will tell anyone what she has seen? Why or why not? [**Infer**]

2. Do you think that Melusina's action violates any or all of the Three Wisdoms? If so how? [**Analyze**]
3. Legends say that mermaids and mermen cannot talk. How has Yolen used this tradition in the story? [**Connect**]

EVALUATE

4. Do you think Melusina's people are right to be so angry, or should they forgive her? [**Make a Judgment**]
5. What punishment do you think would be appropriate for Melusina's crime? Why? [**Connect**]

APPLY

6. Write a moral for the story that would apply in everyday life. [**Relate**]

ane Yolen

from The Wizard of Washington Square

David walked slowly past the chess players in Washington Square Park. He scuffed his shoes on the pavement and kicked at a fallen leaf. He tried balancing on the low wire fence between the grass and the path, but he kept falling off. Each time he fell off, he looked around, hoping someone would notice him. But the old men kept playing chess and never looked up. Then David tried walking on the grass, right by the KEEP OFF THE GRASS sign. But the policeman on the beat had his back turned.

D. Dog, David's Scottish terrier, raced around him in circles, nipping at his heels.

"D.Dog," thought David unhappily, "is the only one in this whole park—in this whole city—who knows I exist. Who cares." And, feeling very sorry for himself, which was something David could do exceptionally well, he walked slowly toward the fountain in the middle of the square.

As he walked, he pulled a rubber ball out of his back pocket. It was shiny and unused. "Because," thought David, "I have no one to use it with—except D. Dog." He threw it into the air with ease. His throwing arm had been appreciated in Connecticut, where David had lived until a week ago with his mother and father and three sisters. But it was definitely *not* appreciated in New York—at least, as far as David could prove by the number of friends he had made in a week.

"Not one," David repeated in his thoughts, "not one person cares." And he threw the ball to D. Dog.

D. Dog jumped into the air, snapping at the ball with his teeth, but he missed. The ball hopped, skipped, and bounced over the low retaining wall, rolled past the wading children, and ended up in the center of the fountain. It stopped there, resting against the silver sprayer.

Now D. Dog, as David knew, was a brave dog under almost any circumstance. But water was definitely one of the almosts. As might be guessed from his matted coat, D. Dog was a coward when it came to water. He just stood at the edge of the fountain and barked.

"Well, now you've done it," said David angrily to D. Dog. "How can I get it out unless they turn off the fountain?" By *they*, David meant all the mysterious people who run the parks and clean the playgrounds and turn on the street lamps at dusk.

D. Dog barked again.

David ignored the question in that bark, which meant, "Why don't you fish out the silly ball yourself?" David felt exactly as D. Dog did on a number of subjects—water and dog biscuits, for example. They both hated the first and loved the second. Besides, David was fully dressed.

"Maybe one of the kids will bring it back," David thought. He thought that anyone under the age of ten was a kid. David was eleven, himself.

"I'll get it for you," came a voice from behind them.

David turned around. A girl just about his age was standing there in a bathing suit, carrying a large bath towel. Her black braids were caught up on top of her head, making her look old and wise. A girl, thought David. It would be! He had no use for silly gigglers. Always talking about adventures and never wanting them once they came.

"I'm Leilah and I'm going into the fountain anyway," the girl said. "I'm going to talk to the Wizard."

"Wizard?" David asked, puzzled. Wasn't that just like a girl to think of a story like that. "Wizards only happen in fairy tales. And only *girls* read fairy tales."

"A wizard," said Leilah calmly, "is just exactly who you believe he is."

"Well, who in the world told you that!" asked David.

"The Wizard," said Leilah.

"Of course," said David. "And I suppose this wizard lives in the fountain."

"Where else?" Leilah stepped over the low wall. She dropped her towel in a dry place. Then, avoiding the babies who played in the puddles, stepping over three pails and two shovels, Leilah walked into the middle of the fountain. She knocked three times on the silver sprayer and said something directly into the gurgling water. Or so it seemed to David.

The Leilah picked up the ball and came out. She deposited it in David's hand.

Shrugging his shoulders in thanks, David looked around to see if anyone was watching them. But no one seemed to care. David wiped the ball on his blue jeans and gave it to D. Dog to carry.

"I certainly didn't see any old wizard," said David. "In fact," he added, "I don't believe there is a wizard at all."

"That's what the Wizard said," Leilah put in. "He said you would never believe in him at all. But I convinced him that seeing is believing. So he promised to meet us by the west side of the Arch." She grinned. "I've never seen him myself," she added.

"Okay," said David nonchalantly. "I wasn't really doing much of anything else." He tried to act reluctant, but actually he was more curious than he would admit. Especially to a girl. Besides, this might be an interesting adventure. Without the girl, of course. She'd never go on with it. It wouldn't be a wizard. Not a real one. David knew they didn't exist. But it might be some interesting nutty old man. And with those thoughts turning over in his head, David joined Leilah in the short walk from the fountain to Washington Square Arch.

It took exactly sixty steps. David counted them out loud as they walked. That included a detour around a hopscotch game and a quick sidestep to avoid a bicycler. David counted out loud to impress Leilah with just how unimpressed he was with meeting her wizard.

When they reached the west side of the Arch, David looked straight up to the top. The Arch rose above them, some five stories high.

"My name is David," said David, squinting into the sun. He didn't want just to stand there saying nothing and it was the first thing that came into his mouth. David often talked that way, bypassing his mind and letting the thoughts just start at his lips. Also, he hated to look at people when he talked to them, which is why he was squinting at the sun. It wasn't very polite but David wasn't very polite either. His father said it came from being an only child. He wasn't, really. He had three older sisters. But since they were five, six, and seven years older, he had always been somewhat spoiled.

"My name is David," David repeated.

"I guessed," said Leilah.

"How did you guess?" David asked the question loudly enough for Leilah to hear, too softly for anyone else to overhear.

Leilah smiled. It was a great grin. "You *look* like a David!"

David thought that was a pretty stupid thing to say, so he ignored it. "My dog is named D. Dog."

"Why?" asked Leilah.

David shrugged. "Because that's his name."

"Oh."

"I mean, why are you named Leilah or why am I named David? It's just our names."

I'm named Leilah because it means 'dark as night.'" explained Leilah. She put her arm next to David's. "See, dark as night."

David was beginning to feel silly and started shifting from one leg to the other. "How do you hapen to know this wizard?" asked David. "Is he a relative? I've got a lot of crazy relatives too. I have one uncle who thinks he's a telephone pole. He's always having trouble with swallows sitting on his wires."

"Don't be silly," answered Leilah. "The Wizard isn't anybody's relative. He's a wizard. And I am the only *older* person who believes in him. Except you, of course."

"I don't believe in him," David protested hotly.

Leilah just grinned.

"You're crazy!" said David.

Just as he said that, four boys almost his age ran past, shouting. At first David thought they were calling Leilah to play with them. But then he realized they were shouting, "Crazy Leilah, Crazy Leilah," as they passed by. It made David feel both angry and sad. Angry that the boys would gang up on a silly girl—even if she *was* crazy. And sad because he was the one stuck with her.

"Don't pay any attention to them," said Leilah softly. "Two of them are my brothers. And they always call me Crazy Leilah. I made the mistake, you see, of trying to convince *them* about the Wizard. So they don't talk to me any more. But that's okay, because I don't talk to them either."

David didn't say anything.

"It's the babies who know about the Wizard," Leilah continued. "Only because they are real little, and don't talk very well, no one pays any attention to them. That's where most people make a mistake. Children know a lot, only they forget most of it when they grow older. My brothers are only nine and ten, but they've forgotten already. I just have an awful good memory and what my granny calls twenty-twenty ear-hear. You have probably just forgotten about wizards."

David didn't answer, but he doubted that very much. He never forgot anything, that he could remember. Then he said, "I've just moved to New York. That's why I haven't heard of your wizard."

Leilah thought about that for a moment. "Probably," she admitted. After a while she continued. "I listened very carefully to all the baby talk about the Wizard. And then I thought about it," she said. "If all the little ones really believed there was a wizard, well, they couldn't *all* be wrong. So I started to wade. No one over six wades in the fountain. They think they're too old. And no one over twelve does, either. That's the law. But I did. I waded and waded and waded half the summer. Until yesterday he gave himself away."

"How did he do that?" asked David. Even though he didn't believe in the Wizard, he had to admire a girl who had so much patience.

"He uses the silver sprayer like a submarine thing—oh, what do you call it?"

"A periscope," said David, scratching a scab on his arm and trying to pretend he was only half interested.

"A periscope," said Leilah.

"And?" David said, not wanting her to slow down the story.

"And then, yesterday, it moved about."

David looked puzzled. "What moved about?"

"The periscope," said Leilah. "And I said, 'I caught you!' And out of the periscope came a sad voice that said, 'So you have.'"

David scratched D. Dog's head. "If that's all true," David said at last, "where is the Wizard now? And what does he look like?"

"He's . . ." Leilah began, when the small black door in the side of the Arch began to open slowly. David stared as it moved inward and a cave darker than midnight appeared.

From behind the door, into the sunlight, stepped the weirdest little man David had ever seen. He had a long, silky white beard that was parted slightly off center and flowed down to his waist. He was no taller than a four-year-old. He wore a robe of inky blue and a pointed hat that sparkled with stars. The stars weren't just painted on and they weren't rhinestones, either. David could see that they moved, floated in the blue-black space of the hat as though it were a window opening on a night sky.

"How do you do," said the little man to David in a voice full of apologies. "I'm the Wizard of Washington Square."

David meant to say "How do you do" back, but he just stood there with his mouth open. Even D. Dog was too surprised to bark.

☑ Check Your Comprehension

1. Why is David feeling unhappy as the story begins?
2. How does David's ball end up in the middle of the fountain in Washington Square?
3. Who does David meet in Washington Square?
4. How does David's new friend find out about the wizard in Washington Square?
5. Where is the wizard hiding?

◆ Critical Thinking

INTERPRET

1. David feels very unhappy as the story begins. How does his behavior demonstrate this? **[Analyze]**
2. Why do you think the narrator says that feeling sorry for himself is something that David does exceptionally well? **[Infer]**

3. Judging from Leilah's personality as Yolen presents it, why do you think that Leilah believed the little children's stories when others would not? **[Draw Conclusions]**
4. What do you think Leilah means when she says, "A wizard is just exactly who you believe he is"? **[Speculate]**

EVALUATE

5. Do you agree that "children know a lot, only they forget most of it when they grow older"? Why or why not? **[Make a Judgment]**

APPLY

6. At the end of the story, David is speechless with surprise. When David recovers from the shock, what do you think he will do or say? **[Predict]**

ane Yolen

Names

from Passager: The Young Merlin Trilogy,
Book One

*Eight-year-old Merlin has been rescued by a kindly woodcutter
from a life in the forest, where the boy has lived like a wild animal.
In this passage, he awakes in a room in his rescuer's cottage.*

Untangling himself from the coverings, the boy crept to the
floor and looked around cautiously. The room was low-ceilinged,
heavily beamed. A grey stone hearth with a large fireplace was on
the north wall. A pair of heavy iron tongs hung from an iron hook
by the hearth. The fire that sat comfortably within the hearth
had glowing red ember eyes that stared wickedly at him.

Suddenly something leaped from the red coals and landed,
smoking, on the stones.

The boy jumped back onto the bed, amongst the tangle of covers, shaking.

The thing on the hearth exploded with a pop that split its
smooth skin, like a newborn chick coming out of an egg. A sweet,
tantalizing, familiar smell came from the thing. The boy watched
as it grew cool, lost its live look. When nothing further happened,
and even the red eyes of the fire seemed to sleep, he ran over,
plucked up the hazelnut from the stones, and peeled it. His
mouth remembered the hot, sweet, mealy taste even before he did.

He ran back to the bed and waited for something more to be
flung out to him from the fire. Nothing more came.

But the nut had rekindled his hunger, and with it, his curiosity. He raised his head and sniffed. Besides the smell of roasted
nut, beyond the heavy scent of the fire itself, was another, softer
smell. The first part of it was like dry grass. He looked over the
side of the bed and saw the rushes and verbena[1] on the floor.
That and the bed matting of heather supplied the grassy smell.
But there was something more.

He scrambled across the wide bed and looked over the side.
There, on a wooden tray, was food. Not mushrooms and berries,
not nuts and silvery fish. But *food*. He bent over the food, as if
guarding it, and looked around, his teeth bared.

He was alone.

He breathed in the smell of the warm loaf.

Bread, he thought. Then he spoke the name aloud.

"Bread!"

---

1. verbena (vǝr bē´ nǝ): A plant grown for its clusters of showy red, pink, or white
flowers.

He remembered how he had loved it. Loved it covered with something. A pale slab next to the loaf had little smell.

Butter. That was it.

"But-ter." He said it aloud and loved the sound of it. "But-ter." He put his face close to the butter and stuck out his tongue, licking across the surface of the pale slab. Then he took the bread and ripped off a piece, dragged it across the butter, leaving a strange, deep gouge.

"Bread and but-ter," he said, and stuffed the whole thing in his mouth. The words were mangled, mashed in his full mouth, but he suddenly understood them with such a sharp insight that he was forced to shout them. The words—along with the pieces of buttered bread—spat from his mouth. He laughed and on his hands and knees picked up the pieces and stuffed them back in his mouth again.

Then he sat down, cross-legged by the tray, and tore off more hunks of bread, smearing each piece with so much butter that soon his hands and elbows and even his bare stomach bore testimony to his greed.

At last he finished the bread and butter and licked the last crumbs from the tray and the floor around it.

There was a bowl of hot water the color of leaf mold on the tray as well. The bread had made him thirsty enough not to mind the color of the water and he bent over and lapped it up. He was surprised by the sweetness of the liquid and then knew—as suddenly as he had known the name of bread and butter—that it was not ordinary water. But he could not recall its name.

"Names," he whispered to himself, and named again all the things that had been given back to him, starting with the bread: "Bread. Butter. Horse. House. Hens. Jerkin. Coat." He liked the sound of these things and said the list of them again.

Then he added, but not aloud, *Master Robin, Mag, Nell.*

Patting his greasy stomach, he grunted happily. He could not remember being this warm and this full for a long time. Maybe not ever.

Going back to the bed, he lay down on it, but he did not close his eyes. Instead he stared for a moment at the low-beamed ceiling where bunches of dried herbs hung on iron hooks. He had not noticed them before.

What else had he not noticed?

He sat up. There were two windows, and the light shining through them reminded him suddenly of the sun through the interlacing of the trees in the forest. This light fell to the floor in strange, dusty patterns. He crawled off the bed and over to the light, where he tried to catch the motes in his hand. Each time he snatched at the dusty beams, they disappeared, and when he opened his hand again, it was empty.

Standing, he looked out the window at the fields and at the forest beyond. There was a strong wind blowing. The trees were bending toward the east. He thrust his head forward, to smell the wind, and was surprised by the glass.

Hard air, he thought at first before his mind recalled the word *window.* He tried to push open the glass, but he could not move it, so he left that window and tried the other. He went back and forth between them, leaving little marks on the glass.

Angry then, he went to the wooden door in the wall next to the hearth and shoved his shoulder against it. It would not open.

So then he knew another name. *Cell.* He was in a cell. The fields he could see through the glass and the tall familiar trees beyond were lost to him. He put his head back and howled.

From the other side of the door came a loud, answering howl. One. Then another.

Dogs!

He ran back to the bed and hid under the covers and shivered with fear. There were no trees for him to climb. It was the first time in a long while that he had felt hopeless. That he had felt fear.

Wrapped in the covers, in the warmth, he fell asleep and did not dream.

☑ Check Your Comprehension

1. What kind of room is the boy in?
2. What is the first thing the boy eats?
3. What are the first two words the boy remembers?
4. What does the boy see through the windows of his room?
5. What word comes to the boy when he realizes the door will not open?

◆ Critical Thinking

INTERPRET

1. In what ways does the boy's behavior suggest that he has not eaten in some time? [Interpret]
2. What evidence is there that someone wants the boy to be comfortable? [Draw Conclusions]

3. The boy drinks some hot water the color of leaf mold. What do you think this liquid is? What evidence makes you think so? [Infer]
4. Why do you think the boy is afraid of the dogs outside the door of the room? [Speculate]

EVALUATE

5. Do you think the author has done a good job of showing how the boy perceives his surroundings? Explain your answer. [Analyze]

APPLY

6. Judging from the evidence in the story, what kind of life does the boy seem to have been living? [Hypothesize]

Jane Yolen

The Golden Stair

I cut my hair last week;
all that long gold gone
in a single silent scissoring
after the king was buried.
5   My husband,
the new king,
wept when he saw it.
But he agreed
that with all I have to do—
10   the royal tea parties,
the ribbon-cuttings,
the hospital visits,
the endless trips
to factories,
15   football games,
day care centers—
a short bob is best.
It has been months
since he has noticed my hair.
20   The golden stair he called it.
It has been years since the tower.
Now that he is king
we cannot risk another fall,
at least until our sons are grown,
25   at least until
they have taken over the kingdom.

☑ Check Your Comprehension

1. What has the speaker in the poem done that makes her husband weep?
2. Why does the speaker think, "a short bob is best"?
3. What recent event has caused a great change in the lives of the speaker and her husband?
4. What kinds of activities occupy the speaker's time?
5. What does the speaker think will happen when her sons are grown?

◆ Critical Thinking

INTERPRET

1. In the fairy tale "Rapunzel," the heroine is locked in a tower and her suitor climbs to her rescue on "the golden stair" of her long hair. What evidence is there in the poem that the speaker is Rapunzel? [Infer]

2. What do you think the speaker means when she says that she and the king "cannot risk another fall?" [Speculate]
3. What does the poem tell you about the life of a queen? [Draw Conclusions]
4. What does the poem suggest about the speaker's expectations for the future? [Deduce]

EVALUATE

5. Do you think the speaker does a good job of being queen? Use evidence from the poem to support your answer. [Assess]

APPLY

6. Sometimes people must give up something important in order to accomplish something else of importance. Relate the sacrifice made by the queen to a sacrifice you have had to make to accomplish a goal. [Relate]

Jane Yolen
Comparing and Connecting the Author's Works

◆ Literary Focus: Fantasy

Realistic fiction consists of stories that might have happened. In **fantasy,** however, the stories contain elements not found in real life. Characters, settings, and events may contain elements of magic or the supernatural, or they may be set in the distant past or far future. Readers of fantasy accept certain unreal conditions about the story, such as when a boy finds a wizard living in a city park. Most successful fantasies, however, have some realistic elements—especially details about the characters' emotions and choices. In this way, as in fairy tales, fantasy fiction can teach the reader much about real life despite the unreal events in the stories.

Many types of literature contain elements of fantasy. Many stories read and told today feature talking animals and imaginary elves, dragons, and ghosts. The hero of *Gulliver's Travels* visits lands inhabited by tiny people, giants, and civilized horses. There are elements of fantasy in science fiction, with its exotic characters and alien worlds.

Jane Yolen's use of fantasy is one element that contributes to the popularity of her writing.

1. In the excerpt from *The Mermaid's Three Wisdoms,* name three details that could not happen in real life.
2. How do you know that *The Wizard of Washington Square* is a fantasy novel?

◆ Drawing Conclusions About Yolen's Work

One way to evaluate literature is to compare and contrast characters, settings, imagery, and themes—either within one selection or as features of different selections. A comparison of the Jane Yolen selections presented here illustrates the wide variety of her subject matter. In a brief essay, compare and contrast at least two of these selections, considering one or more of the following elements: setting, characters, imagery, and theme. Use a graphic organizer such as the one below to organize your ideas.

	Setting	Characters	Imagery	Theme
The Wizard of Washington Square				
The Mermaid's Three Wisdoms				
Names				
The Golden Stair				

◆ Idea Bank

Writing

1. **Letter** Write a letter to Yolen explaining what you liked or disliked about one of the excerpts from her fiction or about the poem "The Golden Stair." Mention specific details in your letter.
2. **Interview** Imagine that you are going to interview one of Yolen's characters. List five questions you would like to ask the character. Then write a dialogue of the interview, supplying the answers you believe the character would give. To write your dialogue, use details from the passages and your own insights into the characters.
3. **Journal Entry** Imagine that you have awakened in a world quite unlike this one. Write a journal entry describing what you see and hear and whom you meet in this place.

Speaking and Listening

4. **Oral Storytelling** In small groups, choose a story that contains elements of fantasy. It might be a fairy tale, science fiction you have read or seen recently, or stories you make up yourselves. Practice telling this tale as a group, experimenting with different ways to keep listeners interested. **[Performing Arts Link; Group Activity]**

5. **Panel Discussion** Yolen was once asked, "What makes a good book?" As part of her answer, she said "I like books that touch my head and my heart at the same time." With a small group, hold a panel discussion in which you discuss how well this statement applies to the stories by Jane Yolen that you have just read. Use details from the stories when you express your opinion. **[Group Activity]**

Researching and Representing

6. **Poster** If you have read Yolen's novel *The Devil's Arithmetic,* watch the 1999 film starring Kirsten Dunst and Brittany Murphy. If you have seen the film, now read the book. Design a poster comparing and contrasting the characters, setting, and plot as presented in the book and the film. **[Media Link; Social Studies Link; Art Link]**

◆ Further Reading, Listening, and Viewing

- *Jane Yolen: A Letter From Phoenix Farm* (Meet the Author Series) (1992). Autobiography.

- ReelLife Productions, *The Children's Writer: Jane Yolen* (1996). This is an interview with Yolen in her home in Massachusetts.

- Tim Podell Productions, *Good Conversations: A Talk with Jane Yolen* (1998). This is a video interview of Jane Yolen in Scotland, where she has a vacation home.

- *The Devil's Arithmetic* (1999). Based on Yolen's prize-winning Holocaust time-travel novel, this film starred Kirsten Dunst and was shot in Lithuania and Montreal.

- Jane Yolen: audiotape recording of the novel *Wizard's Hall,* narrated by Yolen.

On the Web:

http://www.phschool.com/atschool/literature
Go to the student edition *Copper.* Proceed to Unit 4. Then, click Hot Links to find web sites featuring Jane Yolen

Laurence Yep In Depth

"Look at the world from a different angle. This gives freshness to your writing and will make it vivid."

—*Laurence Yep*

LAURENCE YEP, American-born and of Chinese descent, has written dozens of books, many of which explore his Chinese ancestry and the challenges that Chinese Americans face. His works include historical and realistic fiction, science fiction, fantasy, and folktales.

A Difficult Childhood Laurence Yep was born in San Francisco on June 14, 1948. His father, a Chinese immigrant, owned a small grocery store in the neighborhood where the family lived. Yep found it difficult fitting in with playmates, who regarded him, he says, as the "all-purpose Asian" bad guy who had to die when they played war games.

Yep attended school in San Francisco's Chinatown, yet even there he felt out of place since he spoke no Chinese. As a child he read a lot of comic books, which, he says, prepared him for reading other books such as the *Oz* series by L. Frank Baum. "In the *Oz* books, kids are carried away to a faraway place with strange new customs," Yep explains. "They have to adjust to survive." Yep often felt the same way about his own life.

A Fledgling Writer In high school, Yep developed a love of science fiction, which seemed to reflect his own experiences. While a freshman at Marquette University in Wisconsin, he sold his first science-fiction short story. Later he graduated from the University of California, and then earned a Ph.D. in English Literature at the State University of New York in 1975.

While he was still in college, Yep was encouraged by an editor to write a science fiction novel for children. The result was *Sweetwater*, published in 1973, the story of Earth people who struggle to survive on a distant planet. The book reminded Yep of the struggles that Chinese immigrants underwent to survive in America. He decided to make Chinese American identity the topic of his next novel, *Dragonwings*.

A Literary Success Published in 1975, *Dragonwings* is perhaps Yep's most acclaimed work. It required years of painstaking research into his own heritage. "I had grown up as a child in the 1950's, so that my sense of reality was an American one," he says. "Now I had to grow up again, but this time in the 1900's, developing a Chinese sense of reality." His hard work paid off. *Dragonwings* was named a Newbery Honor Book and won more than a dozen other important awards.

A Focus on Heritage After *Dragonwings*, Yep continued to write novels—both realistic and historical— about Chinese culture and tradition. *Child of the Owl*, published in 1977, tells of a Chinese American girl who, like Yep, grew up in San Francisco in the 1960's. "You should always write about what you know," says Yep. "The things you have seen and the things you have thought and, above all, the things you have felt."

Among his most popular historical novels is *Dragon's Gate*, published in 1993. The story's narrator, Otter, joins his father and uncle, both heroes in their Chinese village, as they travel to America to help build the transcontinental railroad in 1867.

A Varied Output Yep has tackled other genres besides the novel. He retold twenty Chinese folktales in *The Rainbow*

People, and published an autobiography of his childhood in *The Lost Garden.* In addition, he has written picture books for young readers, children's plays, and novels for adults.

Yep sometimes writes on topics that are unrelated to Chinese themes. His mysteries include *The Mark Twain Murders* and *The Tom Sawyer Fires.* He also wrote *Shadow Lord,* a novel based on the characters from the television show *Star Trek.*

An Accomplished Career For three decades, Yep has won praise for his well-developed characters, his portrayals of Chinese American culture, and his themes of individual identity. With each book he writes, he imagines seeing things from a different point of view. "Most of my narratives are first person," he explains. "Whatever character I am, I look through the lens of the self."

To Yep, writing is a multisensory experience. "You should learn to use all your senses when you write," he says. "Don't use just visual information. Use smells and sounds, because that helps make the writing more vivid."

◆ The Chinese in California

When the California gold rush began in 1849, thousands of Chinese came to America in an effort to improve their lives. After the rush subsided in the mid-1850's, many Chinese remained in California to work. In the 1860's, even more Chinese were hired as laborers to help build the transcontinental railroad, which was completed in 1869.

By 1870, California's population had soared to half a million, and the next decade brought a depression with high unemployment. Many out-of-work whites blamed their joblessness on the Chinese,

who worked for very low wages. As a result, anti-Chinese riots took place in 1871 in Los Angeles, where a mob of thousands killed twenty Chinese men. In 1877, a riot in San Francisco resulted in the burning of many Chinese stores and businesses.

By the time Laurence Yep was growing up in San Francisco, the city had become much friendlier to Chinese Americans. Today, about 30,000 Chinese live in San Francisco's Chinatown area. Filled with shops, restaurants, and other businesses, it is one of the largest Chinese communities outside of Asia. By the year 2000, Chinese Americans accounted for eighteen percent of the city's population.

◆ Literary Works
Novels

- *Sweetwater* (1973)
- *Dragonwings* (1975)
- *Child of the Owl* (1977)
- *Sea Glass* (1979)
- *Liar, Liar* (1983)
- *The Serpents's Children* (1984)
- *Dragon Steel* (1985)
- *The Star Fisher* (1991)
- *Dragon's Gate* (1993)
- *Hiroshima* (1995)
- *The Case of the Lion Dance* (1999)
- *Dream Soul* (2000)

Folktales

- *The Rainbow People* (1989)
- *Tongues of Jade* (1991)
- *Tree of Dreams: Ten Tales from the Garden of Night* (1995)
- *Kahn's Daughter* (1997)

*L*aurence Yep

The Old Jar

All her life a certain woman never did what anyone wanted. She never asked for charity, but she wouldn't be cheated out of what was hers either.

However, she finally grew too old to work in the fields. She sold her furniture piece by piece until all she had was a pot and one jar full of rice. Although she ate only one meal a day, the rice slowly dwindled until she was down to her last two bowlfuls.

Then she broke the jar. She went to the corner and dug in the dirt and took out her savings. All she had was three *cash*—round coins with holes in the center.

"I was going to buy rice with this, but now I couldn't keep the mice out of the rice. I'll have to buy a new jar," she decided.

So she gathered up the rice from the floor. Carefully she went through the broken pieces of the jar until she had picked up every grain. Then she poured all the rice into a small pouch and put the three coins on top. Satisfied, she closed up the pouch and put it into her sleeve.

Leaving her little house, she took the road into town. She had never been to town before, so the two-story houses looked like mansions to her, and the mansions looked like the palaces of an emperor. From the restaurants came the most delicious aromas: dumplings and duck and a dozen other delicacies. The old woman was so hungry that she almost went in and bought something. But then she bit her lip. "Rice has always been good enough for you before this. It will be good enough now."

She marched straight into a shop that was crammed with every kind of good thing to buy—statues, vases, and all kinds of knickknacks.

A clerk threaded his way through the narrow aisles. He was dressed in a silk robe and a black vest and on his head was a black cap. "What do you want, you old beggar? This isn't a museum." He got ready to throw her out of the store.

The old woman took the pouch from her sleeve and shook it so that her three coins jingled. When the clerk heard the sound and saw how full the pouch was, he thought she was rich.

Instantly he was all smiles and bows. "Why does a rich woman like madam dress like a beggar? Let me show you some silks."

"Silk indeed!" the old woman snorted. "Cotton keeps out the sun and cold just as well."

"Now I know how madam got rich," the clerk sighed. "Well, how can I serve you?"

The old woman folded her hands in front of her. "I need a jar."

"We have some antique jars that go back to the Ming dynasty." The clerk led her over to some bright-blue vases around which dragons curled. "The clay came from the bed of a pure mountain stream, and the potter made only one vase a year."

The old woman pretended to look and shook her head. "That's a bit fancy for what I had in mind."

"Well, we have some excellent celadon vases done in the classic style of the Sung dynasty."[1] The clerk led her over to some green vases.

The old woman tapped a vase with her fingernail. "Not very sturdy."

The clerk showed her almost every vase in the shop, but each time the old woman found something wrong with it. Finally, they wound up in the dim rear of the store. "Madam," the clerk said, "you've seen every vase in the store."

The old woman saw a large, plain earthenware jar on the floor. It was only as high as her knee, but it was solidly made. "What's that?"

The clerk picked up the heavy reddish-brown jar in both arms and dusted off the dirt. "This? It's cracked at the top. We just use it to catch water from the leak in the roof. But it doesn't even do a good job of that. Water pours out of it like it's a well."

The old woman thought to herself, Crack or not, it would still keep out the mice. "It reminds me of something my grandmother had. How much?"

"A hundred cash," the clerk said.

The old woman glared up at the clerk. "Sentiment goes only so far. You just said it had a crack and—"

The clerk thrust the jar at the old woman. "Ten cash then."

However, the old woman did not take the jar. "Humph," she sniffed. "You're awful eager to get rid of it. Why should I take your garbage? It's a big jar and the road home is a long one."

"You've wasted enough of my time," the clerk snapped. "Just take it then. And good riddance to the jar and you."

The old woman laughed to herself, these townfolk don't know how to bargain. But out loud, she asked, "Aren't you going to pay me to take it off your hands?"

"I never met a more contrary[2] person in this whole city than you. Out, out, out!" the clerk shouted angrily.

Still chuckling to herself, the old woman set the jar on her head. Then she walked carefully down the narrow aisles because

---

1. **Sung dynasty** (soong dĭ nəs tē): The Sung dynasty ruled China from 960 to 1279 A.D.
2. **contrary:** Inclined to oppose or disagree stubbornly.

she didn't want to break one of the expensive antiques. She left the city. However, at each step the jar felt heavier and heavier, so she stopped by a farmer's house.

"You're a heavy thing," she said to the old jar. "You must have sides as thick as the city wall."

The farmer's wife was working in the garden. When she saw the jar, she called out to the road. "Hey, Auntie, that jar would be perfect for my garden. I'll just turn it upside down and use it as a stool."

"It's a jar for rice," the old woman panted, "not for people's bottoms."

"But what do you need with that heavy, broken old thing?" the wife asked. "I'll trade you a good jar, and it'll be small enough to carry."

The old woman wiped the sweat from her eyes. She was tempted, but then she thought to herself, It's old and unwanted—just like me. So out loud she said, "It deserves to end its days inside a nice house instead of outside in the mud. Get some pretty pink porcelain stools."

"Humph," the farmer's wife huffed, "you beat the whole district for contrariness."

"That I do," the old woman agreed.

Tipping the jar over on its round side, she began to roll the jar along. But even so, the jar began to grow as heavy. She felt as if she were trying to move a boulder. She began a soft little work chant, "Mice from the rice, mice from the rice, mice from the rice."

Halfway to the village, a cart driver came up behind her. "Is that a jar or a melon, Auntie?"

The old woman looked behind her and went on shoving the jar. "I'm not your auntie—thank Heaven. And this is a jar."

The cart driver slowed down when he reached her. "That's just the thing to break up for paving tiles. I'll give you a hundred cash for it."

The old woman was tempted. The jar kept growing heavier, and the road home was a long one. With the money she could buy not only a smaller jar but rice as well. But then she looked down at the big, cracked jar.

"It's outlived its usefulness—just like me. So I think I'll keep it." And she kept rolling the jar along.

"If they had a contrary contest, you'd take first place in a whole province[3] of contrary people," the driver said, and passed her on the road.

---

3. **province:** District of a country.

At least I'm improving, the old woman thought to herself and she began to shove her jar along. "Mice from the rice, mice from the rice."

As she neared the village, the jar seemed to become bigger and heavier with every step she took. To take her mind off the effort, she began to talk to the jar. "What put the crack in your top?" she puffed. "Where have you been and what's been done to you? Have you carried oils to India? Have you traveled into the desert in an army wagon? You served everybody faithfully, and when they were finished with you, they just threw you away until you wound up in that shop."

And as she struggled along, she kept thinking about the jar until it almost seemed like a friend. She went on pushing the jar until she reached her village. However, the road now wound back and forth up the steep side of the valley. And as she tried to shove the jar along the road, she found herself slipping. For every two steps she took, she slid back one.

The other villagers left the fields and the village to watch and laugh. "What have you got there, Auntie? A new room for your house?"

The old woman would have liked to shout back some insult, but she knew she had to save her breath for the struggle. Mice from the rice, mice from the rice, she murmured to herself.

All the time she worked to get the jar up to the village, her neighbors just stood around and made jokes.

Mice from the rice, mice from the rice, she said over and over.

The old woman tried to ignore them, but by the time she reached the gates, her face was a scarlet red—as much from embarrassment as from the physical effort.

As she rolled the jar down her alley and into her house, she grunted. "Well, this isn't any Indian palace, but it's home." She set it upright against a wall. "I hope you're worth all the work."

She took her three coins and reburied them in the corner. Then she poured the rice into the big jar. The white grains tinkled against the sides. She turned her pouch inside out so that she wouldn't waste one grain. "Just keep the mice from the rice."

She felt so exhausted that she lay down on her straw mat and went right to sleep.

The next day when she woke up, she realized what a fool she was. "I'll run out of rice soon, and then I'll have to use my three cash to buy more rice. When that runs out, I'll have to go out begging. All that work to bring the big jar home, and I won't have anything to put into it."

Grumbling to herself, she went to the jar for that day's bowl of rice. But when she scooped out a handful, she was surprised to see how much rice was still on the bottom. She put her hand in and scooped out another handful. Curious, she looked inside. There was as much rice as before.

She put back most of the rice and cooked her bowlful. Then she had another bowl for lunch and a third for dinner. But there were always the same two handfuls of rice at the bottom of the jar.

"It's magic." The old woman patted the jar wonderingly. "Thank you, friend."

She had three meals every day; and each time she peeked into the jar there were still two handfuls left at the bottom. The amount of rice never increased nor decreased. But she always took the precaution[4] of thanking the jar.

But in a village your neighbors know almost everything about you—or if they don't yet, they soon will. They could see the smoke when the old woman cooked her meals. They knew she was poor and yet she ate three times a day. They began to spy on the old woman, and so one day a neighbor overheard her thanking the magic jar.

In no time, word of the magical jar spread throughout the village. People crowded into her little alley and pounded at her door. When she opened it, they demanded to see the magic jar, but the old woman refused. "You saw it the other day when I was rolling it up the path."

One neighbor wriggled his way into the front. "I'll give you ten pieces of silver for the jar."

A second neighbor shoved the first one out of her way. "He's cheap. I'll give you a hundred pieces of gold."

A third neighbor elbowed his way in front of the others. "I won't cheat you like them. We'll be partners. You provide the jar and I'll provide the gold to put into it. We'll split fifty-fifty."

The old woman shrugged. "What do I need with money now that the jar gives me food? Enough is enough. I have what I want."

"But you could be rich," the neighbor protested. "You're the contrariest woman in the whole country!"

The old woman just eyed all her greedy neighbors. "You all laughed at the jar. But magic is not mocked." She added, "And neither am I."

And she slammed the door shut—right in all their faces.

---

4. **precaution:** An action taken beforehand to avoid danger.

from The Pearl Apartments

Years ago I wrote a book called *Child of the Owl.* It was about a little girl, Casey Young, who had grown up outside of San Francisco. When something happened to her father, she had to move into Chinatown to live with her grandmother. For the first time in her life, she had to think of herself as Chinese.

The title was symbolic of her situation—and of mine and of most Chinese Americans. In Western folklore, owls are usually wise animals. In Chinese folklore, on the other hand, owls are nasty animals. They are disrespectful to their parents and will even kick them out of the nest.

For the same act—such as reading comic books—Casey can feel just as wise as a Western owl and just as disrespectful as a Chinese one. In the late sixties, when I wore my hair long like many other college students, I knew my own grandmother, Marie Lee, would have liked me to cut it short. Again, like so many other students at the time, I wasn't about to give in to convention.[1]

To do my grandmother credit, she did not scold me or throw a tantrum the way many other grandmothers might have. Her solution was unique like much of what she did. As I sat talking with her in her little studio apartment, she would reach over abruptly and unannounced to brush the hair out of my eyes as a hint that it was time to visit the barber. I would try my best to ignore the gesture and go on talking.

I knew that she accepted her strange, American-born grandson—far better than I accepted my China-born grandmother. In many ways, she came to embody what I came to consider my "Chineseness"—that foreign, unassimilable,[2] independent core. Going into Chinatown once a week made me learn about a part of myself that I sometimes wanted to ignore. For a while, she even lived with us while she was recuperating from an operation on her eyes so that for a short time I had to think about my "Chineseness" each day.

Like Casey, I grew up outside of Chinatown. At the end of World War II, my father had bought a small corner grocery and moved into an apartment above the store.

It was an older building so that it even came with a name: the Pearl Apartments. Officially, the Pearl Apartments sat at 1205 Pierce Street. The neighborhood was mixed—not only in people

---

1. convention: Customary practice, rule, or tradition.
2. unassimilible (un ə sim′ əl ə bəl): Not able to be absorbed or incorporated into a main group.

but in architectural styles. The houses were all different—Victorians and stucco postwar houses squatting side by side. However, the Pearl Apartments had their own colorful history. Initially the building had consisted of the store and two sets of apartments. But a second building of three apartments had been jacked up from another location and slowly and painfully brought to the corner where it was joined to the first building by a set of stairs.*

It wasn't a Victorian; but it pretended to be. The bay windows had panes of glass that curved outward—which were always a nuisance for my father to replace when I broke one of them. There was ornate molding on the walls that was great for catching dust; and chandeliers—cheap ones—hung from the ceiling by long chains through which the electric cord wound, its old insulation looking as fuzzy as a stretched-out caterpillar. I always thought of chandeliers as the corpses of fat spiders, their legs kicking up from their round, upturned bodies. They were great earthquake indicators, swaying whenever a tremor hit. However, they were handiest at New Year's because you could throw serpentines, coiled ribbons of paper, over them until there seemed to be a small tree of softly colored ribbons winding upward from the center of the living room floor.

The apartments each had certain features that had been modern once but were now old-fashioned. In the hallway was a little shelf and niche for the old type of phone—the kind that stands up like a candlestick—and each living room had a Murphy bed.

A Murphy bed swung up inside a closet on powerful springs. When the bed was up, it looked like a closet door. In our own apartment, my father had removed the Murphy bed, building instead a homemade captain's bed with drawers that pulled out underneath. The sides curved and over the edge he had put a strip of metal; and it is to that bed I often return in my dreams though I am sleeping some place far different now.

After scrimping and saving, my parents bought the Pearl Apartments, and my father decided to make some small improvements in the other residences. When my father was taking out the Murphy bed from the upstairs unit, one of the springs uncoiled and the sharp tip pierced his cheek. My father combined a steelworker's toughness with the impishness of a small boy, so until the wound healed, he liked to shock people by drinking some water and letting it dribble through the hole in his cheek.

The one drawback to the Pearl Apartments was that there was no heating of any kind. My parents heated one end of the apartment by leaving the door down on the gas stove. The living room

---

* When it was finally torn down to make room for the garage, it took two wrecking balls because it had been so sturdily built.

fireplace had to warm the other half; and one of my chores as a child was chopping up the old wooden fruit crates to use as firewood.

Often, I would lie there in the bed my father had made, snuggled under the many quilts for warmth, watching the shadows of the chandelier dance back and forth over the high ceiling as I slowly fell asleep.

Three flights up from the street was a metal door with a metal latch like some castle gate. Sometimes it stuck; but if you put your shoulder to it and shoved, it would open onto our windy, sun-washed roof.

It was up there my father had also built a sandbox for me, bringing the sand one armload at a time up the three flights of stairs. There I could play under the clotheslines that crossed overhead, their shadows dividing the rooftop into long, even strips. (Sometimes there would be a long line of purple silk boxer shorts handmade by our tenant Mrs. Pauloff for her son. They would flap stiffly like flags.)

Playing in the sandbox was the closest thing to flying. Standing in the sand, I would be high above all the other buildings, as if I were on a sea filled with rafts floating upward into the sky. There was usually a breeze blowing over the rooftop so that I had the illusion I was moving; and if it was a particularly windy day, the clouds would race overhead like huge-hulled, tall-masted yachts, increasing the illusion. Sometimes when I was older, I would dare to go near the edge feeling the electric tingle spread from my toes up my legs as I looked down from the dizzying heights.

It was a wonder that we never flew kites from the rooftop because we flew kites at almost every other windy spot in San Francisco. The Marina Green on the northern edge of San Francisco next to the bay was a favorite place because there were no trees. My father was the master of the winds. As he was fond of saying, a good kite flier shouldn't have to run to get a kite up. With his feet planted firmly in the grass and with just a puff of a breeze, he could coax a kite up high into the sky. In his garden, opposite the fuchsia plants, my father kept the long bamboo poles from which he fashioned kites whenever he had spare time. Since he usually made kites in the shape of butterflies, they were like pets that he teased upward with twitches and tugs of the string. (I usually had to run; and sometimes even that didn't work.)

My father made his kites from scratch, beginning with a section of bamboo that he would cut in half lengthwise with a small hand ax. He would repeat this process until he had long, slender rods that would bend where the now invisible joints had been.

From these rods, he would fashion the outline of a butterfly, complete with wings and body and antennae.

To hold the rods together, my father used his own paste, which he made from ground-up rice and water, and strips of special rice paper that he purchased in a Chinatown stationery store where it lay in a dusty drawer. With larger sheets, he would cover the butterfly itself and then paint it with brightly colored poster paints.

Though I only saw him make butterfly kites, he also created other kites. The sparrow kites interested me the most since they were used for duels. In those battles, the kite string was dipped first into a bowl of rice paste and then into ground glass. The idea was to cut the string of your opponent and send his kite (in my father's time, it would have been men handling the sparrow kites) soaring free up into the clouds. That seems like a kinder and more poetic end than most losers receive—in fact, it hardly seems like a defeat at all except that money might be changing hands if betting is involved.

My father, Yep Gim Lew, or Thomas, was born in China in 1914 in the district of Toisan in the province of Kwangtung. Toisan is a small county to the southwest of the ports of Canton and Hong Kong. Though there are some two million people living in the Toisan district today, there are an estimated four million Toisanese or those of Toisanese ancestry living abroad.

Even though my father was born in China, he had papers that said he was an American citizen because he was the son of a citizen. Immigration laws made it almost impossible for a Chinese to obtain the citizenship that was available to other groups so I'm not sure how his father became a citizen. It is possible that his father was helped by his Irish business partner.

When my father was ten, his father brought him to America. His father's first business had been a restaurant in El Paso. Many Chinese came over in 1849 to work in the gold fields of California and in the 1860's they helped build a railroad across the steep, snowy Sierras, linking the West Coast with the East Coast for the first time by rail. After the transcontinental railroad was built, Chinese then worked on the trunk lines that led to Los Angeles and from there across the Southwest. Some of the men would later settle in those areas. Or, since it was so hard to enter directly into America, there were many Chinese who went to Mexico first and later slipped over the border into America. In any case, I suspect, though I cannot say for sure, that my grandfather had some relatives who lived there. Seeking an opportunity, my grandfather tried to settle in Texas; but it was too hot, according to my father, so he eventually wound up in San Francisco.

☑ Check Your Comprehension

1. In "The Old Jar," how does the old woman plan to use the jar she acquires?

2. Why is the woman unwilling to trade or sell the jar as she travels home?

3. How does the jar turn out to be a magical blessing for the woman?

4. In "The Pearl Apartments," why does the narrator feel uncomfortable with his grandmother?

5. How is the design of the Pearl Apartments similar to the make-up of its residents?

6. What are the main personality traits of Yep's father, as described by the narrator?

◆ Critical Thinking

INTERPRET

1. In "The Old Jar," what does the old woman mean when she tells her neighbors, "Magic is not mocked. And neither am I"? **[Interpret]**

2. In "The Pearl Apartments," why does the narrator see himself as a "child of the owl"? **[Analyze]**

COMPARE LITERARY WORKS

3. Both "The Old Jar" and "The Pearl Apartments" portray strong Chinese personalities—the old woman and Yep's father. Compare these two figures. Is there any similarity in their attitudes and behaviors? **[Compare]**

APPLY

4. "The Old Jar" emphasizes the old woman's stubbornness. Explain whether or not you think stubbornness is a good character trait to possess. Give reasons to support your opinion. **[Evaluate]**

from The Great Silkie

from Sweetwater

The galaxy is an awfully big place so I don't expect you to know about my home world, Harmony; but my ancestors came from Earth. If you go out some cold winter night and look for your constellation Virgo, you might be able to see the tiny pin-prick of light on her left side where her heart ought to be. That's my star, but even if you strained your eyes, you wouldn't be able to see the fifth planet around that star, which is my world.

It's a hard life on a star colony and most humans are too busy trying to survive even to learn where Earth is in the night sky, but that was one of the first things Pa taught me. Pa said that at least his son would remember Earth. He said that in each generation one of us must be able to tell the others about the old Earth ways, and I guess he was right.

But I think it's just as important that we don't forget our city, Old Sion, now that we're about to leave it, and I think it's even more important that we remember how we lost it. Pa says that no one person's responsible, but I figure Pa's just being nice. If I hadn't wanted to play the flute or go mixing with aliens, we wouldn't have had so much trouble. Anyway, I'm going to try to write about what happened during the last few years. And maybe, just maybe, I can save something of what we're losing— for the generations to come on Harmony and for you people back on Earth who don't know what it's like to live on a star colony.

The first thing you ought to know is that our colony here was split into two groups, the ones we call the Mainlanders and my own group, the Silkies. You see, the original colony built a city on what they thought was the coast; but Harmony has a fifty-year cycle of tides and they built Old Sion during the lowest time of the tides. When the sea rose, half submerging the city, a lot of the colonists gave up and moved to the mountain ranges twenty miles to the east where they *knew* it would be dry and built a new city, called New Sion.

But my ancestors stayed on in the city, learning to adjust to the new kind of life, traveling about in the flooded streets in boats. They took so well to the half-flooded city that the other colonists began to call my ancestors Silkies. The Mainlanders meant it as an insult because the mythical Silkies were so ugly on the land,[1] but my ancestors adopted the name with pride because the Silkies were beautiful in their own mysterious sea.

---

1. **the mythical Silkies were so ugly on the land:** Silkies, or selchies, are creatures who take the form of humans on land, but of seals in the sea.

From the very day the colony was founded, my ancestors had never gotten along with the other colonists. My ancestors had been the crews of the starships that had brought the colonists here, and they had never intended to stay; but when their starships broke down, they were stranded. Because of their different background and because of pride, they stayed apart from the other colonists.

And these lonely men fell in love with a city no one else wanted. Each family of Silkies took a house, salvaging more than enough to make their homes comfortable. A lot of the former residents just left things—like chairs and tables—intending to come back for them later and then forgetting about them. Ma got all her pots when Pa found them in a waterproof bag left in someone's flooded basement.

For light they learned to use luminescent mosses, and they took their food from the sea. They turned the flooded alleys into sea gardens by damming them with rubble and then stocking each alley with oysters, clams, and seaweed. (Of course, the oysters and clams and seaweed weren't exactly like the kinds you find on Earth, but we gave Earth names to their counterparts on Harmony.) All the animals grew fat in the slack water of the gardens, but it was a lot of work keeping them inside the dams and keeping the predators out. Households used the food from the sea gardens for a change in their diet; but their main food came from the annual fish run.

Every fall, schools of Sunfish swam from the sea up a river to spawn deep in the interior of the mainland. That was really something to see, too, when the sea turned to gold. It was like the sea was trying to make up for all the hard months by just pouring food into your basements. But don't let me give you the wrong idea. That fish run meant a lot of hard work, so that when we relaxed we really relaxed.

For two weeks of each winter, the whole Commune would do nothing but eat and drink and sing and dance—everyone, that is, except my father. Ever since my father was elected Captain, he hated to be seen wasting time. Though my parents liked music, Pa didn't think they ought to show it in public. Ma's got a beautiful voice but Pa and my litter sister Caley and I were about the only ones who got to hear her. During the winter fête,[2] Pa always made us sit on the side, backs straight against the wall, smiling solemnly while the other folks had fun. It was like Pa didn't want the other Silkies to think he was frivolous.[3] I asked him one time about Great-Great-Grandpa Lamech, who was not only the first Captain of the Silkies but also a great fiddler. All Pa said was that things were different in those days.

---

2. **fête** (fāt): Celebration; party.
3. **frivolous** (friv´ ə les): Interested in things of little importance; trivial.

The only time I saw Pa dance in public was at the winter fête two years ago, when I was eleven. And the marvelous sight of Pa dancing was what got me so interested in music and led to all our trouble. A master fiddler by the name of Jubal Hatcher came to that fête, and his bow work could have matched Great-Great-Grandpa's.

Jubal Hatcher was an old friend of Pa's. They had hunted Hydra together when they were both boys. Jubal ran a resort down south in the marshlands for fishermen and fleet mechanics. During the winter when things were slack, he and his wife Poppy, a little plump partridge of a woman, came up north in their boat, playing music all around the country just for the fun of it.

And the first thing Jubal did when he came to Old Sion was to ask us for a drink of "the only cool, sweet, fresh water for a hundred miles." My family, thanks to Great-Great-Grandpa Lamech, had the only fresh water in Old Sion. The others had to catch rainwater in tanks or distill seawater in evaporating pans. In the very early years of the colony, when the sea began to rise and the colony tried to hold it back with dikes, Great-Great-Grandpa had the foresight to sink a pump down to the water table underneath the house.

Then when the other four families in the house moved out, Great-Great-Grandpa made an imitation well after a story he had read about Earth. He disconnected the pipes to the fourth and fifth floors and then used stones and mortar to form the round walls of a well. Later generations had reinforced the floor beneath the "well" with steel beams during the dry years. It was natural for visitors like Jubal to ask for our fresh water.

Pa had me fetch a bucket of water. The bucket was made of cedar and bought special from the mainland. Jubal dipped a gourd into it and brought the gourd up to his lips while the breeze from the window gently blew his soft gray hair all around like a silver flame. His Adam's apple worked up and down as he swallowed. "Now that is perfection," he said, and gave his wife the gourd.

Then he raised his fiddle and shouted out, "Gonna play 'Sweetwater,' neighbors." It was an old hymn from Earth and Pa's favorite.

He began to tap his boot, the high heel clicking nicely on the concrete roof of the old abandoned warehouse we used for the fête. He settled the fiddle easily between chin and shoulder and he brought the bow down caressingly on the strings and began to play.

Jubal's cheek and lip kind of twitched over the fiddle and his beard jerked up and down. There was Ma nodding her head slowly so that her hair bounced about like a sea. And there was Caley trying to squirm out of Ma's arms to get closer. And there was Pa himself sitting quiet in his chair, his eyes gleaming, his hand softly slapping the table. It put him into just the right mood.

When Jubal started the next song, Pa couldn't take it anymore, so he got up out of his chair. Pa was a big man with a solid, square face and long black hair. In his Captain's uniform he looked even stronger and more impressive. On a public occasion like the fête he usually seemed as if he were just about to be inspected by an admiral, but that night he rolled up the sleeves of his Captain's tunic so that the scars from his Hydra-hunting days showed, and he unbuttoned his collar. Then he turned to Ma with a grin.

Ma was a tall woman with a solid frame, but she could move real light and easy. And when she smiled, she could be as pretty as any girl in the Commune. She was smiling now. She did love music, though out of love for Pa she rarely let it show in public. But now she could forget about being the Captain's wife because the Captain himself had forgotten.

She let Caley slide off her lap and she stood up, gracefully brushing the wrinkles from her formal dress. She and Pa looked fifteen years younger—as fresh as they must have the day they began courting. She let Pa take her in his arms and they danced out there on the floor—No, not danced, they floated out there with hardly any effort. I got to see what Pa must have been like before he became the Captain and had to start taking life so seriously.

And I wanted that music so bad. You might call it hillbilly music and even a mainland foolishness, but that's all right; there was never any kind of music that wouldn't catch you as long as it was done right before you. Music is music, I don't care what type, be it free jazz or a child's off-key singing. It's music if it reaches inside and makes you want to keep time right along from the tapping of your toes to the nodding of your head because you want to be part of that rhythm.

After that night when I saw what music could do, there was nothing for me to do but whittle out a flute. I just had to be a musician.

*L*aurence Yep

from Dragon's Gate

By the summer of 1865, the North has finally defeated the South in the Civil War, and America works for even greater union. During the war, Abraham Lincoln set in motion a plan to build a transcontinental railroad that will effectively join the western half of America to the eastern half. In 1863, one railroad, the Union Pacific, has begun building westward from Omaha. In that same year, the Central Pacific has started eastward from California. However, in two years, it has only built thirty-one miles of track. By February 1865, the railroad is so desperate that it has begun experimenting with using Chinese crews.

At the same time, in China, the boy emperor has survived two more challenges to the rule of his people, the Manchus—a barbarian tribe that has controlled the kingdom for some two hundred years. His generals have crushed two different rebellions. One is the Taiping, or Great Peace, revolt, which has devastated wide areas of China. The other is the Red Turban uprising in southern China in Kwangtung Province, in which over a million people have died during the Manchu suppression.

Seeking revenge for the Manchu reprisals, the local clans in turn have started a genocidal[1] war against an ethnic group known as the Strangers because it is believed the Strangers have provided information and aid to the Manchus. It is estimated that half of the three hundred thousand Strangers have died.

As a result of the turmoil, Chinese men have left Kwangtung in ever-increasing numbers for America.

One

The sixth month of the third year of
the era all in order, or July 1865.
Three Willows Village, Toishan County,
Kwangtung Province, China.

"They're coming!" the servant cried from the pass.

"They're coming!" The cry traveled up the valley faster than the stream.

"They're coming!" the sentry announced from the watchtower.

All over the village of Three Willows, doors and gates slammed as people tumbled into the street. It was a clear day between summer storms, and the sky was a bright blue.

In the schoolroom, I could hear the slap of their feet on the dirt. Though I was only fourteen, I sat in the back of the school-

---

1. **genocidal** (jen ə sīd´ əl): Intended to destroy a whole national or ethnic group.

room with the older boys because I was ahead of my level. I rose eagerly from the school bench.

At the front, Uncle Blacky, our teacher, was lecturing about some ancient words that might occur in the government exams. The exams would qualify you for office.

He was a slender, middle-aged man in a scholar's robes. There were small black marks on his lips, for he had an absentminded habit of licking his brushes to a point. "Yes, Otter."

"Master, may I be excused?" I asked. "I think my father and uncle have arrived."

"Of course." What else was he going to say? Most of the subscription for his new school had come from my own family.

When I got ready to run excitedly, he looked at me sternly. "With dignity," he reminded me. That look was enough to intimidate[2] my other classmates, but not me.

"I'm sorry, master." I started to walk away.

Behind me, I heard Stumpy laugh. He was the sixteen-year-old son of one of our tenants, and he was always trying to play the bully or to mock me when he thought it was safe.

When he wasn't playing one of his pranks, I almost felt sorry for him. His father, Stony, often needed Stumpy in the fields. As a result, Stumpy's schooling was sporadic;[3] but he was sharp enough to make up for the lost time.

Immediately, Uncle Blacky strode down the aisle and grabbed Stumpy's frayed collar. "You should thank Heaven for people like Foxfire and Squeaky. Without their sacrifices, we'd all be starving."

As he lifted Stumpy to his feet, his son, Cricket, brought him his bamboo rod. A young man in his twenties, Cricket acted as his father's assistant while he pretended to study for the government exams.

Uncle Blacky shook the boy as though he were a rat. "I'll teach you some manners, you little pig. Hold out your hand."

Reluctantly, Stumpy held out his hand, palm upward. There were two groups of boys in our school: those whose fathers had stayed here and those whose fathers had gone overseas to *America* to become guests of the Land of the Golden Mountain, as everyone called it. The difference was often between the poor and the rich. Since the guests paid for the school, their sons led a privileged life. The other boys, though, were fair game.

Determined to do the right thing, I turned. "It was my fault, Master. You should hit me."

"Why can't you be a gentleman like Otter?" Uncle Blacky asked. He gave Stumpy six of the best across his palm, even though I had been the insolent one.

---

2. **intimidate:** To make timid; make afraid; daunt.
3. **sporadic** (spə rad´ ik): Happening only from time to time; occasional.

As he sat down, I whispered, "I'm sorry."

Stumpy rested his hand on the table but would not look at me. "I'm used to it."

I felt bad because I could see some of the boys cringing—the ones whose fathers had stayed here. Uncle Blacky might give them six for not volunteering to answer a question; or even if they did, he might punish them if he judged their response a poor one.

What do you do when your family is so powerful that you lead a charmed life and even your teacher won't find fault with you? I tried to bring candy treats on different occasions for all my class-mates. The poorer boys were lucky to get a bite of meat in an entire year, let alone taste sugar. And of course, on festivals, I used my allowance to buy toys and firecrackers for everyone. So I don't think they held it against me that Uncle Blacky treated me as his pet. The other guests' sons led just as protected a life.

Despite Uncle's bamboo rod, the school began to buzz with excitement behind me. When other guests came home, there were banquets and celebrations; but none of them could match one of Uncle Foxfire's homecomings. While Father and Uncle were home, life was one long festival of banquets[4] and entertain-ments and fireworks displays.

I went out of the school into the little courtyard where porce-lain stools sat in the shade of a tree. The entire setting was also the result of my family's donations. My mother was generous with everyone but herself.

As I stepped into the village's main street, I met my mother, Cassia, striding along, too impatient to be carried along in a sedan chair as her sister-in-law wanted her to do. As the clan said, Mother still had mud between her toes.

Mother was tugging self-consciously at her jade necklace. It was her one piece of jewelry—and it had taken Father an entire evening of arguing to make her keep it. Her blouse and pants were clean but plain.

"Look at you." She frowned, "Dirty already." Seizing my arm, she made me stop in the middle of the street. Then, to my cha-grin, she began brushing off my clothes as if I were still a child.

For the homecoming, the Lion Rock lady—Mother referred to her sister-in-law, Uncle Foxfire's wife, only as "that Lion Rock woman"—had insisted on new clothes for herself and her son, whom everyone called the Little Emperor. She had taken me along as well when we went to her hometown, Lion Rock, which was the market town for our area.

---

4. banquets (bang´ kwəts): Fancy meals; feasts.

As we passed by the banquet hall, I saw that folks were already sweeping off the wide porch. The tables and benches were all set out, and the columns and rafters had been freshly painted. The hall had been built five years ago for just such a purpose as this.

In fact, all of Three Willows had been spruced up, and anything that needed a new coat of paint had received one—and the bill was presented to Mother. With the smell of fresh paint tickling my nose, I had gone about pretending that the homecoming was for me.

As we merged with the excited clanspeople, I grinned at Mother. "Are you excited?"

She smiled back. "Are you?"

"Yes," I said, but I couldn't have told her how much. When I was small, I would ask Mother why she had adopted me. And she would stop whatever she was doing, put me on her lap and tell me, "The astrologers say you were born in the hour of fire on the day of fire in the month of fire, so you were bound to join my family, because we've been rebels and troublemakers for seven generations."

Some two centuries ago, a barbarian tribe called the Manchus came thundering down from the north to conquer the Middle Kingdom, or *China*, as it's called in the Land of the Golden Mountain. For two hundred years, our family has been trying to drive them off the dragon throne; and we have paid the price with our blood and our souls.

To hear my mother tell it, when we've carried out the Work, as she calls it, the Middle Kingdom will enter a new age. The universe will be balanced once more, and we will live in harmony and peace with one another.

By the time Mother was finished, I was convinced that once the Work was complete, rice would grow faster. Even the sky would be bluer. And she and I and Uncle and Father were put on this earth to carry out the Work.

As guests of the Golden Mountain, Father and Uncle earned the money that let us further the Work here. And they met with other rebels overseas to make all sorts of plans.

In fact, my Uncle Foxfire had been the first to leave Three Willows some ten years ago. He was famous in the clan not for what he had done for the Work but for his knack of finding gold in places where no one else could. The more superstitious believed that it was magic. They said he had found some object that turned stones into gold. Others thought he had developed some sixth sense that let him smell the nuggets. The more philosophical thought he had some special power of dreaming—that at night the gold would whisper to him and tell him where the various pieces were.

Mother said it was intelligence and not magic that had created his success. However, when she told that to the superstitious folk, they only thought she was covering something up.

I'm afraid that when I was small, I believed all the stories about him—and more because many of the other fairy tales I heard became entwined with his story. There were various times when I had believed he could: 1) fly, 2) kill tigers barehanded and 3) call upon dragons as his friends.

And somehow I pictured that one day he would return from the Golden Mountain to finish the Work and drive out the Manchus. And when he did, Father and Mother and I would be right by his side.

In the meantime, the clan elders had collected by the gates. Uncle Pine, the oldest of the elders, was rehearsing his speech, his lips moving as he mumbled softly. Everyone was dressed in holiday finery. The actors and acrobats and even the man with the trained monkey were there as well to watch the spectacle.

Halfway up one side of the valley, Three Willows sat behind its ancient brick wall. To the left and right were orchards and ter-raced fields, while down below, on the valley floor, the rice fields gleamed among the dikes like bits of polished shell in a wooden lattice.[5] And along the dirt dikes I saw a procession of people the size of ants.

The Lion Rock lady made quite an entrance in a sedan chair borne by servants. And when she stepped out of the chair, she wore an elegant robe embroidered with birds, and her hair had been wrapped around an elaborate wire frame. Bright semi-precious stones and pearls had been hung among her tresses. Her son, my cousin, tagged along behind like a miniature peacock.

"She looks like her head rammed a trellis,"[6] Mother whispered disapprovingly to me.

There was nothing wrong, though, with the hearing of that Lion Rock lady. Her plucked eyebrows formed an irritated wedge. "How splendid you look today, my dear. Why, you'd think you were selling your prize pig."

Bristling, Mother gathered herself for one of her lectures on waste, but Aunt Diligence shoved between them. "How happy you must be to be united with your husbands."

Both Mother and her sister-in-law remembered their manners. "Yes," Mother said.

"Quite," the Lion Rock lady agreed, and her features became as smooth and cold as those of a marble statue.

---

5. **lattice:** A structure formed of crossed strips or bars.
6. **trellis:** A lattice upon which plants are trained to grow.

Over the gate, two men hastily unfurled a welcome banner, while above the gate, people lined the walls for a glimpse of the two fabled heroes. "They're here!" someone shouted.

I stood on my toes as if that would help me see better. I had been ten when they had last visited the village, and I remembered that their homecoming was worthy of kings. And they didn't disappoint me this time. The procession was led by musicians, in robes as brightly colored as parrots, who played horns in a triumphant air. Next came a pair of men staggering beneath the weight of a trunk hanging from a pole between them. And behind them stumbled more such pairs carrying more trunks and baskets. Finally came the chairs, gilded and lacquered and fit for an emperor.

When Father and Uncle climbed out of their chairs, I saw that beneath their elegant embroidered silk robes, they were wearing heavy western boots of leather rather than normal shoes. They were boots for storming the gates of Heaven. And as the roar went up from the village, they stood there, hands on their hips, mighty as lords.

☑ Check Your Comprehension

1. In "The Great Silkie," how does the narrator come to be on the planet Harmony? Give a brief history.
2. Why is the colony split into two groups? How are the groups different from each other?
3. In Dragon's Gate, how and why does the teacher treat some students better than others?
4. Why do the narrator's father and uncle travel back and forth to America? What do they do with the money they earn there?
5. How do the residents of Three Rock regard Squeaky and Foxfire? What do they do to show their regard?

◆ Critical Thinking

INTERPRET

1. In "The Great Silkie," why does the narrator feel it is important to remember how the city of Old Sion was lost? [Infer]

2. In Dragon's Gate, what does the narrator's mother mean by "the Work"? Why is it important to her and her people? [Interpret]

COMPARE LITERARY WORKS

3. In both "The Great Silkie" and Dragon's Gate, people struggle to survive in their surroundings. What parallels do you find between the people who left Earth for the planet Harmony, and the people who were conquered by the Manchus? How are their situations similar and different? [Analyze]

APPLY

4. Yep writes about the challenges that immigrants face after moving to a new home. How are those challenges similar to those of immigrants who come to America today? [Connect]

◆ Literary Focus: Point of View

A key element in Yep's stories is point of view. **Point of view** is the perspective, or viewpoint, from which a story is told. Most of Yep's narratives are told from the *first-person point of view*, meaning the narrator is a character in the story and refers to himself or herself with the pronoun *I*. For example, *Dragon's Gate* is told by the narrator, Otter, who participates in the story's action. Everything you learn about the characters and events stems from the way Otter relates them to you. Another character might relate the same story in a significantly different way.

Other stories are told from a *third-person* point of view, in which the narrator is not a part of the action and uses third person pronouns such as *he* and *she* to refer to characters. There are two kinds of third-person narration. In *omniscient third person point of view*, the narrator knows and tells about what each character feels and thinks. In *limited third person point of view*, the narrator relates the inner thoughts and feelings of only one character.

1. Identify the point of view used to narrate "The Old Jar." Provide details from the selection to support your answer.

2. How does the first-person narration of "The Pearl Apartments" affect the reader's impressions of the narrator's grandmother and father?

3. Imagine that "The Great Silkie" had been narrated in first person by one of the Mainlanders instead of one of the Silkies. How might that have affected the reader's feelings about the Silkies?

4. Imagine that *Dragon's Gate* had been narrated in omniscient third person instead of first person. How might that have changed your general impressions of Three Willows and its people?

◆ Drawing Conclusions About Yep's Work

In his stories, Yep often writes of the struggles of individuals or a group to adjust to a new society. He details the challenges that newcomers face, and shows how they work to overcome their conflicts.

Work with a partner to create a sunburst organizer like the one that follows. The center of the organizer refers to the theme of Yep's stories. Redraw the organizer. Then, in each box surrounding the center circle, provide key details relating to the theme. Above each box, write the name of the story in which the details apply.

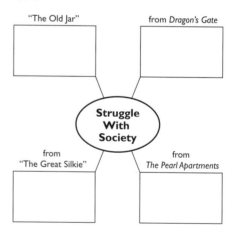

◆ Idea Bank
Writing

1. **Letter** Write a letter to Laurence Yep in which you comment on the stories you have read. Identify what

you especially like or dislike about his work, and submit questions about his writing. Send the letter in care of one of his publishers.

2. **Dialogue** The excerpt from *Dragon's Gate* ends with the dramatic entrance of Father and Uncle. Write dialogue that tells what those two characters might discuss with Otter, the Lion Rock lady, or other characters in the story after they arrive in Three Willows.

3. **Speech** Imagine you are the young Laurence Yep on his first day in a new school. Write a speech introducing yourself to your new classmates, and telling about yourself, your family, and your home. **[Performing Arts Link]**

4. **Dramatic Presentation** Working with a group, prepare and perform "The Old Jar" as a play. Characters will include the old woman, the clerk, various townspeople, and a narrator. One or more students can gather or make props, including the jar and the rice. After preparing a script and rehearsing, perform the play for classmates. **[Performing Arts Link; Group Activity]**

Researching and Representing

5. **Oral Report** Research an aspect of Chinese-American history, such as the growth of San Francisco's Chinatown, Chinese crews on the transcontinental railroad, or prominent Chinese-Americans. Prepare an oral report on your topic. **[Social Studies Link]**

6. **Book Review** Read *The Lost Garden, Dragon's Gate, Sweetwater,* or *The Rainbow People* in its entirety. Prepare a book report that summarizes the story and offers a critical evaluation of the content and the author's writing style. Present your report to the class. **[Media Link]**

◆ **Further Reading, Listening, and Viewing**

• *The Lost Garden* (1991). This autobiography tells of the author's childhood and writing experiences.

• *Dragonwings* (1979). This Miller-Brody record, cassette, and filmstrip depict Yep's novel.

• *The Curse of the Squirrel* (1989). This Random House cassette adapts Yep's 1987 novel.

On the Web:

http://www.phschool.com/atschool/literature
Go to the student edition *Copper*. Proceed to Unit 5. Then, click Hot Links to find Web sites featuring Laurence Yep.

Jean Craighead George In Depth

> "Her books are distinguished by authentic detail and a blend of scientific curiosity, wonder, and concern for the natural environment, all described in a manner . . . both unsentimental and lyrical."
>
> —*Polly A. Vedder*

JEAN CRAIGHEAD GEORGE has been creating fiction and nonfiction works about nature since the late 1940's. Basing much of her writing on personal experience and exploration, George captures the appeal of the natural world for her audiences. Through careful observations and an engaging writing style, she provides fascinating insights into the plant and animal world all around us.

A Happy Outdoor Youth Jean Craighead was born in Washington, D. C., in 1919, and spent her childhood summers on the family farm in southern Pennsylvania. On land her ancestors had held since 1742, George learned as a young girl to love both nature and literature. Her scientist father had a great influence on her, but so did her twin brothers John and Frank. Even as teenagers the two boys were actively involved with natural pursuits. For example, their love of falcons, or hunting hawks, led them to introduce the sport of falconry into the United States. Later, they would do some of the earliest tracking of grizzly bears in Yellowstone National Park by installing radio tags on the bears' necks. As George has written, "With two such brothers, a younger sister *had* to be a writer to find her niche and survive."

Marriage and Early Books Jean Craighead graduated from Pennsylvania State University in 1941 and for a time was a reporter for the *Washington Post*. In 1944 she married John L. George. John George shared her interest in nature, and soon they published their first book, *Vulpes, The Red Fox*. The two worked together on five other books, mostly animal biographies based on wild creatures they had taken into their home. John brought his research and his observations to the books, but Jean did most of the writing and illustrating.

At this time, the Georges lived near Vassar College in New York State, where John was a teacher. Eventually they had three children: Carolyn (called "Twig" because she had been such a tiny baby), Craig, and Luke.

Awards and Hardships In the 1950's George began writing on her own. She worked for several years on her first novel, *My Side of the Mountain*, which was very successful when it was published in 1959. Set in the Catskill Mountains in New York, the novel tells of young Sam Gribley, who lives alone in the wilderness for a year. Sam survives by making a comfortable home in a hollow tree and by developing his skills in wild cookery. As with many of her books, George spent time in the Catskills in order to give the events in the story authentic details. *My Side of the Mountain* received several awards when it was published.

One summer George took her son Luke to Alaska to find out more about wolf behavior. She studied life in wolf packs and how wolves communicate. She used this information in her novel *Julie of the Wolves* and in her later books *Julie* and *Julie's Wolf Pack*. *Julie of the Wolves*, one of George's best known books, won the Newbery Award in 1975.

A Life Devoted to Writing Today, George lives in a rambling house in New York and continues to write, usually publishing at least one book a year. Her house is filled with souvenirs from her nature trips, including Eskimo masks from Alaska. Her children, now adults, have followed in her footsteps: Craig and Luke are environmental scientists (one lives in Alaska) and Carolyn is a writer.

In 1990 George published a sequel to *My Side of the Mountain* called *On the Far Side of the Mountain,* and in 1999 wrote another related book, *Frightful's Mountain,* which was highly praised. Lately she has worked with a composer to create music to accompany some of her books.

◆ Nature Writers in America

As a nature writer, Jean Craighead George fits into a strong American tradition. For example, some of the earliest Native American accounts that we have are poems about the beauty of the prairies and mountains.

When Europeans came to the North American continent, many wrote descriptions of the land they explored. Much early writing of this type was done to help other explorers find their way around. By the 1700's, however, several writers were focusing on the plants and wildlife they found, often including carefully made drawings. Thomas Jefferson, our third President, wrote a nature book called *Notes on the State of Virginia,* describing the Blue Ridge Mountains and the Shenandoah Valley.

One of the most important American nature books of the 1800's was *Walden.* Its author, Henry David Thoreau, spent two years alone in a cabin on Walden Pond in Connecticut. Though Thoreau expressed his views on life and politics in this book, many parts of it are wonderful nature descriptions. One passage, for example, describes a battle between red and black ants.

In the 1900's, some American nature writing began to focus, as much of Jean Craighead George's writing does, on preserving the environment. John Muir, the founder of the Sierra Club, wrote beautiful descriptions of West Coast landscapes, and he also worked actively to keep them from harm. All nature writers have this in common with Jean Craighead George: They want readers to appreciate the wonder and diversity of the natural world.

◆ Literary Works

Novels
- *My Side of the Mountain* (1959)
- *Julie of the Wolves* (1972)
- *On the Far Side of the Mountain* (1990)
- *Julie's Wolf Pack* (1997)
- *Frightful's Mountain* (1999)

Nonfiction Series
The "Thirteen Moons" Series
- *The Moon of the Mountain Lions* (1991)
- *The Moon of the Salamanders* (1992)
- *The Moon of the Owls* (1993)

The "One Day" Series
- *One Day in the Desert* (1983)
- *One Day in the Woods* (1988)
- *One Day in the Tropical Rain Forest* (1990)

Recent Writings
- *The Tarantula in My Purse: And 172 Other Wild Pets* (1996)
- *Dear Katie, The Volcano Is a Girl* (1998)
- *Incredible Animal Adventures* (1999)
- *Snow Bear* (1999)

Jean Craighead George

from The Tarantula in My Purse

My children, Twig, Craig, and Luke, were the third generation of Craighead children who brought home wild birds and beasts to have and to contemplate. In their grandfather's day, and even in mine, wild animals were considered pests. There was no need for permits to keep them, as there is today. Hawks, owls, and falcons were shot. Crows and coyotes were poisoned. Songbird nests were raided for eggs. Anyone was free to bring home the earth's creatures to nurture and think about—and bring them home we did.

My father had started the tradition. He had lined his room with bottles of insects, raised snakes, and fed treats to a friendly skunk in the meadow. When called upon to dress up in his hated, lace-trimmed Lord Fauntleroy suit to go to town with his mother, he teased his wild friend until she sprayed him—to his delight. When he arrived at the back door, his mother ordered him to stay home and not come inside the house all day. So he didn't. Eyes sparkling, he fished the creek that ran through the backyard of his Pennsylvania home, caught frogs, ate dinner on the back porch, and stayed out until bedtime. How he loved that skunk.

When Frank and John, my twin brothers, and I were young, Dad encouraged in us that love of animals innate in all children. He found us walking sticks and assassin bugs, praying mantises, opossums, snakes, and owls. He taught us the plants they lived with and the environments where they could be found. To Dad all birds, beasts, and plants were works of art.

I must have learned this early. My first pet was a baby turkey vulture, a carrion eater fit for witches and monsters and associated with graveyards and death. He was a work of art. I loved him on sight.

Nod was about the size of a chicken and covered—all but his neck, head, and feet—with fluffy white down. His featherless head hung between protruding shoulders. He resembled a gargoyle on the Cathedral of Notre Dame.[1]

Dad had found him sitting in the middle of a footpath in the Potomac River bottomlands near our home in Washington, D.C. The vulture had greeted him with a rasping hiss. Seeing no parents anywhere, Dad put the gawky chick in his pack and brought him home to me.

---

1. **a gargoyle on the Cathedral of Notre Dame:** A stone waterspout carved to look like a monster on the roof of Notre Dame Cathedral in Paris, France.

Dad was an entomologist, but he did not concentrate on insects alone. He studied the whole forest or an entire ecosystem to find explanations for the behavior of a beetle or a wasp. He spent as much time as possible outdoors. The answers were all out there, he would say, not in books or at a desk. My mother, my brothers, and I went with him. He taught us the plants and animals and why birds migrate. He taught us how to hunt and fish, to make shelters and fire, but primarily he infused in us an enthusiasm for the ingenuity of nature.

No sooner had Dad put Nod in my hands than I hugged the awkward baby and asked what kind of a nest he had come from. That was a standard question in our household when new forms of life came to visit.

"A hollow log on the ground or the foot of a big tree," he answered.

"And what does he eat?"

"Carrion—dead things. Turkey vultures are the forest's sanitation department."

After Dad had fed him bites of a catfish he had caught in the Potomac River that day, I put a cardboard box on its side and lined it with newspaper. Nod waddled into it. I carefully pushed him under the kitchen table, then crawled in beside the box. He looked sideways at me out of bluish eyes set in wrinkled gray-blue skin. I patted his naked cheeks, and he sank to his heels. He closed his eyes and slept.

Nod throve on all manner of meat and fish, cooked and raw, and presently he was two feet tall with nearly six feet of wingspan. Mother grew nervous. When he flapped, her recipes flew across the room and flour puffed up from the cake-mixing bowl. This took her from nervousness to protest. Dad suggested we put Nod on the top of the kitchen door, where he could exercise without rearranging the kitchen.

High overhead he gave his full attention to Mother. His primordial instincts made him concentrate on her for two reasons. Turkey vultures roost together at night because they are safer in a group, and—the best reason—in the morning the young can follow experienced elders to food. Mother was Nod's elder. She brought chickens, roasts, and fish to the kitchen table. He followed her with his eyes from sink to stove to table.

Although Mother was also a naturalist, she was primarily a mother and the maestro[2] of life in our home.

"Jean," she said one day, "Nod has to go. I can't stand a turkey vulture watching me cook another minute."

---

2. **maestro** (mīs′ trō): A master in any art, especially in music.

My father called his friend, the director of the National Zoo in Washington, D.C., and they made arrangements to ship Nod to a zoo in Scotland that did not have an American turkey vulture. When he was taken away, I cried until Dad pointed out that I had come to know a truly remarkable creature. Indeed I had.

When I grew up, I went right on bringing wild animals home; and when I had children, they did too. . . .

The Screech Owl Who Liked Television

Twig's favorite pet was a small gray screech owl. Had he not fallen from his nest before he could fly, he would have lived in the open woodland, deciduous forest, park, town, or river's edge. But he had landed on a hard driveway instead and ended up in our house. He was round eyed and hungry. He looked up at Twig and gave the quivering hunger call of the screech owl. Twig named him Yammer.

Yammer quickly endeared himself to us. He hopped from his perch to our hands to eat. He rode around the house on our shoulders and sat on the back of a dining-room chair during dinner.

Before the green of June burst upon us, Yammer had become a person to Twig, who felt all wild friends were humans and should be treated as such.

Wild animals are not people. But Twig was not convinced. One Saturday morning she and Yammer were watching a cowboy show on television. They had been there for hours.

"Twig," I said, "you've watched TV long enough. Please go find a book to read, or do your homework." My voice was firm. I kept the TV in my bedroom just so the children wouldn't be constantly tempted to turn it on as they had when it was downstairs.

Reluctantly, Twig got to her feet. At the door she turned and looked at her little owl. He was on top of the headboard, staring at the screen. A rider on a horse was streaking across the desert. From an owl's point of view the pair were mouse sized.

"How come Yammer can watch TV and I can't?" she asked, pouting.

Hardly had she spoken than Yammer pushed off from the headboard, struck the prey with his talons, and dropped to the floor, bewildered.

Twig rushed to his rescue. She gathered him up and hugged him to her chest. With a scornful glance at me, she hurried to her room. The small owl's round yellow eyes were peering from between her gently curled fingers.

Twig was right: This otherworldly creature was a person. Wasn't his menu of mice and crickets included on the shopping list? Didn't he have his own bedroom in the gap between the Roger Tory Peterson field guides in the living-room bookcase?

Didn't he run down into the cozy blanket-tunnels made by Twig at bedtime and utter his note of contentment? And didn't he like TV just as she did?

Most scientists are taught not to read human emotions into animals, but sometimes they wonder about the truth of it. When you live with animals, they often seem quite humanlike.

Later that morning of the TV incident, I looked in on Twig and Yammer. The owl was perched on the top of her open door, preening his feathers. She was sitting with her chin in her hands, looking at him.

"I feel sorry for Yammer," she said. "He's stuck in this house. He needs to see things that move like they do in the woods."

"So?" I said.

"So, I've finished my homework and made my bed. Can Yammer and I watch TV?"

I heard myself whisper, "Yes."

Letting Yammer Go

When I told Twig she could watch TV that day of the cowboy incident, she stood on her desk and held up her hand to Yammer. He stepped onto her finger. As she climbed down, she touched his toes and the talons curled around her forefinger.

"I wish I had Yammer's feet," she said. "Then I could sit on the teeny tiny branches of the apple tree."

Suddenly her brother Craig shouted, "*Road Runner's* on."

"Yammer loves *Road Runner*," Twig said, and dashed to the TV in my bedroom. Yammer flapped his wings to keep his balance, and the two joined Twig's brothers, Craig and Luke, before the television. Luke, not quite four, patted the pillow next to him.

"Put him here," he said. A chord of music sounded, lights flashed, and all eyes—particularly Yammer's—were riveted on that zany bird running on and off the screen.

Second to *Road Runner* was Yammer's love for the shower. He would fly into the bathroom when he heard one of us turn on the spray, sit on the top of the shower-curtain rod to orient himself, then drop into the puddles at our feet. Eyes half closed, he would joyfully flip the water up and into his wings and dunk his breast until he was soaked. A wet screech owl is as helpless as an ant in an ant lion's trap. Having bathed, Yammer couldn't climb out of the tub. We would have to pick him up and put him on a towel by the hot-air vent to dry.

This was a perfectly satisfactory arrangement until we failed to tell a visitor about Yammer's passion. In the morning, unaware of his quiet presence, she showered, stepped out of the tub, and left him there. It was almost noon before we discovered him.

Craig promptly put up a sign: "Please remove the owl after showering." It hung over the shower faucets for as long as Yammer lived with us.

Yammer was devoted to Twig. He sat on her shoulder at breakfast, flew to her hand for food when she whistled for him, and roosted on the window-curtain rod of her room when he was not watching TV.

He did like Craig's train set, however.

He had reason to. It moved like a garter snake. The tracks that Craig balanced on his big wooden blocks ran under the bed, then out across the floor past the chest of drawers, over the mainline, and back under the bed again. When Yammer heard the train start up, he would fly to the back of the chair in Craig's room. Crouched to drop on this prey, he watched engine and cars ply the precarious route. The blocks would shudder as the little black locomotive swung around a curve or speedily crossed a ravine into the open stretch between the wall and the door. Yammer never struck this prey. The train was not the right size. Yammer was programmed to eat mice, insects, small snakes, and arthropods. The big owls, like the great horned, barred, and barn owls—pets of my childhood—might have pounced on Craig's train, but not Yammer. He just sat and watched. In a house that lacked diving blue jays and scurrying chipmunks, "Black Darling," as Craig called the Lionel train, was biological diversity to Yammer. His head fairly spun off his shoulders as his eyes followed the speeding engine around the room, under the bed, and out again.

Often the train wrecked. Craig ran it on the bleeding edge of disaster, and when the building blocks shifted too much, Black Darling would jump the tracks, knock down the trestles, and career through the air before coming to rest on its side, wheels spinning. With every crash, Yammer took off for Craig's door top, where he would study the dead engine until its wheels stopped turning. Then he would look away. When the train didn't move, it wasn't there.

One evening, a screech owl's plaintive call of spring floated through our windows as we were going to sleep. The voice came from the spruce trees on the other side of the lane.

The next day at breakfast I put down my fork and leaned toward Twig, Craig, and Luke, smiling. They put down their forks and looked at me with that oh-boy-here-it-comes expression on their faces.

"It's time . . ." I said. The eyes widened, the fingers tightened on the table edge.

". . . to set Yammer free."

"NO."

"NO."

"NO NO NO NO." The third voice in the round came in. "Don't let him go."

"He'll stay around," I said. "It will be lovely to have Yammer in our woods, flying, calling to us at night and coming to the window for a mouse or two."

"NO NO NO NO NO NO."

"Maybe he'll even have owlets and bring them to us."

Silence, as they thought about that.

"I'm going to feed him on the windowsill of my bedroom for a few days," I said. "When he knows he can always get food there, I'll open the window and he'll fly off. I'll whistle and he'll come back."

"NO, NO," said Twig. "He won't."

"Yes, he will," I said. "Don't you remember Bubo, Twig?"

"No," she said. "I was just born when we had Bubo."

"Bubo was a great horned owl," I explained. "She lived with us for four years at Vassar College, and then we let her go."

"Don't let Yammer go," said Twig.

"Bubo came back every evening to be fed," I went on. "When she found a male great horned owl in the nearby woodsy graveyard, she moved off the campus and into the woods with him. They raised two owlets in an old crow's nest."

"NO, NO," shouted Luke and Craig.

"Don't let Yammer go," said Twig.

A week later we met in the bedroom.

"Yammer has been eating mice and chicken on the windowsill for a long time now," I said. "The moment has come to open the window." They looked at me as if I were an owl executioner.

"He'll be back. He's very hungry."

Eyes widened in disbelief. No one spoke.

"He'll fly to the basswood tree to get his bearings," I said quickly. "Then I'll whistle the 'come get the food' call and he'll be right back."

"No, don't," said Twig.

"We'll feed him just a little bit tonight," I continued. "He'll still be hungry tomorrow, and he'll come back for more. We'll do this every night until he can hunt on his own."

I was facing an audience of skeptics. I had to convince them. "When I was a kid," I hastened to say, "we had a barn owl named Windy."

"He was Uncle John and Uncle Frank's lovable owl. They set him free, and he came to the sleeping porch every night to be fed. Yammer will too."

"Yammer's not a barn owl," said Craig.

That evening we let Yammer go. Twig was hopeful—she trusted that Yammer would come back. Craig was still skeptical. But

Luke was brightened by a new awareness rising in him—freedom. The owl would go free. He liked that.

As we opened the window, Yammer blinked his golden eyes and swung his head in a wide circle. He saw the basswood tree, Mr. Ross's spruces, the sky, and the rising moon. Spreading his wings, he floated into the twilight.

We never saw him again.

☑ **Check Your Comprehension**

1. How did young Jean George get the turkey vulture?
2. What kind of an animal was Yammer?
3. What happened to Yammer at the end of the story?

◆ **Critical Thinking**

INTERPRET

1. What kinds of things did Yammer do to show he was a wild animal? What kinds of things did he do that seemed human? **[Classify]**

2. Were your surprised at what Yammer did when he was freed? Why or why not? **[Interpret]**

EVALUATE

3. Reread to find George's father's advice to her when she has to give up the turkey vulture. How could his comment also be a lesson for George's children? **[Evaluate]**

APPLY

4. Why do you think people are so attached to their pets? List as many reasons as you can think of. **[Relate]**

$\mathscr{J}$ean Craighead George

from The Wild, Wild Cookbook

Introduction

When the flicker returns to my lawn in spring and the flowers of the shadbush shine like frost in the dark woodland, I am reminded that it is time to whip up a batch of Dandelion Fritters or a Fiddlehead Pie. It is April, and another foraging season has begun.

A penknife, a bag, and fingers are the tools of the craft. The wild crops are found along roadsides and waterways, in fields, forests, city parks, vacant lots, and even on city sidewalks where acorns fall and purslane pushes up through cracks in the cement.

I am the third of four generations of wildfood gatherers who take to the hills and fields in spring, summer, and autumn to harvest the free-growing plants, cook, and eat them. Grandfather taught my father, my father taught me, and I taught my children where the violets bloom and the lamb's-quarters flourish.

We do not necessarily wander far from our doors. My daughter who now lives in the city finds chicory and plantain in parks and abandoned lots. I pick tasty weeds along roadsides or in fields and marshes near my suburban home. My own lawn is a weed feast. The grasslands and desert of my youngest son's southwest home offers a variety of pot herbs for his table.

And there is the serendipity[1]—the unsought gifts of foraging: learning the names and families of plants and the birds and beasts they support. As a bonus we discover wondrous habitats: cool waterfalls, fern-luminous groves. Sometimes we are diverted by an ant collecting aphids for her tribe or a Baltimore oriole pulling threads from a grapevine to weave into a basket nest. Most important, we see the interdependency of plant, bird, beast, and human. We understand why we must protect our vanishing wilderness and farmlands. And we have joined conservation societies to fight for them. Once you have learned from a knowledgeable person how to identify wild plants, you can use this book to increase the knowledge that you already have. When in doubt do not taste a plant. Knowing your plants is the best insurance against accidental poisoning. Make sure that you know what you are gathering before you use any of the recipes in this book. If you are not sure about the identity of a plant take it to an expert such as a teacher or a naturalist at a nature center for identifica-

---

1. **serendipity** (ser ən dip´ ə tē): Finding something good accidentally.

tion before doing anything further. Most plants are safe, but certainly not all are safe, nutritious, or tasty.

Begin foraging by only picking a plant you know well: The dandelion is a good one since most people learned it with their ABC's; it is nationwide in distribution and a "weed." No one will stop you from picking dandelions. Violets, cacti, garlic, and oxalis are good followup plants once you know how to identify them; they can be learned at a glance and all but violets are unloved.

Mushrooms I pass by. They are difficult to identify and so dangerous that a professor of mycology once told me that he himself would never pick and eat wild mushrooms, expert as he was. "They are too confusing," he said, "even when examined under a microscope." So I, too, leave them alone.

The recipes are written for the modern kitchen, but many can be made over a campfire or in a rock oven, a method that tenderizes and flavors not only wild plants but game and fish as well.

ROCK OVEN

1. Dig a saucer-shaped hole in the ground about three feet across and a foot and a half deep. Line it with hand-sized rocks. Keep the dirt.

2. Build a fire in the rock saucer and let it burn until the rocks are hot and sizzle when water is dropped on them.

3. Remove the logs and embers with a shovel, and either douse them or add wood to make a campfire.

4. Line the pit with a bed of green grass or moistened leaves such as arrowhead or corn husks.

5. Wrap plants, fish, or game in aluminum foil or leaves, after seasoning with salt, pepper, and herbs. Breads and pies should be placed in lidded pots with room for them to rise.

6. Place foods on the grass bed.

7. Cover with grass, corn husks, or leaves.

8. Cover with damp cloth, dish towels, or burlap bag.

9. Shovel the dirt over the cloth.

10. In about two hours the meal is ready to eat. My twenty-one-pound Thanksgiving turkey cooked in three hours.

THE FEAST

Our family serves wild foods on linen tablecloths with the best china and silver. In the back country we dine around a campfire or sit before an inspiring view of forest, prairie, or mountain. No matter where we are, the banquet table is permeated[3] with a sense of achievement and freedom. I know of no other pursuit with such rewards.

---

3. **permeated** (pər´ mē āt əd): Spread through; filled with.

Day Lily: DESCRIPTION AND HABITAT

Perky orange and yellow flowers with six petals. They bloom in high summer face up to the sun. The flowers are clustered on the top of a naked stalk. They last but one day, opening at dawn and closing in the evening. The leaves are long and lancelike. This is not a lily with a bulb, as are the trillium, onion, tulip and hyacinth, etc., but a member of the Lily Family with a root, an alien of Asiatic origin. The plant came to America via Europe, and escaped from gardens to the roadsides and woodland meadows across the eastern United States. It has migrated[4] now to moist western wastelands.

The buds, the open flowers, the wilted flowers, and the roots are good to eat, and are considered delicacies in Japan and China. Boil roots in salt water and serve with butter, or use in Fiddlehead Pie.

---

4. migrated: Moved from one place to another.

LEMON DAY LILIES

Ingredients

2 dozen day lily buds or wilted
  flowers
4 cups water
¾ cup sugar
½ cup white vinegar
I cup canned chicken broth
I lemon, juice and grated rind
I tablespoon cornstarch
2 tablespoons water
  Cooked rice
  Candied ginger

Utensils

Measuring cup
Measuring spoon
3-quart saucepan
Colander
Grater
Lemon squeezer
Bowl

Directions

 1. Boil day lilies in water for 15 minutes.
 2. Drain.
 3. Pour sugar and vinegar in saucepan. Heat until dissolved.
 4. Add chicken broth. Stir.
 5. Add lemon juice and grated rind. Stir.
 6. Simmer for 5 minutes.
 7. Dissolve cornstarch in 2 tablespoons water. Add to sauce.
 8. Over low heat, stir constantly until thickened and clear.
 9. Add day lilies. Heat briefly.
10. Serve over rice with sliced candied wild ginger.

DAY LILY FRITTERS

Ingredients

12 buds or wilted flowers of day
   lilies
4 cups water
1 cup biscuit mix
¾ cup water or milk (enough to
   make pastry mixture)

or in lieu of[5] *biscuit mix*
1 cup flour
2 eggs, well beaten
⅔ cup milk
1 teaspoon baking powder
¼ teaspoon salt
   Pepper
½ inch cooking oil in skillet

Utensils
Measuring cup
Measuring spoons
3-quart saucepan
Bowl
Mixing spoon
Skillet
Paper toweling or brown paper bag

Directions
1. Place day lilies and water in saucepan and bring to boil.
2. Simmer for 15 minutes.
3. Drain cooked lilies and pat dry. Dip into batter.
4. Drop into hot fat and cook until golden brown.
5. Turn and cook other side.
6. Drain on paper toweling or brown paper bag.
7. Serve as vegetable or snack.

---

5. **in lieu** (lo͞o) **of:** Instead of.

Wild Cherry: DESCRIPTION AND HABITAT

The flowers of the wild black cherry open from the end of March in Texas to June in the North, are about one half inch in diameter, and hang in clusters. They appear when the leaves are half grown. The fruits ripen from June to October in drooping clusters and are round and bright red when fully grown, and almost black when ripe.

The bark is broken into scaly small irregular plates that are dark cherry red.

This tree grows from Nova Scotia westward to Lake Superior and southward to Florida, Nebraska, South Dakota, Kansas, Oklahoma, and the Rio River, Texas, usually in rich soil. They were once abundant in the Appalachian Mountains.

CHERRY CORN BREAD

TO PREPARE CHERRIES:

Ingredients
1 cup cherries
2 cups water
2 tablespoons honey

Utensils
Measuring cup
Measuring spoons
3-quart saucepan
Colander

Directions
1. Place cherries and water in saucepan.
2. Bring to a boil and simmer for 20 minutes.
3. Drain juice through colander and reserve.
4. Pit the cherries—give a little squeeze and the seeds pop out.
5. Combine pitted cherries and honey.

THE BREAD:
Oven: 425°F   *Time: 20–30 minutes*

Ingredients
1 cup cornmeal
1 cup whole wheat flour
2 teaspoons baking powder
1 teaspoon salt
1 egg
1 tablespoon honey
2 tablespoons melted margarine,
   butter, or cooking oil
1 tablespoon sugar
   Juice from 1 cup of cooked
   cherries
   Water
1 cup cherries, prepared as above

Utensils
9" cake pan
2 mixing bowls
Measuring cup
Measuring spoons

Directions

1. Grease a 9" cake pan and put in oven to heat.
2. Combine cornmeal, flour, baking powder, and salt.
3. In second bowl, stir together egg, honey, and melted margarine or cooking oil.
4. Pour cherry liquid into measuring cup and add water to make ¾ cup. Add to egg mixture.
5. Mix dry ingredients with egg mixture.
6. Stir in cherries.
7. Pour batter into hot pan and bake at 425°F for 20 to 30 minutes, or when browned and toothpick comes out clean after being inserted.

Also use raspberries, gooseberries, blueberries and relatives; rose hips, high bush cranberries, manzanitas.

Wild black cherries may be used as a substitute fruit in elderberry recipes.

WILD CHERRY BREAKFAST CAKE

Oven: 425°F, or put in coals
or rock oven

Time: 20–25 minutes

Ingredients
2 cups biscuit mix
⅔ cup milk
2 tablespoons sugar
I egg
I cup wild cherries, pitted and
　sweetened with honey
Honey, butter, or maple syrup

Utensils
Bowl
Measuring cup
Measuring spoons
Mixing spoon
Cake pan

Directions
1. Pour biscuit mix into bowl.
2. Add milk. Stir.
3. Add sugar. Stir.
4. Stir in egg.
5. Fold in wild cherries.
6. Bake 20 to 25 minutes.
7. Serve with honey, butter, or maple syrup.

☑ **Check Your Comprehension**

1. At what time of year does the author begin to gather food outdoors?
2. What two kinds of plants does she give recipes for?

◆ **Critical Thinking**

INTERPRET
1. Why do you think George's family "serves wild foods on linen tablecloths with the best china and silver"? **[Draw Conclusions]**

EVALUATE
2. What safety rules does George set out for the gathering of wild foods? Why must these be strictly followed? **[Evaluate; Health Link]**

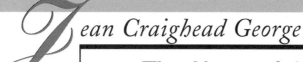

ean Craighead George

from The Moon of the Mountain Lions

The young mountain lion opened his mouth and rolled out his tongue in a waking yawn. Lying in his summer den at timberline,[1] he turned his gaze upon his home on the side of Mount Olympus in Washington. Snowcapped peaks speared the darkness above him. An alpine meadow splattered with flowers lay below, and far down the mountain shaggy forests hugged the slopes and glacial valleys. Below them the northern rain forest reached to the Pacific Ocean.

Stretching and cupping his whiskers forward, the noble cat arose and quietly stepped into the moonlight. He stood beneath the moon of August, the moon of change.

The hummingbirds, sippers of flower nectar, had already sensed the force of this moon. They were ready to migrate. The temperature had dropped only one or two degrees across North America and had actually risen that much on the Pacific Coast, yet the flower birds were ready to go. The sun was setting earlier and rising later. The days were growing shorter. Snow and darkness were coming to the mountains.

At the dawn of this day several male rufous hummingbirds, some of the tiniest birds in the world, had darted past the lion's den as they spun south on whirling wings. No bigger than daisy heads, they were off toward winter homes on the plateaus[2] of Mexico three thousand miles away. Their females stayed behind to hurriedly feed the last brood of nestlings. They would see their bud-sized youngsters out of the nests and onto their wings, teach them how to sip the nectar of the last lilies and bellflowers, then all would follow the males to the sunny winter lands where flowers bloomed.

The swallows also felt the change of the August moon. Great flocks were gathering by the thousands and tens of thousands over lakes, marshes, and seacoasts. Almost always on the wing, these agile birds have tiny, feeble feet that they rarely use. Before the moon would wane they would climb high into the sky and, out of sight of man and beast, circle and rest on their wings. Then, on a cue from the sun, they would turn south and speed away. The next day the swallows would be gone, leaving the skies strangely empty, like beaches when winter comes.

---

1. **timberline:** The line above which trees do not grow.
2. **plateaus** (pla tōz´): Elevated areas of level land; mesas.

Other animals were responding differently to the change. In the deserts, on the August-dry prairies, and in forests from Mexico up through Canada, the chipmunks, toads, and frogs were asleep. This was not the sleep of hibernation but of estivation,[3] summer's torpor. In this quiet state these animals were avoiding the adversities of the month, dryness and heat.

One beast, however would combine the sleeps of summer and winter. In the rockslides, the Olympic marmots, the whistlers of high country, were getting ready for the longest sleep of all the mammals—the nine months from mid-August to mid-May. Some of the marmots were already taking naps that lasted a day or two. Fat and drowsy, they slept longer and longer with each snooze. As they did so, their hearts beat more slowly and their bodies cooled. Eventually they would not be able to awaken until spring. Those that were still running across the rockslides whistled to each other, like children calling their dogs.

The lion tasted the wind with his tongue and nose. It tasted of another change, the change of aging and ripening. The wind bore the scent of sweet huckleberries, ripe gooseberries, and twinberries. This change did not interest the mountain lion, for he was a meat eater, or carnivore. Having looked, smelled, and tasted, the young lion now listened. He rotated his ears. The elk and deer had changed their direction. They were no longer climbing among the peaks but were moving downward. He heard them snapping branches in the forest below.

Since spring they had been wandering upward toward the alpine meadows as the melting snow uncovered sweet grasses. Now the grasses were dying, the growing season of the high country was ending and like the birds, the deer and elk were on migration. Their migration, however, was not south but down the mountain, and this concerned the lion. The deer and elk were his staff of life. He had moved up the mountain with them in the spring, harvesting the weak and infirm as he went. At about five thousand feet above sea level, where the trees stopped and the rocks, ice, and alpine prairies took over, the young lion had denned for the summer. His shelter was a twisted thicket of alpine firs, the last trees to withstand the driving wind and stunting cold at the tops of the mountains. They mark the timberline beyond which no trees grow.

Tonight the elk and deer were two thousand feet below the lion in a lower and, therefore, different kind of forest. On mountains the forests change with the altitude, the tougher trees braving the rugged heights. The lion could smell the pungent[4] cedars

---

3. **estivation:** To pass the summer in a dormant state.
4. **pungent:** Sharply odorous.

the herds were trampling lower down the mountain. He must follow.

Before he entered the forest, he stopped in the last alpine meadow and tipped his ears forward. An elk had injured his foot in a crevasse several days ago and was limping through the trees, *da, thump, thump, thump.* The lion swished his tail. This animal was wounded. In the scheme of things he would falter and eventually be harvested.

Slowly the lion crossed the meadow. Beneath his feet a different sort of change was taking place. Spring was beginning. Under the leaf stems of the tiny alpine willow trees, no taller than a thumb, new buds were forming. This was happening not only on the mountain but all across the northern United States and Canada. Next year's willows, elm, maple, beech, and apple leaf buds were forming. As they emerged, the cells that brought food and water to the old leaves shut down. When these were sealed off, the leaves would lose their chlorophyll, turn yellow, red, orange, or gold and fall to the ground.

The young lion stopped at the edge of the forest and listened. He had lost sight and sound of the limping elk, so he climbed a leaning cedar to search for him. Lean and muscular, the lion was magnificently beautiful. Tawny in color, he had black smudges under his eyes and along his nose. His back was as straight as a leveling rod, his paws immense. His tail was tipped with black and almost as long as he. It touched the ground and curled up at the end. He weighed more than two hundred pounds. He was a cougar, or mountain lion, of North America. Almost as large as African lions, cougars are the second largest species of cat in the New World. Only jaguars surpass them in length and weight.

A hundred years ago mountain lions were abundant in all the mountains of the United States and Canada. Now they are rare in the United States and found only in the lonely wilderness areas of the West, Southwest, and Florida. Washington's Olympic Peninsula, a land barely touched by humans, still has its appropriate number of mountain lions. Because of their presence the elk and deer do not become so numerous that they ravage trees, bushes, grasses, and the wildlife that depend on them for shelter and food. The lions keep the herds in balance with their environment.

From the tree, the young lion could see the Hoh River valley where he had been born and raised. Turning his head he glanced up the mountain. The snow-covered peaks of the Olympic Mountains shone like silver saw blades against the purple-black sky. In the moonlight the mountain glaciers looked like Rocky Mountain goats sleeping on the dark rocks. Some of the spots may even have been goats. The goats lived at timberline and above all year round.

The lion's sensitive ears could hear the largest glacier, Blue Glacier, moan as its tons of ice moved great boulders, slowly grinding them to dust. In the August heat, all sixty glaciers were melting. The melt spilled down the mountain, forming waterfalls, streams, and the many rivers that joined the sea.

The lion could not locate the lame elk. Silently he leaped to the ground and slipped into the forest.

☑ Check Your Comprehension

1. Where exactly does the mountain lion live?
2. What animal is the first to migrate from this area in late summer?
3. Name three other animals (besides the mountain lion) discussed in the selection.
4. Summarize the activities of the mountain lion in the selection.

◆ Critical Thinking

INTERPRET

1. How would you describe the natural changes going on during this selection, noticeable or not so noticeable? Give examples to support your answer. **[Analyze]**

2. For what reason do you think the author focuses on these changes in such detail? **[Infer]**

COMPARE LITERARY WORKS

3. Both *The Moon of the Mountain Lions* and *The Tarantula in My Purse* deal with animal behavior, but in different ways. What are some differences in the way the story is told in the two selections? **[Compare and Contrast]**

EXTEND

4. People as well as animals make preparations for when the winter comes. What things do people do to get ready for winter? Are any of these things similar to the preparations animals make? **[Classify; Social Studies Link]**

Jean Craighead George
Comparing and Connecting the Author's Works

◆ Literary Focus: Similes

In order to present her ideas strongly and vividly, Jean Craighead George often uses language that compares things in new ways. To do this, she often uses **similes,** which are comparisons that use the word *like* or *as,* to point out similarities between two unlike things. For example, at the beginning of *The Wild, Wild Cookbook,* she says that " ... the flowers of the shadbush shine like frost in the dark woodland." Here, the two unlike things that are being compared are flowers and frost. You may not be familiar with the flowers of the shadbush, but after you read this simile you can make a good guess that they are white.

Similes often work particularly well in descriptions of nature. George uses a number of them in *The Moon of the Mountain Lions.* When she tells about the swallows leaving the area, for example, she says that they "[leave] the skies strangely empty, like beaches when winter comes." This simile reinforces not only the emptiness, but also the coldness and barrenness, of an autumn sky. Later, in describing the mountain lion, she says that "His back was as straight as a leveling rod." Through this simile the reader gets a strong picture of the magnificent stance and posture of the mountain lion.

1. In *The Tarantula in My Purse,* George says that her son Craig's "train set ... moved like a garter snake." What are some things this simile suggests about the train?

2. Explain what makes the comparison in this simile, from the last portion of *The Moon of the Mountain Lions,* seem appropriate: "The snow-covered peaks of the [mountains] shone like silver saw blades against the purple-black sky."

3. Find another simile in the same paragraph of *The Moon of the Mountain Lions.* Tell what two things it compares and why these things are unlike.

◆ Drawing Conclusions About George's Work

According to Jean Craighead George, in order to be a good nature writer, one must "listen and watch and observe." She might have added that sometimes good observation takes a long time. When George was researching *Julie of the Wolves,* she spent a whole summer in Alaska learning all she could about life in a wolf pack. Especially when writing about how animals learn and grow, she understands that it is important to watch and then carefully record the changes that take place over time.

Choose one of the events in the list below. Then fill in the chart with information about it. Include as much detail as you can.

- Yammer lives with the family in *The Tarantula in My Purse*

- The marmot hibernates in *The Moon of the Mountain Lions*

- The wild cherry goes from flower to fruit in *The Wild, Wild Cookbook*

Event	Start Time/ End Time	Observable Changes

◆ Idea Bank

Writing

1. **Animal Activity Summary** Sit and watch an outdoor animal such as a bird, squirrel, possum, or raccoon for at least five minutes. Write a summary of the animal's activities.

2. **Persuasive Letter** Imagine that you are Twig. Write a short letter to your mother trying to persuade her to let you keep Yammer. Use specific details and information that you think will convince her. Before you begin, outline your response. Organize your arguments from least persuasive to most persuasive.

3. **Descriptive Writing** Write a description of the natural changes in your community when one season moves to another—for example, when winter changes to spring. Use two or three similes in your description.

Speaking and Listening

4. **Poster** Make a poster offering to give a screech owl away to a good home. Use details about Yammer to list the advantages and disadvantages of owl ownership. Do research to illustrate your poster realistically. **[Art Link]**

5. **Mixed Media Oral Reading** With a group of classmates, prepare an oral reading of a section of *The Moon of the Mountain Lions* to be preformed for a group of younger students. Choose members of the group to prepare appropriate illustrations for the reading. Choose two or three readers, and have the illustrators work with them to display the pictures at the appropriate times. **[Performing Arts Link; Art Link; Group Activity]**

Researching and Representing

6. **Animal Research** Find out all you can about an animal that Jean Craighead George discusses in these selections. Your research should cover such things as the animal's size, physical appearance, diet, natural habitat, and life span. Prepare a chart showing your findings. **[Science Link]**

◆ Further Reading, Listening, and Viewing

- George, Jean Craighead. *Acorn Pancakes, Dandelion Salad and 38 Other Wild Recipes* (1995). A new edition of *The Wild, Wild Cookbook,* with even more natural treats.

- George, Jean Craighead. *The Tarantula in My Purse: And 172 Other Wild Pets* (1996). Read stories of other wild animals cared for by Jean Craighead George and her family.

- *A Visit with Jean Craighead George* (1994). View this videocassette to spend a day with George in her home and in the mountain area where her novel *My Side of the Mountain* is set.,

On the Web:

http://www.phschool.com/atschool/literature
Go to the student edition *Copper*. Proceed to Unit 6. Then, click Hot Links to find Web sites featuring Jean Craighead George.

Gary Soto In Depth

"I don't think I had any literary aspirations when I was a kid. We didn't have books, and no one encouraged us to read. So my wanting to write poetry was a sort of fluke."

—*Gary Soto*

When **GARY SOTO** was growing up during the 1950's and 1960's, he noticed that very few books for young people featured Mexican American characters. In the 1970's, when Soto became a writer, he set out to fill that gap. He says, "Because I believe in literature and the depth of living it adds to our years, my task is to start Chicanos reading." He pursues this goal by writing about characters to whom Chicanos can relate. Today, thanks to Soto and others, there exist many books for young people that feature Mexican American characters, use everyday Spanish phrases, and give readers a sense of Chicano culture.

A Working-Class Neighborhood

Gary Soto was born in Fresno, California, in 1952. His family had lived in the area since the 1930's, when his grandparents emigrated from Mexico during the Great Depression and found work as farm laborers. When Soto was five years old, his father died as the result of a factory accident. With the help of the children's grandparents, Soto's mother raised young Gary and his siblings. Soto describes his family as illiterate. They kept no books or magazines in the house, and the adults were too busy working to encourage a love of reading in their children.

Soto performed his own share of hard work when he was young. In addition to his household chores, he helped support his family by mowing lawns, picking grapes, painting house numbers on street curbs, and washing cars. As he grew up, Soto wanted at various times to become a priest, a hobo, and a paleontologist. He never dreamed he would become a writer.

A Change of Plans

After high school, Soto enrolled at California State University at Fresno. He planned to study geography, but then he discovered poetry. One day, when he was supposed to be researching a paper on continental drift, Soto spotted a poetry anthology that looked interesting. He sat down to read, and the poems seemed to leap off the page at him. He spent the next few weeks reading poetry, and felt that his life had been changed.

Excited by this discovery, Soto changed his major from geography to English and, in 1973, started writing poetry. Three years later, he won the United States Award of the International Poetry Forum for his collection of poems, *The Elements of San Joaquin.*

Branching Out

Soto published his next poetry collection, *The Tale of Sunlight,* in 1977. His work continued to win many awards, and he became a professor of English and Ethnic Studies at the University of California.

In 1985, Soto decided to broaden his career as a writer. In *Living Up the Street,* he wrote short stories about growing up in Fresno. After writing about his youth, Soto found that writing for young people was a natural step. In *Baseball in April and Other Stories,* Soto depicts daily life in a Mexican American community. He addresses the idea of cultural pride and awareness in many of his stories and novels.

A Writer's Life Today, Soto lives with his wife and daughter in Berkeley, California. In addition to his writing career, Soto has been a teacher at the college level since 1976. He is also a volunteer English teacher at his church.

Soto loves to meet his readers. He enjoys playing baseball and basketball with the young people he meets at schools, and he hopes that his visits will excite students about reading and writing. "I figure if they meet me, they will be curious to read what I write," he says. "If that inspires them to read what other people write, all the better!"

Supporting the Arts Soto works hard to support and encourage young Chicano writers. He says, "I'm 47, and I'm thinking I would like to produce writers who actually could take over my job. Not many Hispanic youth are going into creative writing as a field." To this end, he edits the Chicano Chapbook Series, which presents the works of young Chicano writers. He purchased land for Arté Americas, a Mexican Arts center, and he serves on several boards, including those of La Galería de la Raza and Arté Americas.

◆ Migrant Farm Workers

After immigrating to the United States, Gary Soto's grandparents became migrant farm workers. These workers move from one region to another, doing temporary, seasonal jobs such as picking crops. Their work is manual and easy to learn.

Migrant farm workers tend to have low wages, poor working conditions, and a lower standard of living than that of other groups of workers. They are constantly moving to find available work, so they do not develop stable relationships with employers. As a result, these workers often remain on the outskirts of communities, and are denied access to local agencies such as health services and the courts.

In the 1960's, conditions began to improve for migrant farm workers when a man named Cesar Chavez worked to organize them into unions. A former migrant worker himself, Chavez dreamed of ending the suffering of farm workers. He organized a union called the United Farm Workers, which has used peaceful strikes and boycotts to gain power. Today, the UFW has about 100,000 members. Cesar Chavez died in 1993, but the UFW continues to work to improve conditions for farm workers.

◆ Literary Works

Poetry

- *The Elements of San Joaquin* (1977)
- *The Tale of Sunlight* (1978)
- *Where Sparrows Work Hard* (1981)
- *Black Hair* (1985)
- *Who Will Know Us?* (1990)
- *A Fire in My Hands* (1991)
- *Home Course in Religion* (1991)
- *Neighborhood Odes* (1992)
- *Canto Familiar/Familiar Song* (1995)
- *New and Selected Poems* (1995)

Essays

- *Living Up the Street* (1985)

Short Story Collections

- *Baseball in April and Other Stories* (1990)
- *Local News* (1993)
- *Petty Crimes* (1998)

Novels for Young Adults

- *Taking Sides* (1991)
- *Pacific Crossing* (1992)
- *The Skirt* (1992)
- *Crazy Weekend* (1994)
- *Jesse* (1994)
- *Off and Running* (1996)
- *Boys at Work* (1996)
- *Buried Onions* (1997)

Gary Soto

Baseball in April

The night before Michael and Jesse were to try out for the Little League team for the third year in a row, the two brothers sat in their bedroom listening to the radio, pounding their fists into their gloves, and talking about how they would bend to pick up grounders or wave off another player and make the pop-up catch. "This is the year," Michael said with the confidence of an older brother. He pretended to scoop up the ball and throw out a man racing to first. He pounded his glove, looked at Jesse, and asked, "How'd you like that?"

When they reached Romain playground the next day there were a hundred kids divided into lines by age group: nine, ten, and eleven. Michael and Jesse stood in line, gloves hanging limp from their hands, and waited to have a large paper number pinned to their backs so that the field coaches would know who they were.

Jesse chewed his palm as he moved up the line. When his number was called he ran out onto the field to the sound of his black sneakers smacking against the clay. He looked at the kids still in line, then at Michael who yelled, "You can do it!" The first grounder, a three-bouncer, spun off his glove into center field. Another grounder cracked off the bat, and he scooped it up, but the ball rolled off his glove. Jesse stared at it before he picked it up and hurled it to first base. The next one he managed to pick up cleanly, but his throw made the first baseman leap into the air with an exaggerated grunt that made *him* look good. Three more balls were hit to Jesse, and he came up with one.

His number flapped like a broken wing as he ran off the field to sit in the bleachers and wait for Michael to trot onto the field.

Michael raced after the first grounder and threw it on the run. On the next grounder, he lowered himself to one knee and threw nonchalantly to first. As his number, a crooked seventeen, flapped on his back, he saw a coach make a mark on his clipboard.

Michael lunged at the next hit but missed, and it skidded into center field. He shaded his eyes after the next hit, a high pop-up, and when the ball came down he was there to slap it into his glove. His mouth grew fat from trying to hold back a smile. The coach made another mark on his clipboard.

When the next number was called, Michael jogged off the field with his head held high. He sat next to his brother, both dark and serious as they watched the other boys trot on and off the field.

Finally, the coaches told them to return after lunch for batting tryouts. Michael and Jesse ran home to eat a sandwich and talk about what to expect in the afternoon.

"Don't be scared," Michael said with his mouth full of ham sandwich, though he knew Jesse's batting was no good. He showed him how to stand. He spread his legs, worked his left foot into the carpet as if he were putting out a cigarette, and glared at where the ball would come from, twenty feet in front of him near the kitchen table. He swung an invisible bat, choked up on the handle, and swung again.

He turned to his younger brother. "Got it?"

Jesse said he thought he did and imitated Michael's swing until Michael said, "Yeah, you got it."

Jesse felt proud walking to the playground because the smaller kids were in awe of the paper number on his back. It was as if he were a soldier going off to war.

"Where you goin'?" asked Rosie, sister of Johnnie Serna, the playground bully. She had a large bag of sunflower seeds, and spat out a shell.

"Tryouts," Jesse said, barely looking at her as he kept stride with Michael.

At the diamond, Jesse once again grew nervous. He got into the line of nine-year-olds and waited for his turn at bat. Fathers clung to the fence, giving last-minute instructions to their kids.

By the time it was Jesse's turn, he was trembling and trying to catch Michael's eye for reassurance. He walked to the batter's box, tapped the bat on the plate—something he had seen many times on television—and waited. The first pitch was outside and over his head. The coach laughed.

He swung hard at the next pitch, spinning the ball foul. He tapped his bat again, kicked the dirt, and stepped into the batter's box. He swung at a low ball. Then he wound up and sliced the next ball foul to the edge of the infield grass, which surprised him because he didn't know he had the strength to send it that far.

Jesse was given ten pitches and got three hits, all of them grounders to the right side. One grounder kicked up into the face of a kid trying to field the ball. The kid tried to hang tough as he trotted off the field, head bowed, but Jesse knew tears were welling up in his eyes.

Jesse handed the bat to the next kid and went to sit in the bleachers to wait for the ten-year-olds to bat. He was feeling better than after that morning's fielding tryout because he had gotten three hits. He also thought he looked strong standing at the plate, bat high over his shoulder.

Michael came up to the plate and hit the first pitch to third base. He sent the next pitch into left field. He talked to himself as he stood in the box, bouncing slightly before the next pitch, which he smacked into the outfield. The coach marked his clipboard.

After his ten hits, he jogged off the field and joined his brother in the bleachers. His mouth was again fat from holding back a smile. Jesse was jealous of his brother's athletic display. He thought to himself, Yeah, he'll make the team, and I'll just watch from the bleachers. He imagined Michael running home with a uniform under his arm while he walked home empty-handed.

They watched other kids come to the plate and whack, foul, chop, slice, dribble, and hook balls all over the field. When a foul ball bounced into the bleachers, Jesse got it. He weighed the ball in his palm, like a pound of bologna, and then hurled it back onto the field. An uninterested coach watched it roll by his feet.

After it was over, they were told to expect a phone call by the end of the week if they had made the team.

By Monday afternoon they were already anxious for the phone to ring. They slouched in the living room after school and watched "Double Dare" on TV. Every time Jesse went into the kitchen, he stole a glance at the telephone. Once, when no one was looking, he picked it up to see if it was working and heard a long buzz.

By Friday, when it was clear the call would never come, they went outside to the front yard to play catch and practice bunting.

"I should have made the team," Michael said as he made a stab at Jesse's bunt. Jesse agreed with him. If anyone should have made the team, it should have been his brother. He was the best one there.

They hit grounders to each other. A few popped off Jesse's chest, but most disappeared neatly into his glove. Why couldn't I do this last Saturday? he wondered. He grew angry at himself, then sad. They stopped playing and returned inside to watch "Double Dare."

Michael and Jesse didn't make Little League that year, but Pete, a friend from school, told them about a team of kids from their school that practiced at Hobo[1] Park near downtown. After school Michael and Jesse raced to the park. They laid their bikes on the grass and took the field. Michael ran to the outfield, and Jesse took second base to practice grounders.

"Give me a baby roller," Danny Lopez, the third baseman, called. Jesse sidearmed a roller, which Danny picked up on the third bounce. "Good pickup," Jesse yelled. Danny looked pleased, slapping his glove against his pants as he hustled back to third.

Michael practiced catching pop-ups with Billy Reeves until Manuel, the coach, arrived in his pickup. Most of the kids ran to

---

1. **Hobo:** Vagrant, wanderer.

let him know they wanted to play first, to play second, to hit first, to hit third. Michael and Jesse were quiet and stood back from the racket.

Manuel pulled a duffel bag from the back of his pickup and walked over to the palm tree that served as a backstop. He dropped the bag with a grunt, clapped his hands, and told the kids to take the field.

The two brothers didn't move. When Pete told the coach that Michael and Jesse wanted to play, Jesse stiffened up and tried to look strong. Because he was older, and wiser, Michael stood with his arms crossed over his chest.

"You guys are in the outfield," the coach shouted before turning to pull a bat and a ball from the bag.

Manuel was middle-aged, patient, and fatherly. He bent down on his haunches to talk to the kids, spoke softly and listened to what they had to say. He cooed "Good" when they made catches, even routine ones. The kids knew he was good to them because most of them didn't have fathers, or had fathers who were so beaten from hard work that they came home and fell asleep in front of the TV set.

The team practiced for two weeks before Manuel announced their first game.

"Who we playing?" asked Pete.

"The Red Caps," he answered. "West Fresno kids."

"What's our name?" two kids asked.

"The Hobos," the coach said, smiling.

In two weeks Jesse had gotten better. But Michael quit the team because he found a girlfriend, a slow walker who hugged her books against her chest while gazing dreamily into Michael's equally dazed face. What fools, Jesse thought as he rode off to practice.

Jesse was catcher and winced behind his mask when the batter swung, because he had no chest protector or shin guards. Balls skidded off his arms and chest, but he never let on that they hurt.

His batting, however, did not improve, and the team knew he was a sure out. Some of the older kids tried to give him tips: how to stand, follow through, and push his weight into the ball. Still, when he came up to bat, the outfielders moved in, like wolves moving in for the kill.

Before their first game, some of the team members met early at Hobo Park to talk about how they were going to whip the Red Caps and send them home crying to their mothers. Soon, others showed up to field grounders while they waited for the coach. When they spotted him, they ran to his pickup and climbed the sides. The coach stuck his head from the cab and warned them to be careful. He waited for a few minutes for the slow kids, and waved for them to get in the front with him. As the team drove slowly to the West Side, the wind running through their hair, they thought they looked pretty neat.

When they arrived, they leaped from the pickup and stood by the coach, who waved to the other coach as he hoisted his duffel bag onto his shoulder. Jesse scanned the other team: most were Mexican like his team, but they had a few blacks.

The coach shook hands with the other coach. They talked quietly in Spanish, then roared with laughter and patted each other's shoulder. They turned around and furrowed their brows at the infield, which was muddy from a recent rain.

Jesse and Pete warmed up behind the backstop, throwing gently to each other and trying to stay calm. Jesse envied the Red Caps, who seemed bigger and scarier than his team and wore matching T-shirts and caps. His team wore jeans and mismatched T-shirts.

The Hobos batted first and scored one run on an error and a double to left field. Then the Red Caps batted and scored four runs on three errors. On the last one, Jesse stood in front of the plate, mask in hand, yelling, "I got a play! I got a play!" But the ball sailed over his head. By the time Jesse picked up the ball, the runner was already sitting on the bench, breathing hard and smiling. Jesse carried the ball to the pitcher.

He searched his face and saw that Elias was scared. "C'mon, you can do it," Jesse said, putting his arm around the pitcher's shoulder. He walked back to the plate. He was wearing a chest protector that reached almost to his knees and made him feel important.

The Red Caps failed to score any more that inning.

In their second turn at bat, the Hobos scored twice on a hit and an error that hurt the Red Caps' catcher. But by the sixth inning, the Red Caps were ahead, sixteen to nine.

The Hobos began arguing with each other. Their play was sloppy, nothing like the cool routines back at their own field. Fly balls to the outfield dropped at the feet of openmouthed players. Grounders rolled slowly between their legs. Even the pitching stank.

"You *had* to mess up, *menso*,"[2] Danny Lopez shouted at the shortstop.

"Well, you didn't get a hit, and *I* did," the shortstop said, pointing to his chest.

From the dugout, the coach told them to be quiet when they started cussing.

Jesse came up to bat for the fourth time that afternoon with two men on and two outs. His teammates moaned because they

---

2. *menso* (men´ sō): Dummy.

were sure he was going to strike out or hit a pop-up. To make matters worse, the Red Caps had a new pitcher and he was throwing hard.

Jesse was almost as scared of the pitcher's fast ball as he was of failing. The coach clung to the fence, cooing words of encouragement. His team yelled at Jesse to swing hard. Dig in, they shouted, and he dug in, bat held high over his shoulder. After two balls and a strike, the pitcher threw low and hard toward Jesse's thigh. Jesse stood still because he knew that was the only way he was going to get on base.

The ball hit with a thud, and he went down holding his leg and trying to hold back the tears. The coach ran from the dugout and bent over him, rubbing his leg. A few of the kids on his team came over to ask, "Does it hurt?" "Can I play catcher now?" and "Let me run for him, coach!"

Jesse rose and limped to first. The coach shooed the team back into the dugout and jogged to the coach's box at first. Although his leg hurt, Jesse was happy to be on base. He grinned, looked up, and adjusted his cap. So this is what it's like, he thought. He clapped his hands and encouraged the next batter, their lead-off man. "C'mon, baby, c'mon, you can do it!" The batter hit a high fly ball to deep center. While the outfielder backpedaled and made the catch, Jesse rounded second on his way to third, feeling wonderful to have gotten that far.

Hobo Park lost, nineteen to eleven, and went on to lose against the Red Caps four more times that season. The Hobos were stuck in a two-team league.

Jesse played until the league ended. Fewer and fewer of the players came to practice and the team began using girls to fill in the gaps. One day Manuel didn't show up with his duffel bag. On that day, it was clear to the four boys who remained that the baseball season was over. They threw the ball around, then got on their bikes and rode home. Jesse didn't show up the next day for practice. Instead he sat in front of the TV watching Superman bend iron bars.

He felt guilty though. He thought that one of the guys might have gone to practice and discovered no one there. If he had, he might have waited on the bench or, restless for something to do, he might have practiced pop-ups by throwing the ball into the air, calling, "I got it! I got it!" all by himself.

☑ Check Your Comprehension

1. As the story opens, what are Michael and Jesse doing?
2. (a) Describe Jesse's performance at Little League tryouts. (b) Describe Michael's performance.
3. What do Jesse and Michael do when they learn they have not made the team?
4. Describe the personality of Manuel, the coach of the Hobos. Support your answer with details from the story.
5. Why does Michael quit the team?
6. How does Jesse know the season is over?

◆ Critical Thinking

INTERPRET

1. At Little League tryouts, why does Michael have so much trouble holding back his smiles? **[Infer]**
2. How does Jesse feel during tryouts? Support your answer with details from the story. **[Analyze]**

3. Michael is one of the best players at tryouts. Why do you think he doesn't make the team? **[Speculate]**
4. Name two things Manuel does to make the Hobos feel good about themselves and their team. **[Analyze Causes and Effects]**
5. Why does the season end early for the Hobos? **[Infer]**

EVALUATE

6. Soto writes that when they rode in Manuel's pickup, the Hobos "thought they looked neat." Why is this an important moment in the story? **[Evaluate]**

APPLY

7. Do you think Manuel and Jesse make the right decision when they don't show up for practice at the end? What would you have done in this situation? **[Make a Judgment]**

Mother and Daughter

$\mathbf{Y}$ollie's mother, Mrs. Moreno, was a large woman who wore a muumuu[1] and butterfly-shaped glasses. She liked to water her lawn in the evening and wave at low-riders,[2] who would stare at her behind their smoky sunglasses and laugh. Now and then a low-rider from Belmont Avenue would make his car jump and shout *"Mamacita!"* But most of the time they just stared and wondered how she got so large.

Mrs. Moreno had a strange sense of humor. Once, Yollie and her mother were watching a late-night movie called "They Came to Look." It was about creatures from the underworld who had climbed through molten lava to walk the earth. But Yollie, who had played soccer all day with the kids next door, was too tired to be scared. Her eyes closed but sprang open when her mother screamed, "Look, Yollie! Oh, you missed a scary part. The guy's face was all ugly!"

But Yollie couldn't keep her eyes open. They fell shut again and stayed shut, even when her mother screamed and slammed a heavy palm on the arm of her chair.

"Mom, wake me up when the movie's over so I can go to bed," mumbled Yollie.

"OK, Yollie, I wake you," said her mother through a mouthful of popcorn.

But after the movie ended, instead of waking her daughter, Mrs. Moreno laughed under her breath, turned the TV and lights off, and tiptoed to bed. Yollie woke up in the middle of the night and didn't know where she was. For a moment she thought she was dead. Maybe something from the underworld had lifted her from her house and carried her into the earth's belly. She blinked her sleepy eyes, looked around at the darkness, and called, "Mom? Mom, where are you?" But there was no answer, just the throbbing hum of the refrigerator.

Finally, Yollie's grogginess cleared and she realized her mother had gone to bed, leaving her on the couch. Another of her little jokes.

But Yollie wasn't laughing. She tiptoed into her mother's bedroom with a glass of water and set it on the nightstand next to the alarm clock. The next morning, Yollie woke to screams. When her mother reached to turn off the alarm, she had overturned the glass of water.

---

1. muumuu (mōō´ mōō): A loose, often long dress with bright colors and patterns.
2. low-riders: People riding in a car with a lowered suspension, so that the body is very close to the road.

Yollie burned her mother's morning toast and gloated. "Ha! Ha! I got you back. Why did you leave me on the couch when I told you to wake me up?"

Despite their jokes, mother and daughter usually got along. They watched bargain matinees together, and played croquet in the summer and checkers in the winter. Mrs. Moreno encouraged Yollie to study hard because she wanted her daughter to be a doctor. She bought Yollie a desk, a typewriter, and a lamp that cut glare so her eyes would not grow tired from hours of studying.

Yollie was slender as a tulip, pretty, and one of the smartest kids at Saint Theresa's. She was captain of crossing guards, an altar girl, and a whiz in the school's monthly spelling bees.

"*Tienes que estudiar mucho,*"[3] Mrs. Moreno said every time she propped her work-weary feet on the hassock.[4] "You have to study a lot, then you can get a good job and take care of me."

"Yes, Mama," Yollie would respond, her face buried in a book. If she gave her mother any sympathy, she would begin her stories about how she had come with her family from Mexico with nothing on her back but a sack with three skirts, all of which were too large by the time she crossed the border because she had lost weight from not having enough to eat.

Everyone thought Yollie's mother was a riot. Even the nuns laughed at her antics. Her brother Raul, a nightclub owner, thought she was funny enough to go into show business.

But there was nothing funny about Yollie needing a new outfit for the eighth-grade fall dance. They couldn't afford one. It was late October, with Christmas around the corner, and their dented Chevy Nova had gobbled up almost one hundred dollars in repairs.

"We don't have the money," said her mother, genuinely sad because they couldn't buy the outfit, even though there was a little money stashed away for college. Mrs. Moreno remembered her teenage years and her hardworking parents, who picked grapes and oranges, and chopped beets and cotton for meager pay around Kerman. Those were the days when "new clothes" meant limp and out-of-style dresses from Saint Vincent de Paul.[5]

The best Mrs. Moreno could do was buy Yollie a pair of black shoes with velvet bows and fabric dye to color her white summer dress black.

"We can color your dress so it will look brand-new," her mother said brightly, shaking the bottle of dye as she ran hot water

---

3. *Tienes que estudiar mucho* (tē en´ ās kā es tōō d´ ē är mōō´ chō): You have to study a lot.
4. **hassock:** A footrest.
5. **Saint Vincent de Paul:** A charitable society that provides used items at low prices.

into a plastic dish tub. She poured the black liquid into the tub and stirred it with a pencil. Then, slowly and carefully, she lowered the dress into the tub.

Yollie couldn't stand to watch. She *knew* it wouldn't work. It would be like the time her mother stirred up a batch of molasses for candy apples on Yollie's birthday. She'd dipped the apples into the goo and swirled them and seemed to taunt Yollie by singing *"Las Mañanitas"*[6] to her. When she was through, she set the apples on wax paper. They were hard as rocks and hurt the kids' teeth. Finally they had a contest to see who could break the apples open by throwing them against the side of the house. The apples shattered like grenades, sending the kids scurrying for cover, and in an odd way the birthday party turned out to be a success. At least everyone went home happy.

To Yollie's surprise, the dress came out shiny black. It looked brand-new and sophisticated, like what people in New York wear. She beamed at her mother, who hugged Yollie and said, "See, what did I tell you?"

The dance was important to Yollie because she was in love with Ernie Castillo, the third-best speller in the class. She bathed, dressed, did her hair and nails, and primped until her mother yelled, "All right already." Yollie sprayed her neck and wrists with Mrs. Moreno's Avon perfume and bounced into the car.

Mrs. Moreno let Yollie out in front of the school. She waved and told her to have a good time but behave herself, then roared off, blue smoke trailing from the tail pipe of the old Nova.

Yollie ran into her best friend, Janice. They didn't say it, but each thought the other was the most beautiful girl at the dance; the boys would fall over themselves asking them to dance.

The evening was warm but thick with clouds. Gusts of wind picked up the paper lanterns hanging in the trees and swung them, blurring the night with reds and yellows. The lanterns made the evening seem romantic, like a scene from a movie. Everyone danced, sipped punch, and stood in knots of threes and fours, talking. Sister Kelly got up and jitterbugged with some kid's father. When the record ended, students broke into applause.

Janice had her eye on Frankie Ledesma, and Yollie, who kept smoothing her dress down when the wind picked up, had her eye on Ernie. It turned out that Ernie had his mind on Yollie, too. He ate a handful of cookies nervously, then asked her for a dance.

"Sure," she said, nearly throwing herself into his arms.

They danced two fast ones before they got a slow one. As they circled under the lanterns, rain began falling, lightly at first. Yollie loved the sound of the raindrops ticking against the leaves. She leaned her head on Ernie's shoulder, though his sweater was

---

6. *Las Mañanitas* (läs män yän ē′ täs): Mexican birthday song.

scratchy. He felt warm and tender. Yollie could tell that he was in love, and with her, of course. The dance continued successfully, romantically, until it began to pour.

"Everyone, let's go inside—and, boys, carry in the table and the record player," Sister Kelly commanded.

The girls and boys raced into the cafeteria. Inside, the girls, drenched to the bone, hurried to the restrooms to brush their hair and dry themselves. One girl cried because her velvet dress was ruined. Yollie felt sorry for her and helped her dry the dress off with paper towels, but it was no use. The dress was ruined.

Yollie went to a mirror. She looked a little gray now that her mother's makeup had washed away but not as bad as some of the other girls. She combed her damp hair, careful not to pull too hard. She couldn't wait to get back to Ernie.

Yollie bent over to pick up a bobby pin, and shame spread across her face. A black puddle was forming at her feet. Drip, black drip. Drip, black drip. The dye was falling from her dress like black tears. Yollie stood up. Her dress was now the color of ash. She looked around the room. The other girls, unaware of Yollie's problem, were busy grooming themselves. What could she do? Everyone would laugh. They would know she dyed an old dress because she couldn't afford a new one. She hurried from the restroom with her head down, across the cafeteria floor and out the door. She raced through the storm, crying as the rain mixed with her tears and ran into twig-choked gutters.

When she arrived home, her mother was on the couch eating cookies and watching TV.

"How was the dance, *m'ija?*[7] Come watch the show with me. It's really good."

Yollie stomped, head down, to her bedroom. She undressed and threw the dress on the floor.

Her mother came into the room. "What's going on? What's all this racket, baby?"

"The dress. It's cheap! It's no good!" Yollie kicked the dress at her mother and watched it land in her hands. Mrs. Moreno studied it closely but couldn't see what was wrong. "What's the matter? It's just little bit wet."

"The dye came out, that's what."

Mrs. Moreno looked at her hands and saw the grayish dye puddling in the shallow lines of her palms. Poor baby, she thought, her brow darkening as she made a sad face. She wanted to tell her daughter how sorry she was, but she knew it wouldn't help. She walked back to the living room and cried.

The next morning, mother and daughter stayed away from each other. Yollie sat in her room turning the pages of an old *Seventeen*,

---

7. **m'ija** (mē´ hä): Abbreviation for *mi hija,* which means "my daughter."

while her mother watered her plants with a Pepsi bottle.

"Drink, my children," she said loud enough for Yollie to hear. She let the water slurp into pots of coleus and cacti. "Water is all you need. My daughter needs clothes, but I don't have no money."

Yollie tossed her *Seventeen* on her bed. She was embarrassed at last night's tirade. It wasn't her mother's fault that they were poor.

When they sat down together for lunch, they felt awkward about the night before. But Mrs. Moreno had made a fresh stack of tortillas and cooked up a pan of *chile verde*,[8] and that broke the ice. She licked her thumb and smacked her lips.

"You know, honey, we gotta figure a way to make money," Yollie's mother said. "You and me. We don't have to be poor. Remember the Garcias. They made this stupid little tool that fixes cars. They moved away because they're rich. That's why we don't see them no more."

"What can we make?" asked Yollie. She took another tortilla and tore it in half.

"Maybe a screwdriver that works on both ends? Something like that." The mother looked around the room for ideas, but then shrugged. "Let's forget it. It's better to get an education. If you get a good job and have spare time then maybe you can invent something." She rolled her tongue over her lips and cleared her throat. "The county fair hires people. We can get a job there. It will be here next week."

Yollie hated the idea. What would Ernie say if he saw her pitching hay at the cows? How could she go to school smelling like an armful of chickens? "No, they wouldn't hire us," she said.

The phone rang. Yollie lurched from her chair to answer it, thinking it would be Janice wanting to know why she had left. But it was Ernie wondering the same thing. When he found out she wasn't mad at him, he asked if she would like to go to a movie.

"I'll ask," Yollie said, smiling. She covered the phone with her hand and counted to ten. She uncovered the receiver and said, "My mom says it's OK. What are we going to see?"

After Yollie hung up, her mother climbed, grunting, onto a chair to reach the top shelf in the hall closet. She wondered why she hadn't done it earlier. She reached behind a stack of towels and pushed her chubby hand into the cigar box where she kept her secret stash of money.

"I've been saving a little every month," said Mrs. Moreno. "For you, *m'ija*." Her mother held up five twenties, a blossom of green that smelled sweeter than flowers on that Saturday. They drove to Macy's and bought a blouse, shoes, and a skirt that would not bleed in rain or any other kind of weather.

---

8. *chile verde* (chē´ lā vār´ dā): A stew-like dish.

☑ Check Your Comprehension

1. Soto writes that Yollie's mother had a "strange sense of humor." Give one example of this.
2. Describe the relationship between Yollie and her mother. Support your answer with details from the story.
3. How does Yollie's mother help her prepare for the eighth-grade fall dance?
4. What happens to Yollie's dress at the dance?
5. What does Yollie's mother do for Yollie at the end of the story?

◆ Critical Thinking

INTERPRET

1. Find two details that show that Mrs. Moreno cares about Yollie's future. **[Support]**
2. Mrs. Moreno comes up with the idea to dye Yollie's old dress to make it look new. What does this suggest about her personality? **[Analyze]**

3. The morning after the dance, Yollie feels "embarrassed about last night's tirade." Why do you think she feels embarrassed? **[Infer]**
4. Why does Yollie tell her mother that the county fair would not hire them? **[Infer]**
5. Why do you think Mrs. Moreno decides to give Yollie the money she's been saving? **[Draw Conclusions]**

EVALUATE

6. Do you think Yollie is justified in feeling angry with her mother about what happened to the black dress? Why? **[Make a Judgment]**

COMPARE LITERARY WORKS

7. In both "Baseball and April" and "Mother and Daughter," young people get support from a caring adult. Find one example of this in each story. **[Connect]**

Gary Soto

Ode to Mi Perrito

He's brown as water
Over a stone,
Brown as leaves and branches,
Brown as pennies in a hand.
5   He's brown as my mitt
On a bedpost,
And just as quick:
A baseball rolls
His way and his teeth
10 Chatter after it.
Mi perrito[1] rolls
His tongue for the taste
Of a dropped *chicharrón*,[2]
For the jawbreaker
15 That fell from my pocket,
For a potato chip bag
Blowing across a lawn.
He's brown as earth
But his days are yellow
20 As the sun at noon.
Today he rode
In my father's car,
His paws on the dash
As he looked around
25 At the road giving way
To farms and countryside.
He barked at slow drivers
And Father barked back.
Where did they go?
30 Fishing. Ten miles
From town, and they crossed
A river, blue with the
Rush of water.
Fish lurked beneath
35 The surface, the big
O of their mouths
Gulping bubbles.
Father threw his line
There, and waited,
40 His hands in his pockets.

---

1. **Mi perrito** (mē per ē′ tō): My little dog.
2. **chicharrón** (chē chä rōn′): Fried pork rind.

Mi perrito didn't wait.
He jumped into the river,
And jumped back out—
The water was icy
45   Cold. Father fished
And *mi perrito*
Walked along the riverbank,
Sniffing for birds
And cool-throated mice.
50   *Mi perrito* was a hunter.
He crept in the low brush,
His ears perked up.
When he jumped,
His paws landed on a cricket.
55   The cricket chirped
And jumped into
The gray ambush of grass.
He barked and returned
To my father, who
60   Returned to the car:
The fish would have
Nothing of hook and sinker.
They drove back
To town through the curve
65   Of hills. When
My father turned
Sharply, *mi perrito* barked
Because it's his job
To make noise
70   Of oncoming danger.
He had his paws
Up on the dash,
With a good view
Of the hills
75   Where cows sat down on the job.
When one cow dared
To moo, *mi perrito* barked
And showed his flashing teeth.
Mi perrito is a chihuahua—[3]
80   Smaller than a cat,
Bigger than a rubber mouse.
Like mouse and cat,
He goes running
When the real dogs
85   Come into the yard.

---

3. chihuahua (chi wä′ wä): Any of an ancient Mexican breed of very small dog
with large, pointed ears.

ary Soto

Where We Could Go

Happy that this is another
Country, we're going to
Sit before coffees and croissants
On Rue Lucerne
5   And watching the working fathers
Labor up the street,
A stiff loaf of bread
In each roughed-up hand.
Some nod to us;
10   Others pass with the moist eyes
Of a strict wind.
This is France, daughter.
This is the autumn of calendars.
The sparrows are like
15   Those back home fighting
With the lawn,
Squealing and transparent
As their hunger.
They play at our feet,
20   Then climb to our knees
To hop like windup toys,
Until they're on the table
That's scratched with more
History than either of us—
25   Their beaks tap for crumbs.
But the waiter shoos them
With a dish towel.
This is a cafe for people,
Not birds, he says,
30   And so we leave because
We're like birds,
Transparent at love and deceit.
We hunger; we open our mouths . . .
We walk up the street, our shoes
35   Ringing against the stones,
To stare into a store window—
Clocks, coffee pots, an accordion
Longing for the sea.
But we're miles from the sea.
40   There are no boats or salt
Climbing our arms.

This is a country town,
And straw is what makes things
Go here—or so says our guidebook.
45 And it says that there
Is a church, lit with gold
And rare paintings,
And we start off
Hand in hand, smiling
50 For no reason other than
Everything is new—
The stone buildings, straw
Whacked into bundles.
What's that? my daughter
55 Asks, and there's no greater
Pleasure than saying,
Beats me. Let's go see.

Tortillas Like Africa

When Isaac and me squeezed dough over a mixing bowl,
When we dusted the cutting board with flour,
When we spanked and palmed our balls of dough,
When we said, "Here goes,"
5 And began rolling out tortillas,
We giggled because ours came out not round, like Mama's,
But in the shapes of faraway lands.

Here was Africa, here was Colombia and Greenland.
Here was Italy, the boot country,
10 And here was México, our homeland to the south.

Here was Chile, thin as a tie.
Here was France, square as a hat.
Here was Australia, with patches of jumping kangaroos.

We rolled out our tortillas on the board
15 And laughed when we threw them on the *comal*,[1]
These tortillas that were not round as a pocked moon,
But the twist and stretch of the earth taking shape.

---

1. *comal* (cō mäl´): Griddle.

So we made our first batch of tortillas, laughing.
So we wrapped them in a dish towel.
20   So we buttered and rolled two each
And sat on the front porch—
Butter ran down our arms and our faces shone.

I asked Isaac, "How's yours?"
He cleared his throat and opened his tortilla.
25   He said, "¡*Bueno!*2 Greenland tastes like México."

---

2. *Bueno* (bwā´ nō): Good.

☑ Check Your Comprehension

1. In "Ode to Mi Perrito," where do the speaker's father and the dog go?
2. Find two details in "Ode to Mi Perrito" that show the dog is curious about his surroundings.
3. Where are the speaker and his daughter in "Where We Could Go"?
4. In "Where We Could Go," what gives the speaker the greatest pleasure?
5. In "Tortillas Like Africa," what do the tortillas look like? Why?

◆ Critical Thinking

INTERPRET

1. Explain the meaning of these lines from "Ode to Mi Perrito": "He's brown as earth / But his days are yellow / As the sun at noon." **[Interpret]**

2. Were you surprised that the dog in "Ode to Mi Perrito" is a chihuahua? Explain your answer. **[Analyze]**
3. In "Where We Could Go," how would you characterize the relationship between the father and daughter? Use details from the poem to support your answer. **[Infer]**
4. What do you think Isaac means when he says, "Greenland tastes like México"? **[Interpret]**

EVALUATE

5. Why do you think the father in "Where We Could Go" gets so much pleasure from exploring new places with his young daughter? **[Relate]**

APPLY

6. In what way can you relate to the boys' experience in "Tortillas Like Africa" even if you have never made tortillas? **[Relate]**

Gary Soto

Comparing and Connecting the Author's Works

◆ Literary Focus: Imagery

One of Gary Soto's greatest strengths as a writer is his use of sensory language to create powerful descriptions. **Sensory language** is the use of words and phrases to create pictures in the reader's mind. These pictures, or images, help the reader respond to the experience being described by appealing to our sense of sight, hearing, smell, taste, or touch. In "Ode to Mi Perrito," for example, we can almost see the "potato chip bag / blowing across the lawn."

1. Reread the first six lines of "Ode to Mi Perrito." Name three visual images Soto uses to describe the color of the dog.
2. Read aloud the first paragraph of both stories. List images that can be appreciated by your senses. Next to each image, write the sense it appeals to.
3. With a partner, look through all three poems for examples of language that appeals to each of your senses. Write them in a chart like this one:

Sight	Hearing	Smell	Taste	Touch

◆ Drawing Conclusions About Soto's Work

Gary Soto writes, "As with much of my work, I like to place young people in small, everyday problems. I like to see them…right something that goes wrong." He understands that young people face problems, and admires their determination in overcoming them.

For example, in "Baseball in April,"

Jesse joins the Hobos and tries to enjoy himself despite the fact that he doesn't make the Little League team. Soto shows that he is a resilient character who tries to make the best of things.

In the left-hand column of the chart below, describe two difficult situations that Yollie faces in "Mother and Daughter." In the right, explain how she tries to overcome each problem.

Problem	Solution
Jesse doesn't make the Little League team.	He joins the Hobos and tries to enjoy himself.

After you complete the chart, write a paragraph about the ways Yollie confronts problems. Explain what this tells you about her character.

◆ Idea Bank

Writing

1. **News Article** Write a news article about a game between the Hobos and the Red Caps. In your article, make sure to include the five W's (who, what, when, where, and why). Before you begin, read an account of a baseball game from your school or local newspaper and use it as a model. **[Media Link]**
2. **Journal Entry** Imagine that you are Yollie, and write a journal entry about your experience with the dress. What did your learn from the experience?

What did you learn about your mother? When you finish, share your entry with a classmate.

3. **Poem** Write a poem about a pet. It can be a pet that belongs to you or a friend, or it can be a pet that you would like to have. Try to use sensory language to describe it. Use "Ode to Mi Perrito" as a model.

Speaking and Listening

4. **Dramatic Presentation** With a small group, present one of the stories by Soto as a play. First, rewrite the story in the form of a script. Then, choose roles and rehearse the script. You might want to use costumes or props to add visual interest to your presentation. Perform your play for the class, either live or on tape. **[Performing Arts Link; Group Activity]**

5. **Poetry Reading** In the library or on the Internet, look for another poem by Soto that you find interesting. After rehearsing, read it aloud to your class, emphasizing the words and lines you think are important. Explain why you like the poem. **[Performing Arts Link]**

Researching and Representing

6. **Multimedia Presentation** With a small group of classmates, create a multimedia presentation based on a topic mentioned by Soto in one of the poems. Here are some examples: having a pet, chihuahuas, fishing, France, and preparing Mexican foods. Enhance your presentation by including photos, charts, audio and video recordings, or other media. Make sure each member of the group contributes to the research and the presentation. **[Social Studies Link, Art Link; Group Activity]**

◆ Further Reading, Listening, and Viewing

- Soto, Gary, ed. Chicano Chapbook Series.

- Carlson, Lori M., ed. *Cool Salsa: Bilingual Poems on Growing Up Latino in the United States* (1994).

- Collins, David. *Farmworker's Friend: The Story of Cesar Chavez* (1996).

- Fernandez-Shaw, Carlos. *The Hispanic Presence in North America from 1492 to Today* (1991).

- Hoyt-Goldsmith, Diane. *Day of the Dead: A Mexican-American Celebration* (1994).

- Jimenez, Francisco. *The Circuit: Stories from the Life of a Migrant Child* (1996).

- Sinnott, Susan. *Extraordinary Hispanic Americans* (1991).

- *The Corn Woman: Audio Stories and Legends of the Hispanic Southwest* (1995), Libraries Unlimited.

- *The Pool Party* (1992). Gary Soto produced this film, which won the 1993 Andrew Carnegie Medal for Excellence in Children's Video.

On the Web:

http://www.phschool.com/atschool/literature
Go to the student edition *Copper.* Proceed to Unit 7. Then, click Hot Links to find Web sites featuring Gary Soto.

Norton Juster In Depth

> "The way I see things and think about things is as an architect, and my writing is totally influenced by this."
>
> *—Norton Juster*

NORTON JUSTER spent his professional life primarily as an architect, designing buildings and other structures. However, with the 1961 publication of his first novel, *The Phantom Tollbooth,* Juster suddenly found himself also a celebrated author of children's books. His love of mathematics, geometry, and aesthetics (the study of art and of people's reactions to it) is evident in his writings.

An Able Student

Norton Juster was born on June 2, 1929, in Brooklyn, New York. His father, Samuel, was an architect who encouraged his son's interest in the world of design.

Juster attended James Madison High School in Brooklyn. He enjoyed writing for his classes, but never imagined writing for a living. He graduated from the University of Pennsylvania with a bachelor's degree in architecture in 1952. After college he won a Fulbright scholarship to study city planning at the University of Liverpool in England.

An Ambitious Architect

Upon completing his graduate studies, Juster put his architectural skills to work. From 1954 to 1957, he served in the U.S. Naval Reserve as an engineer. During that time, he constructed airfields in Morocco and Newfoundland.

Juster demonstrated great aptitude and ambition as an architect. In 1960, he received a Ford Foundation grant for work in urban aesthetics. The same year, he joined the architectural firm of Juster & Gugliotta. In addition, he became a professor at the Pratt Institute in Brooklyn, where he worked for the next decade.

A Literary Surprise

As if being a full-time architect and professor weren't enough, Juster found himself doing creative writing in his spare time "as a relaxation" from a difficult planning project, he says. He began writing what he thought was only going to be a short story for his own pleasure. Yet before long, Juster says, "it had created its own life and I was hooked."

The result was *The Phantom Tollbooth*, a fantasy about a boy named Milo who travels to the Lands Beyond, where Dictionopolis, the kingdom of words, is at war with Digitopolis, the kingdom of numbers. Critics hailed the book as a children's classic, comparing it in style and wordplay to Lewis Carroll's *Alice in Wonderland.* Young readers formed the Phantom Phan Club.

The Output Continues

The huge success of his first novel did not encourage Juster to quit work as an architect and pursue writing full-time. However, he did continue to write on the side. In 1963 his second book, *The Dot and the Line,* was published. It is an allegory describing the romance between a round dot and a straight line who learn to accept their differences and work together to create beautiful and complex designs.

In 1965, Juster produced his third children's book, *Alberic the Wise and Other Journeys.* His trilogy of fantasies focuses on people searching for fulfillment in life.

A Move to the Country

Married in 1964, Juster and his wife, Jeanne, moved five years later to an old farm in western Massachusetts. He established a new architectural firm and became a professor of architectural design at Hampshire College in Amherst. A daughter, Emily, was born in 1971.

To the great disappointment of his Phantom Phans, the 1970's brought a temporary halt to Juster's fiction for children. Working on a farm proved a time-consuming task for Juster. He was amazed by the amount of labor required to maintain a farm. He began pondering how early American farmers, especially women, managed to run farms. His research resulted in a new book in 1979, this one nonfiction and for adults: *So Sweet to Labor: Rural Women in America, 1865-1895*. It is a collection of essays, poetry, and letters written by, for, and about farm women in the late nineteenth century.

A Return to Children's Books The 1980's saw Juster write two new books for children. In 1982, he produced *Otter Nonsense*, a playful collection of puns based on animals' names, such as "lemming meringue pie," "crocoduel," and "pupsicle." In 1989, he published *As: A Surfeit of Similes*, the story of two men who travel the world to collect similes such as "fresh as a daisy" and "hot as a griddle."

A Man of Two Worlds Like many of his fictional characters, Juster has journeyed to a variety of places in life. As a city person who moved to the country, he has managed successfully to meld his two worlds. "My love of the country is influenced and heightened by my city experience," he says, "and, conversely, my appreciation of the city has grown through the time spent here [in the country]."

Juster's career has also straddled two worlds, though he remains modest about his writing. "My sense of myself is as an architect, and I am always a little embarrassed to call myself a writer, since I don't engage in it with the same consistency and commitment," he admits.

◆ The Renaissance

The Renaissance was a great cultural movement that began in Italy during the 1300's, spread to other countries in Europe in the 1400's, and lasted until about 1600. The Renaissance marked a great change in philosophy, art, and architecture from the styles used during the Middle Ages. The word *renaissance* means rebirth or renewal, and during this time many European scholars and artists worked to recapture the spirit of ancient Greece and Rome, which had emphasized learning, beauty, justice, and harmony in all things.

Renaissance architects designed their buildings to help make people aware of human dignity and potential.

"Alberic the Wise" is set during the Renaissance. Alberic's attempts to find fulfillment through excellence in his craft reflect the Renaissance spirit.

Milo's struggle in *The Phantom Tollbooth* to bring peace and harmony to the Kingdom of Wisdom, and by doing so improve himself, also reflects Renaissance ideals.

◆ Literary Works

Books for Children
- *The Phantom Tollbooth* (1961)
- *The Dot and the Line: A Romance in Lower Mathematics* (1963)
- *Alberic the Wise and Other Journeys* (1965)
- *Otter Nonsense* (1982)
- *As: A Surfeit of Similes* (1989)

Books for Adults
- *So Sweet to Labor: Rural Women in America, 1865-1895* (1979)

Norton Juster

It's All in How You Look at Things
from The Phantom Tollbooth

Milo is so bored that he has lost all interest in the world around him, until one day when he suddenly finds himself traveling in the Lands Beyond. With his companions Tock the Watch Dog (whose mission is to make sure no one wastes time) and the Humbug (a highly untrustworthy insect indeed) Milo explores the Kingdom of Wisdom.

Soon all traces of Dictionopolis had vanished in the distance and all those strange and unknown lands that lay between the kingdom of words and the kingdom of numbers stretched before them. It was late afternoon and the dark-orange sun floated heavily over the distant mountains. A friendly, cool breeze slapped playfully at the car, and the long shadows stretched out lazily from the trees and bushes.

"Ah, the open road!" exclaimed the Humbug, breathing deeply, for he now seemed happily resigned to the trip. "The spirit of adventure, the lure of the unknown, the thrill of a gallant quest. How very grand indeed." Then, pleased with himself, he folded his arms, sat back, and left it at that.

In a few more minutes they had left the open countryside and driven into a dense forest.

THIS IS THE SCENIC ROUTE:
STRAIGHT AHEAD TO POINT OF VIEW

announced a rather large road sign; but, contrary to its state-ment, all that could be seen were more trees. As the car rushed along, the trees grew thicker and taller and leafier until, just as they'd hidden the sky completely, the forest abruptly ended and the road bent itself around a broad promontory.[1] Stretching below, to the left, the right, and straight ahead, as far as anyone could see, lay the rich green landscape through which they had been traveling.

"Remarkable view," announced the Humbug, bouncing from the car is if he were responsible for the whole thing.

"Isn't it beautiful?" gasped Milo.

"Oh, I don't know," answered a strange voice. "It's all in the way you look at things."

"I beg your pardon?" said Milo, for he didn't see who had spoken.

"I said it's all in how you look at things," repeated the voice.

---

1. promontory: A peak of high land.

Milo turned around and found himself staring at two very neatly polished brown shoes, for standing directly in front of him (if you can use the word "standing" for anyone suspended in mid-air) was another boy just about his age, whose feet were easily three feet off the ground.

"For instance," continued the boy, "if you happened to like deserts, you might not think this was beautiful at all."

"That's true," said the Humbug, who didn't like to contradict anyone whose feet were that far off the ground.

"For instance," said the boy again, "if Christmas trees were people and people were Christmas trees, we'd all be chopped down, put up in the living room, and covered with tinsel, while the trees opened our presents."

"What does that have to do with it?" asked Milo.

"Nothing at all," he answered, "but it's an interesting possibility, don't you think?"

"How do you manage to stand up there?" asked Milo, for this was the subject which most interested him.

"I was about to ask you a similar question," answered the boy, "for you must be much older than you look to be standing on the ground."

"What do you mean?" Milo asked.

"Well," said the boy, "in my family everyone is born in the air, with his head at exactly the height it's going to be when he's an adult, and then we all grow toward the ground. When we're fully grown up, or as you can see, grown down, our feet finally touch. Of course, there are a few of us whose feet never reach the ground no matter how old we get, but I suppose it's the same in every family."

He hopped a few steps in the air, skipped back to where he started, and then began again.

"You certainly must be very old to have reached the ground already."

"Oh no," said Milo seriously. "In my family we all start on the ground and grow up, and we never know how far until we actually get there."

"What a silly system." The boy laughed. "Then your head keeps changing its height and you always see things in a different way? Why, when you're fifteen things won't look at all the way they did when you were ten, and at twenty everything will change again."

"I suppose so," replied Milo, for he had never really thought about the matter.

"We always see things from the same angle," the boy continued. "It's much less trouble that way. Besides, it makes more sense to grow down and not up. When you're very young, you can never hurt yourself falling down if you're in mid-air, and you certainly can't get into trouble for scuffing up your shoes or marking the floor if there's nothing to scuff them on and the floor is three feet away."

"That's very true," thought Tock, who wondered how the dogs in the family liked the arrangement.

"But there are many other ways to look at things," remarked the boy. "For instance, you had orange juice, boiled eggs, toast and jam, and milk for breakfast," he said, turning to Milo. "And you are always worried about people wasting time," he said to Tock. "And you are almost never right about anything," he said, pointing at the Humbug, "and, when you are, it's usually an accident."

"A gross exaggeration," protested the furious bug, who didn't realize that so much was visible to the naked eye.

"Amazing," gasped Tock.

"How do you know all that?" asked Milo.

"Simple," he said proudly. "I'm Alec Bings; I see through things. I can see whatever is inside, behind, around, covered by, or subsequent[2] to anything else. In fact, the only thing I can't see is whatever happens to be right in front of my nose."

"Isn't that a little inconvenient?" asked Milo, whose neck was becoming quite stiff from looking up.

"It is a little," replied Alec, "but it is quite important to know what lies behind things, and the family helps me take care of the rest. My father sees to things, my mother looks after things, my brother sees beyond things, my uncle sees the other side of every question, and my little sister Alice sees under things."

"How can she see under things if she's all the way up there?" growled the Humbug.

"Well," added Alec, turning a neat cartwheel, "whatever she can't see under, she overlooks."

"Would it be possible for me to see something from up there?" asked Milo politely.

"You could," said Alec, "but only if you try very hard to look at things as an adult does."

Milo tried as hard as he could, and, as he did, his feet floated slowly off the ground until he was standing in the air next to Alec Bings. He looked around very quickly and, an instant later, crashed back down to earth again.

"Interesting, wasn't it?" asked Alec.

"Yes, it was," agreed Milo, rubbing his head and dusting himself off, "but I think I'll continue to see things as a child. It's not so far to fall."

"A wise decision, at least for the time being," said Alec. "Everyone should have his own point of view."

---

2. subsequent (sub´ si kwent): After; following.

"Isn't this everyone's Point of View?" asked Tock, looking around curiously.

"Of course not," replied Alec, sitting himself down on nothing. "It's only mine, and you certainly can't always look at things from someone else's Point of View. For instance, from here that looks like a bucket of water," he said, pointing to a bucket of water; "but from an ant's point of view it's a vast ocean, from an elephant's just a cool drink, and to a fish, of course, it's home. So, you see, the way you see things depends a great deal on where you look at them from. Now, come along and I'll show you the rest of the forest."

He ran quickly through the air, stopping occasionally to beckon Milo, Tock, and the Humbug along, and they followed as well as anyone who had to stay on the ground could.

"Does everyone here grow the way you do?" puffed Milo when he had caught up.

"Almost everyone," replied Alec, and then he stopped a moment and thought. "Now and then, though, someone does begin to grow differently. Instead of down, his feet grow up toward the sky. But we do our best to discourage awkward things like that."

"What happens to *them?*" insisted Milo.

"Oddly enough, they often grow ten times the size of everyone else," said Alec thoughtfully, "and I've heard that they walk among the stars." And with that he skipped off once again toward the waiting woods.

Check Your Comprehension

1. Where do Milo, Tock, and the Humbug stop on their journey?

2. What is unusual about the boy that Milo, Humbug, and Tock meet?

3. What does Alec mean when he says that people in his family "grow down" instead of up?

4. Name three of the special talents of Alec's family members.

5. What must Milo do in order to rise to Alec's point of view?

◆ Critical Thinking

INTERPRET

1. How are Milo and Alec different from each other? **[Contrast]**

2. Explain why Alec will always have the same point of view about things his whole life. **[Analyze]**

EVALUATE

3. Why does Milo prefer to continue to see things from his own point of view rather than as an adult would, for the time being? **[Speculate]**

4. Do you think it would be better if everyone always shared the same point of view? Explain. **[Connect]**

5 What causes different points of view between people, even between those people who agree most of the time? **[Analyze Cause and Effect]**

orton Juster

Alberic the Wise

More than many years ago when fewer things had happened in the world and there was less to know, there lived a young man named Alberic who knew nothing all. Well, almost nothing, or depending on your generosity of spirit, hardly anything, for he could hitch an ox and plow a furrow straight or thatch a roof or hone his scythe[1] until the edge was bright and sharp or tell by a sniff of the breeze what the day would bring or with a glance when a grape was sweet and ready. But these were only the things he had to know to live or couldn't help knowing by living and are, as you may have discovered, rarely accounted as knowledge.

Of the world and its problems, however, he knew little, and indeed was even less aware of their existence. In all his life he had been nowhere and seen nothing beyond the remote estate on which he lived and to whose lands he and his family had been bound back beyond the edge of memory. He planted and harvested, threshed and winnowed,[2] tended the hives and the pigs, breathed the country air, and stopped now and again to listen to the birds or puzzle at the wind. There were no mysteries, hopes or dreams other than those that could be encompassed by his often aching back or impatient stomach. This was the sum of his existence and with it he was neither happy nor sad. He simply could not conceive of anything else.

Since the days were much alike he measured his life by the more discernible[3] seasons—yet they too slipped easily by, and would have continued to do so, I'm sure, had it not been for the lone traveler who appeared unaccountably one chill morning at the close of winter. Alberic watched him make his weary way along the road until, when they stood no more than a glance apart, he paused to rest before continuing on his journey. A curious old man—his tattered tunic was patched on patches and his worn shoes left hardly a suggestion of leather between himself and the cold ground. He carried a massive bundle on his back and sighed with the pleasure of letting it slide gently from his shoulder to the ground—then just as gently let himself down upon it. He nodded and smiled, mopped his face carefully with a handkerchief easily as old as himself, then acknowledged Alberic's timid greeting and finally began to speak, and when he did it was of many, many things.

---

1. scythe (sīthe): A tool with a long, sharp blade used for cutting grain by hand.
2. threshed and winnowed: Separated grain from the stalk on which it grows.
3. discernible (di zurn´ ə bl): Recognizable; perceivable.

Where he had come from and where he was bound, what he had seen and what there was yet to discover—commonwealths, kingdoms, empires, counties and dukedoms—fortresses, bastions and great solitary castles that dug their fingers into the mountain passes and dared the world to pass—royal courts whose monarchs dressed in pheasant skins and silks and rich brocades of purple and lemon and crimson and bice all interlaced with figures of beasts and blossoms and strange geometric devices—and mountains that had no tops and oceans that had no bottoms.

There seemed no end to what he knew or what he cared to speak about, and speak he did, on and on through the day. His voice was soft and easy but his manner such that even his pauses commanded attention. And as he spoke his eyes sparkled and his words were like maps of unknown lands. He told of caravans that made their way across continents and back with perfumes and oils and dark red wines, sandalwood and lynx hides and ermine and carved sycamore chests, with cloves and cinnamon, precious stones and iron pots and ebony and amber and objects of pure tooled gold—of tall cathedral spires and cities full of life and craft and industry—of ships that sailed in every sea, and of art and science and learned speculation hardly even dreamed of by most people—and of armies and battles and magic and much, much more.

Alberic stood entranced, trying desperately to imagine all these wonderful things, but his mind could wander no further than the fields that he could see and the images soon would fade or cloud.

"The world is full of wonders," he sighed forlornly, for he realized that he could not even imagine what a wonder was.

"It is everything I've said and even more," the stranger replied, and since it was by now late afternoon he scrambled to his feet and once more took up his heavy bundle. "And remember," he said with a sweep of his arm, "it is all out there, just waiting." Then down the road and across the stubble fields he went.

For weeks after the old man had gone Alberic brooded, for now he knew that there were things he didn't know, and what magic and exciting things they were! Warm wet breezes had begun to blow across the land and the frozen fields had yielded first to mud and then to early blossoms. But now this quiet hillside was not enough to hold his rushing thoughts. "It is all out there, just waiting," he said to himself again and again, repeating the old man's words. When he had repeated them often enough, they became a decision. He secretly packed his few belongings and in the early morning's mist left his home and started down into the world to seek its wonders and its wisdom.

For two days and nights and half another day again he walked—through lonely forests and down along the rushing mountain streams that seemed to know their destination far better than he knew his. Mile after mile he walked until at last the trees and vines gave way to sweeps of easy meadowland and in the distance, barely visible, the towers of a city reflected back the sun's bright rays. As he approached, the hazy form became a jumble of roofs and chimney pots spread out below, and each step closer embellished them with windows, carved gables, domes and graceful spires. All this in turn was circled by a high wall which seemed to grow higher and wider as he descended towards it until at last it filled his vision and hid all else behind it. The stream which only days before had been so gay and playful now broadened and as if aware of its new importance assumed a slow and dignified pace as it passed through the city. Alberic paused for a moment to catch his breath, then, with a slight shiver of anticipation, passed beneath the cool dark gates and entered the city too.

What a teeming, busy place! Houses and shops, music and movement, all kinds of noises, signs and smells, and more people than he ever knew existed. He wandered along the cobbled streets delighted by each new discovery and noting with care the strange new sights and sounds so unfamiliar to his country senses. He soon learned too that he had come to a city famous above all others for the beautiful stained glass manufactured in its workshops.

"A noble and important profession," he decided soberly, "for surely beauty is the true aim of wisdom!" Without delay he went off to apprentice himself to the greatest of the master glassmakers.

"Well, well," growled the old craftsman after examining Alberic carefully, "so you want to make glass. Very well, we shall see. Your duties will be few and simple. Each morning you'll rise before the birds and with the other apprentices fetch sixty barrows of firewood from the forest. Then in each furnace bank a fire precisely hot enough to melt the lead and fuse the glass, and keep them tended constantly so that none goes out or varies even slightly in its heat. Then, of course, work the bellows, fetch the ingots[4] from the foundry, run errands, assist the journeymen as they need, sharpen and repair all the chisels, files, knives, scrapers, shears, mallets and grozing irons so that each is in prefect order, make deliveries quickly and courteously, grind and mix the pigments, work the forge, sweep out the shop, fetch, carry, stoop, haul and bend, and in your spare time help with the household chores. You can of course eat your fill of the table scraps and sleep on the nice warm floor. Well, don't just stand there, you've only started and you're already hours behind in your work."

---

4. **ingot** (ing´ get): A mass of metal cast into a bar or other shape.

When he finished he smiled a benevolent smile, for he was known for his generous nature.

Alberic applied himself to his new tasks with diligence, working from early morning until late at night when he would curl up in one corner of the shop to dream happily of the day's accomplishments and carefully sort and pack into his memory everything he'd learned. For some time he did only the menial jobs, but soon under the watchful eye of the master he began taking part in more important and exacting procedures. He learned to chip and shape the glass into pieces often no larger than the palm of his hand and then apply the colors mixed in gum or oil with a delicate badger brush and fire these to permanence in the glowing kilns. Then from measurements and patterns he learned to set each piece in the grooved strips of lead and solder them carefully at each joint. For almost two years he worked and watched as all these small and painstaking operations took form in great windows and medallions of saintly lives or tales of moral instruction which glowed in deep splendid blues and vivid rubies.

Finally the time came for Alberic to prove his skill and take his place among the glassmakers—to create a work entirely on his own. He was determined that it would be a rare and lovely thing and he set about it with quiet intensity.

"What will it be, Alberic?" they all asked eagerly.

"Beautiful," he replied with never a moment's doubt, and that was all he'd say.

And for weeks he worked secretly in one corner of the shop until the day came when his work was to be judged. Everyone gathered to see it. The master looked long and carefully. He stood back to view it in the light and squinted close at matters of fine detail, and then he rubbed his chin and then he tapped his finger and then he swayed and then he sighed and then he frowned.

"No," he said sadly and slowly, "certainly not. You will never be a glassmaker." And everyone agreed, for despite the best of intentions Alberic's work was poor indeed.

How miserable he was! How thoroughly miserable! Why wasn't it beautiful when he had tried so hard? How could he have learned so much and yet still fail? No one knew the answer. "There is no reason now for me to stay," he said quietly, gathering up his bundle, and without even as much as a last look back he walked out into the lonely countryside. For several days he wandered aimlessly, seeing nothing, heading nowhere, his thoughts turned inward to his unhappy failure. But it was spring and no one who has ever worked the land can long ignore the signs this season brings. Sweet promising smells hung gently in the warm air, and all around the oxlips, daisies and celandine splashed the fields in lively yellow. A graceful bird and then another caught Alberic's eye. The busy buzz and click of smaller things were reassuring to his ear and even the bullfrogs' heavy thump set his heart beating once again. His spirits and then his hope revived. The world seemed large and inviting once again.

"There are other places and other things to learn," he thought. "Beauty isn't everything. The true measure of wisdom is utility. I'll do something useful." He hurried now and before long came to a city whose stonecutters and masons were renowned throughout the world for the excellence of their work. His thoughts turned to castles and cloisters, massive walls, towering vaults and steeples which only miracles of skill could hold suspended in the air.

"Everything of use and value is made of stone," he concluded and rushed to seek employment with the master stonecutter.

And for two more years he busied himself learning the secrets of this new vocation—selecting and cutting only the finest stone from the quarry—matching, marking and extracting the giant blocks to be moved on heavy wheeled carts to each new building— and then noting carefully how each shaped stone was fitted in its place so that walls and buttresses grew and arches sprang from pier to pier with such precision that no blade however sharp could slip between the joints. Soon he learned to mix and measure mortar and operate the windlasses whose ingenious ropes and pulleys allowed one man to lift for fifty. Then to make his first careful cuts with bolster and chisel and then stop and watch again as surer hands than his cut and shaped the graceful moldings and intricate tracery which brought the stone to life. As he worked he questioned and remembered everything he saw and heard, and as each day passed, his confidence and his knowledge grew and he began to think of his future life as a great and skillfull stonecutter.

When the time came for him to prove his skill to masons and sculptors of the guild, Alberic chose a piece of specially fine, delicately veined marble and set to work. It was to be the finest carving they had ever seen. With great care he studied and restudied the block and planned his form, then cut into the stone in search of it. He worked in a fever of excitement, his sharp chisels biting off the unwanted material in large chips and pieces. But the image he saw so clearly in his mind seemed always to be just out of sight, a little deeper in the stone. The block grew smaller and the mound of dust and chips larger, and still, like a phantom, the form seemed to recede and still he chased it. Soon there was nothing left at all. The great block of stone had disappeared and soon afterwards, the stonecutter too. For again, without a word, Alberic gathered up his belongings and passed through the city gate. He had failed once more.

"Usefulness isn't everything," he decided after roaming about disconsolately for several days. "Innovation is surely a measure of wisdom. I'll do something original."

The opportunity presented itself in the very next town, where the goldsmiths, it was said, produced objects of unsurpassed excellence and fancy. Bowls and magic boxes, mirrors, shields and scepters, crowns, rings, enchanted buckles and clasps, and candlesticks and vases of incredible grace and intricacy[5] spilled from these workshops and found their way to every royal court and market in the land. It was here that Alberic learned to draw and shape the fine gold wire and work the thin sheets of metal into patterns and textures of light and shape and then inlay these with delicate enamels and precious stones. It was here also that he worked and hoped for the next two years of his life and it was here that for the third time he failed and for the third time took his disappointment to the lonely countryside.

And so it went, from town to town, from city to city, each noted for its own particular craft or enterprise. There were potters who turned and shaped their wet clay into graceful bowls and tall jugs fire-glazed with brilliant cobalt, manganese and copper oxides. Leather finishers who transformed smooth soft skins into shoes and boots, gloves, tunics, bombards, bottles and buckets. There were weavers and spinners who worked in wools and silks, carpenters and cabinetmakers, glassblowers, armorers and tinkers. There were scholars who spent their days searching out the secrets of ancient books, and chemists and physicians, and astronomers determining the precise distances between places that no one had ever seen. And busy ports which offered men the sea and all it touched, and smiths and scribes and makers of fine musical instruments, for anyone with such a bent. Alberic tried them all— and watched and learned and practiced and failed and then moved on again. Yet he kept searching and searching for the one thing that he could do, the secret of the wisdom and skill he so desired.

The years passed and still he traveled on—along the roads and trails and half-forgotten paths—across plains and deserts and forests whose tangled growth held terrors that were sometimes real and sometimes even worse—over hills and cruel high mountain passes and down again perhaps along some unnamed sea— until at last, alone and old and tired, he reached the ramparts of the great capital city.

"I will never find wisdom," he sighed. "I'm a failure at everything."

At the edge of the market square Alberic set his bundle down and watched longingly as all the students, artisans and craftsmen went unconcernedly about their business. He wiped the dust from his eyes and sat for a moment, thinking of his future and his

---

5. **intricacy** (in´ tri kə sē): The quality of being elaborately detailed; complex.

past. What a strange sight he was! His beard has now quite long and grey and the cloak and hat and shoes bore evidence of some repair from every place he'd been. His great bundle bulged with the debris of a lifetime's memories and disappointments and his face was a sad scramble of much the same. As he rummaged through his thoughts, a group of children, struck by his uncommon look, stopped and gathered close around him.

"Where have you come from?"

"What do you do?"

"Tell us what you've seen," they eagerly asked, and poised to listen or flee as his response required.

Alberic was puzzled. What could he tell them? No one had ever sought his conversation before, or asked his opinion on any question. He scratched his head and rubbed his knees, then slowly and hesitantly began to speak, and suddenly the sum of all those experiences, which lay packed up in his mind as in some disordered cupboard, came back to him. He told them of a place or two he'd been and of some lands they'd never known existed and creatures that all their wildest fancies could not invent, and then a story, a legend and three dark mysterious tales remembered from a thousand years before. As he spoke, the words began to come more easily and the pleasure of them eased away his weariness. Everything he'd ever seen or heard or touched or tried was suddenly fresh and clear in his memory, and when the children finally left for home, their faces glowing with excitement, it was to spread the news of the wonderful old man who knew so much.

Since he had no place else to go, Alberic returned to the square each day, and each day the crowds grew larger and larger around him. At first it was only the children, but soon everyone, regardless of age or size, crowded close to listen—and patiently he tried to tell them all they wished to hear. For many of their question his own experience provided the answers, and for those he could not directly answer he always had a tale or story whose point or artifice[6] led them to answers of their own. More and more he began to enjoy the days and soon he learned to embellish his tales with skillful detail, to pause at just the right time, to raise his voice to a roar or lower it to a whisper as the telling demanded. And the crowds grew even larger.

Workmen came to listen and stayed to learn the secret ways and methods of their own crafts. Artisans consulted him on questions of taste or skill and when they left they always knew more than when they came. Alberic told them everything he had learned or seen through all his failures and his wanderings, and

---

6. artifice: Skill; ingenuity.

before very long he became known throughout the realm as Alberic the Wise.

His fame spread so far that one day the King himself and several of his ministers came to the square to see for themselves. Cleverly disguised so as not to alert the old man to his purpose, the King posed several questions concerning matters of state and situations in far—off corners of the kingdom. Everything he asked, Alberic answered in great detail, enlarging each reply with accounts of the lore and customs of each region, condition of the crops and royal castles, local problems and controversies, reports on the annual rainfall and the latest depredations[7] by various discontented barons. And for added measure, two songs and a short play (in which he acted all the parts) which he had learned before being dismissed from a traveling theater company.

"You are the wisest man in my kingdom," the astonished King proclaimed, throwing off his disguise, "and you shall have a palace of your own with servants and riches as befits a man of your accomplishments."

Alberic moved into the new palace at once and was more than content with his new life. He enjoyed the wealth and possessions he had never known before, slept on feather beds, ate nothing but the most succulent and delicate foods and endlessly put on and took off the many cloaks, robes and caps the King had graciously provided. His beard was trimmed and curled and he spent his time strolling about the gardens and marble halls posing with proper dignity before each mirror and repeating to himself in various tones and accents, "Alberic the Wise, ALBERIC THE WISE, A-L-B-E-R-I-C-T-H-E W-I-S-E!" in order to become accustomed to his new title.

After several weeks, however, the novelty began to wear thin, for a sable cloak is just a sable cloak and a *poulet poêle à l'estragon* is really just another roast chicken. Soon doubts began to crowd out pleasures and by degrees he grew first serious, then sober, then somber and then once again thoroughly discouraged. "How is it possible to be a failure at everything one day and a wise man the next?" he inquired. "Am I not the same person?"

For weeks this question continued to trouble him deeply, and since he could not find a satisfactory answer he returned to the square with his doubts.

"Simply calling someone wise does not make him wise!" he announced to the eager crowd. "So you see, I am not wise." Then, feeling much better, he returned to the palace and began to make ready to leave.

"How modest," the crowd murmured. "The sign of a truly great man." And a delegation of prominent citizens was sent to prevail on him to stay.

---

7. **depredations:** Robberies; plunderings.

Even after listening to their arguments Alberic continued to be troubled and the very next day he returned to the square again.

"Miscellaneous collections of fact and information are not wisdom," he declared fervently. "Therefore I am not wise!" And he returned and ordered workmen to begin boarding up the palace.

"Only the wisest of men would understand this," the people all agreed and petitions were circulated to prevent his leaving.

For several more days he paced the palace corridors unhappily and then returned for a third time.

"A wise man's words are rarely questioned," he counseled gently. "Therefore you must be very careful whom you call wise."

The crowd was so grateful for his timely warning that they cheered for fully fifteen minutes after he had returned to the palace.

Finally, in desperation, he reappeared that very afternoon and stated simply, "For all the years of my life I have sought wisdom and to this day I still do not know even the meaning of the word, or where to find it," and thinking that would convince them he ordered a carriage for six o'clock that afternoon.

The crowd gasped. "No one but a man of the most profound wisdom would ever dare to admit such a thing," they all agreed, and an epic poem was commissioned in his honor.

Once again Alberic returned to the palace. The carriage was canceled, the rooms were opened and aired. There was nothing he could say or do to convince them that he wasn't what they all thought him to be. Soon he refused to answer any more questions or, in fact, to speak at all and everyone agreed that because of the troubled times this was certainly the wisest thing to do. Each day he grew more morose and miserable, and though his fame continued to grow and spread he found no more satisfaction in his success than he had in all his failures. He slept little and ate less and his magnificent robes began to hang like shrouds. The bright optimism that had shone in his eyes through all his travels and hardships began to fade and as the months passed he took to spending all his time at the top of the great north tower, staring without any interest at nothing in particular.

"I am no wiser now that I was before." he said one afternoon, thinking back across the years. "For I still don't know what I am or what I'm looking for." But as he sat there remembering and regretting, he sensed in the air the barest suggestion of some subtle yet familiar scent that drifted in on the freshening breeze. What it was he didn't know—perhaps the pungent tangled aroma of some far eastern bazaar or the sharp and honest smell of a once-known workshop, or it might have been simply the sweet clean air of an upland field the memory of which had long been lost in detail yet retained in some more durable way; but whatever it was it grew stronger and stronger, stirring something deep within him and taking hold of all his thoughts and feelings. His spirit suddenly quickened in response and each breath now came faster than the one before. And then for just a moment he sat quite still—and then at last he knew.

"I am not a glassmaker nor a stonecutter, nor a goldsmith, potter, weaver, tinker, scribe or chef," he shouted happily and he leaped up and bounded down the steep stone stairs. "Nor a vintner, carpenter, physician, armorer, astronomer, baker or boatman." Down and around he ran as fast as he could go, along the palace corridors until he reached the room in which all his old things had been stored. "Nor a blacksmith, merchant, musician or cabinetmaker," he continued as he put on the ragged cloak and shoes and hat. "Nor a wise man or a fool, success or failure, for no one but myself can tell me what I am or what I'm not." And when he'd finished he looked into the mirror and smiled and wondered why it had taken him so long to discover such a simple thing.

So Alberic picked up his bundle, took one last look through the palace and went down to the square for the last time.

"I have at last discovered one thing," he stated simply. "It is much better to look for what I may never find than to find what I do not really want." And with that he said goodbye and left the city as quietly as he'd come.

The crowd gasped and shook their heads in disbelief.

"He has given up his palace!"

"And his wealth and servants!"

"And the King's favor!"

"And he does not even know where he is going," they buzzed and mumbled. "How foolish, how very foolish! How could we ever have thought him wise?" And they all went home.

But Alberic didn't care at all, for now his thoughts were full of all the things he had yet to see and do and all the times he would stop to tell his stories and then move on again. Soon the walls were far behind and only his footsteps and the night were there to keep him company. Once again he felt the freedom and the joy of not knowing where each new step would take him, and as he walked along his stride was longer and stronger than was right somehow for a man his age.

☑ Check Your Comprehension

1. How is Alberic affected by the old man who travels through his town?
2. At what various professions does Alberic try his hand?
3. What happens when Alberic tells the townspeople about his experiences?
4. Why does Alberic insist that he is not a wise man, even when he is widely admired for his wisdom?
5. What has Alberic learned by the end of the story?

◆ Critical Thinking

INTERPRET

1. Why do you think Alberic fails at each job he works so hard to master? **[Speculate]**

2. Even after winning the people's respect, Alberic still insists that he is not wise. Do you agree with him? Why or why not? **[Analyze]**
3. Why does Alberic at last feel joyful, despite the fact that he does not know where his new journey will lead him? **[Draw Conclusions]**

COMPARE LITERARY WORKS

4. How does Alec Bings' philosophy about point of view apply to the characters and events in "Alberic the Wise"? **[Apply]**
5. Based on your own experiences and observations, what would you say most makes a person wise? **[Connect]**

Norton Juster

Comparing and Connecting the Author's Works

◆ Literary Focus: Allegory

The Phantom Tollbooth and *Alberic the Wise* are both allegories. An allegory is a story in which people, things, and events have a hidden or symbolic meaning. The characters usually personify, or represent, abstract qualities. Allegories use narrative to teach ideas.

For example, in *The Phantom Tollbooth*, Milo is bored by everything, including his toys and his schoolwork. In this allegory, Milo is a symbol for those people who have lost interest in the world around them. What he learns from his journey, and how it changes him, is the hidden message, or theme, of the story.

1. In "It's All in How You Look at Things," Milo meets Alec, a boy who grows down instead of up. Describe the idea that Alec personifies. Support your answer using details of his words and actions.

2. Through example and demonstration, Alec manages to influence Milo's thoughts about point of view. Explain the underlying message that is implied by Alec's speech and actions.

3. Think about things that Alberic thinks, says, and does in "Alberic the Wise." As a class, speculate about the ideas that Alberic personifies. How are they the same or different from those personified by Milo?

4. Alberic's years of struggle lead him to make a discovery about his own fulfillment. Explain the underlying message that this allegory expresses. How is it similar to or different from the message implied in "It's All in How You Look at Things"?

◆ Drawing Conclusions About Juster's Work

Often in Juster's works, characters change significantly as the result of a chance meeting with a stranger. Characters may change in their general attitude or outlook about life, or in the way they view one particular issue or idea. For example, after meeting the stranger on the road, Alberic changes his mind about the possibilities that life has to offer.

Create a character chart like the one shown below. In the first box, identify a main character from each of the selections. In the second box, briefly describe the character's personality or philosophy before meeting a stranger. In the third box, identify the stranger whom the character meets. In the last box, explain how the character's attitudes or ways of thinking change as a result.

Character:
Character's Attitude Before:
Stranger:
Character's Attitude Afterward:

◆ Idea Bank

Writing

1. **Diary** Imagine that Milo or Alberic kept a diary. Write a diary entry that describes one of his experiences and expresses his personal feelings about it.

2. **Flow Chart** Create a flow chart that shows the different places to which Alberic traveled. For each place, write a brief phrase or sentence that identifies what Alberic did there.

3. **Pros and Cons** Choose an issue on which there are two differing points of view. Make a list of arguments that support one of the two points of view. Then make a list of arguments supporting the other point of view.

Speaking and Listening

4. **Interview** Work with a partner to perform an interview with Alberic, Milo, or Alec. Compose questions for your subject and record the character's likely response to each, based on what you know about him from the selection. Then perform your interview for classmates. **[Performing Arts Link]**

5. **Radio Play** Working with a group, perform "It's All in How You Look at Things" as a radio play. Roles will include the Humbug, Tock, Milo, and Alec. Prepare a script using the dialogue in the selection plus more of your own. Add sound effects as well. After sufficient rehearsal, perform your play for the class. **[Performing Arts Link; Group Activity]**

Researching and Representing

6. **Oral Report** Do research in the library or on the Internet to learn more about the Renaissance period. Find out how Renaissance philosophy affected Europe in terms of politics, philosophy, and the arts. Present your findings in an oral report. **[Social Studies Link]**

7. **From Book to Film** Read *The Phantom Tollbooth* in its entirety, and then watch the 1970 MGM full-length feature cartoon based on the book. Create a chart that compares and contrasts the characters, events, and settings of the book and the film. **[Media Link]**

◆ Further Reading, Listening, and Viewing

- Norton Juster: *Alberic the Wise and Other Journeys* (1965). Includes "She Cries No More" and "Two Kings."

- Norton Juster: *The Dot and the Line: A Romance in Lower Mathematics* (1963). A dot and a line learn to accept their differences and cooperate in the creation of beautiful designs.

- Norton Juster: *Otter Nonsense* (1982). A collection of puns based on animals' names.

- Norton Juster: *As: A Surfeit of Similes* (1989). Two men travel the world to collect colorful and unusual similes.

- *The Phantom Tollbooth* (1970) MGM. This animated full-length feature film is based on Juster's book.

- *The Dot and the Line* (1965) MGM. This animated short film is based on Juster's book of the same name.

On the Web:

http://www.phschool.com/atschool/literature
Go to the student edition *Copper*. Proceed to Unit 8. Then, click Hot Links to find Web sites featuring Norton Juster.

Lewis Carroll In Depth

"Charles Dodgson was born on January 27, 1832. He lived his life and eventually died on January 14, 1898. 'Lewis Carroll' was born on March 1, 1856, and is still very much alive."

—Karoline Leach

LEWIS CARROLL's life was filled with contradictions. Some reports suggest that he was so shy he could sit at a party for hours without adding a word to the conversation. Others say that he was a sociable, charming man who had many friends. One undisputed fact about him, however, is that his two *Alice* books are among the most entertaining children's stories ever written.

Childhood and Oxford Lewis Carroll was born Charles Lutwidge Dodgson in 1832 in Daresbury, Cheshire, England. He was the third of the eleven children of the Reverend Charles Dodgson and his wife, Frances Jane Lutwidge.

In Dodgson's early years, he was educated at home. His "reading lists" show that he was very intelligent. He entertained his brothers and sisters by creating his own magazines full of poetry, stories, and drawings.

After the age of twelve, Dodgson was educated at private schools. He went on to Christ Church, a college at Oxford University, in 1851. He was a brilliant student, especially in mathematics. After graduating in 1854, he became a lecturer in mathematics at Christ Church. Despite reports that his lectures were extremely boring, he held this position for the next twenty-six years.

Alice Dodgson was a shy man who sometimes stuttered when he was nervous. However, among children, he was thoroughly at home. Some stories about him say that he lost his stutter when he was with children. One of his young friends, the dainty Alice Liddell, was his

favorite. She was one of the three daughters of the dean of Christ Church.

On July 4, 1862, Dodgson and his friend, the Reverend Robinson Duckworth, rowed the three Liddell girls up the Thames River from Oxford for a picnic. To entertain the girls, Dodgson made up the story of a girl named Alice, and her adventures in a marvelous underground world. When they returned home, Alice said, "Oh, Mr. Dodgson, I wish you would write out Alice's adventures for me!" Dodgson produced a handwritten copy with his own illustrations. He called it *Alice's Adventures Underground* and gave it to Alice for Christmas in 1864.

Lewis Carroll Children's author George MacDonald, a friend of Dodgson's, read the handwritten book. He took it home to read to his six-year-old son, Greville, who declared that he "wished there were 60,000 volumes of it." Encouraged by this enthusiastic response, Dodgson decided to publish the book. He made a number of changes, including doubling the story's length and altering its title. He then chose John Tenniel, a magazine cartoonist, to illustrate it.

Finally, the book was ready to be published. Dodgson put his pen name, "Lewis Carroll," on the cover. To get this name, he first changed his birth name, Charles Lutwidge, into Latin, to get Carolus Ludovicus. Then he changed the order of the names and retranslated them into English, to get Lewis Carroll.

By the following year, the book was so successful that Dodgson started planning the sequel. Six years later, he published *Through the Looking- Glass and What Alice Found There.*

A Fine Photographer In addition to writing for children, Dodgson took fine photographs. At the time, photography was a young art, and it took thirty to forty seconds to expose the film. Even though the subjects had to remain still during that time, Dodgson managed to make them look relaxed and natural. Among his subjects were the actress Ellen Terry, the poet Alfred, Lord Tennyson, and the poet and painter Dante Gabriel Rossetti. Dodgson is considered one of the best amateur photographers of his time.

Later Years Dodgson tried to write other whimsical stories like the *Alice* books later in life. His two attempts, *Sylvie and Bruno* and *Sylvie and Bruno Concluded*, were unsuccessful. In fact, *Sylvie and Bruno Concluded* has been called "one of the most interesting failures in English literature."

Dodgson died suddenly in 1898 after contracting pneumonia. At that time, the *Alice* books were the most popular children's books in England. By 1932, the hundredth anniversary of Dodgson's birth, they were perhaps the most famous children's books in the world.

◆ Education During the Victorian Era

Throughout the *Alice* books, Alice refers to the lessons she has learned in school. She takes great pride in the knowledge she has acquired, and considers it a defining part of her character. However, the information she retains is often unhelpful or wrong. For example, in the excerpt from *Alice's Adventures in Wonderland,* she knows the words *latitude* and *longitude,* but has no idea what they mean.

The *Alice* books can teach us about the role of education in Victorian England. During that time, traditional public schools emphasized Greek and Latin. In addition, they focused on improving character and on molding students into young men and women with strict morals.

This approach can be seen in the *Alice* books, since her knowledge consists largely of maxims and morals about obedience, politeness, and safety. In "Humpty Dumpty," for example, Alice tries hard to hide her true thoughts for the sake of making pleasant conversation. She often says things "hoping to turn her remark into a sort of compliment," or "not wishing to begin an argument."

Often, Alice cannot stop herself from revealing her true thoughts. In this way, Carroll gently satirizes the Victorian goal of training children to be mild and obedient above all else. His whimsical, nonsensical stories show that he values creativity and imagination—especially that of a child.

◆ Literary Works
Books by "Lewis Carroll"
- *Alice's Adventures in Wonderland* (1865)
- *Phantasmagoria and Other Poems* (1869)
- *Through the Looking- Glass and What Alice Found There* (1871)
- *The Hunting of the Snark* (1876)
- *Alice's Adventures Underground* (facsimile) (1886)
- *The Nursery Alice* (1889)
- *Sylvie and Bruno* (1889)
- *Eight or Nine Words About Letter Writing* (1890)
- *Sylvie and Bruno Concluded* (1893)

Books by Charles Dodgson
- *A Syllabus of Plane Algebraical Geometry* (1860)
- *Euclid and His Modern Rivals* (1879)
- *Curiosa Mathematica* (1888–1893)
- *Symbolic Logic, Part I* (1896)
- *Symbolic Logic, Part II* (1897)

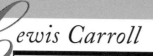

from Alice's Adventures in Wonderland

Down the Rabbit-hole

Alice was beginning to get very tired of sitting by her sister on the bank, and of having nothing to do; once or twice she had peeped into the book her sister was reading, but it had no pictures or conversations in it, "and what is the use of a book," thought Alice, "without pictures or conversations?"

So she was considering in her own mind (as well as she could, for the hot day made her feel very sleepy and stupid), whether the pleasure of making a daisy-chain would be worth the trouble of getting up and picking the daisies, when suddenly a White Rabbit with pink eyes ran close by her.

There was nothing so *very* remarkable in that: nor did Alice think it so *very* much out of the way to hear the Rabbit say to itself, "Oh dear! Oh dear! I shall be too late!" (When she thought it over afterwards, it occurred to her that she ought to have wondered at this, but at the time it all seemed quite natural); but when the Rabbit actually *took a watch out of its waistcoat-pocket,* and looked at it, and then hurried on, Alice started to her feet, for it flashed across her mind that she had never before seen a rabbit with either a waistcoat-pocket or a watch to take out of it, and burning with curiosity,[1] she ran across the field after it, and was just in time to see it pop down a large rabbit-hole under the hedge.

In another moment down went Alice after it, never once considering how in the world she was to get out again.

The rabbit-hole went straight on like a tunnel for some way, and then dipped suddenly down, so suddenly that Alice had not a moment to think about stopping herself before she found herself falling down what seemed to be a very deep well.

Either the well was very deep, or she fell very slowly, for she had plenty of time as she went down to look about her, and to wonder what was going to happen next. First, she tried to look down and make out what she was coming to, but it was too dark to see anything: then she looked at the sides of the well, and noticed that they were filled with cupboards and book-shelves: here and there she saw maps and pictures hung upon pegs. She took down a jar from one of the shelves as she passed: it was labelled "ORANGE MARMALADE," but to her great disappointment it was empty: she did not like to drop the jar for fear of killing somebody underneath, so managed to put it into one of the cupboards as she fell past it.

---

1. **curiosity:** Eager desire to know or find out.

"Well!" thought Alice to herself. "After such a fall as this, I shall think nothing of tumbling down-stairs! How brave they'll all think me at home! Why, I wouldn't say anything about it, even if I fell off the top of the house!" (Which was very likely true.)

Down, down, down. Would the fall *never* come to an end? "I wonder how many miles I've fallen by this time?" she said aloud. "I must be getting somewhere near the centre of the earth. Let me see: that would be four thousand miles down, I think—" (for, you see, Alice had learnt several things of this sort in her lessons in the schoolroom, and though this was not a *very* good opportunity for showing off her knowledge, as there was no one to listen to her, still it was good practice to say it over) "—yes, that's about the right distance—but then I wonder what Latitude or Longitude I've got to?" (Alice had not the slightest idea what Latitude was, or Longitude either, but she thought they were nice grand words to say.)

Presently she began again. "I wonder if I shall fall right *through* the earth! How funny it'll seem to come out among the people that walk with their heads downwards! The Antipathies, I think—" (she was rather glad there *was* no one listening, this time, as it didn't sound at all the right word) "—but I shall have to ask them what the name of the country is, you know. Please, Ma'am, is this New Zealand? Or Australia?" (And she tried to curtsey as she spoke—fancy *curtseying* as you're falling through the air! Do you think she could manage it?) "And what an ignorant little girl she'll think me for asking! No, it'll never do to ask: perhaps I shall see it written up somewhere."

Down, down, down. There was nothing else to do, so Alice soon began talking again. "Dinah'll miss me very much to-night, I should think!" (Dinah was the cat.) "I hope they'll remember her saucer of milk at tea-time. Dinah, my dear! I wish you were down here with me! There are no mice in the air, I'm afraid, but you might catch a bat, and that's very like a mouse, you know. But do cats eat bats, I wonder?" And here Alice began to get rather sleepy, and went on saying to herself, in a dreamy sort of way, "Do cats eat bats? Do cats eat bats?" and sometimes, "Do bats eat cats?", for, you see, as she couldn't answer either question, it didn't much matter which way she put it. She felt that she was dozing off, and had just begun to dream that she was walking hand in hand with Dinah, and was saying to her very earnestly, "Now, Dinah, tell me the truth: did you ever eat a bat?", when suddenly, thump! thump! down she came upon a heap of sticks and dry leaves, and the fall was over.

Alice was not a bit hurt, and she jumped up on to her feet in a moment: she looked up, but it was all dark overhead: before her was another long passage, and the White Rabbit was still in sight, hurrying down it. There was not a moment to be lost: away went Alice like the wind, and was just in time to hear it say, as it turned a corner, "Oh my ears and whiskers, how late it's getting!" She was close behind it when she turned the corner, but the Rabbit was no longer to be seen: she found herself in a long, low hall, which was lit up by a row of lamps hanging from the roof.

There were doors all round the hall, but they were all locked; and when Alice had been all the way down one side and up the other trying every door, she walked sadly down the middle, wondering how she was ever to get out again.

Suddenly she came upon a little three-legged table, all made of solid glass: there was nothing on it but a tiny golden key, and Alice's first idea was that this might belong to one of the doors of the hall; but, alas! either the locks were too large, or the key was too small, but at any rate it would not open any of them. However, on the second time round, she came upon a low curtain she had noticed before, and behind it was a little door about fifteen inches high: she tried the little golden key in the lock, and to her great delight it fitted.

Alice opened the door and found that it led into a small passage, not much larger than a rat-hole: she knelt down and looked along the passage into the loveliest garden you ever saw. How she longed to get out of that dark hall, and wander about among those beds of bright flowers and those cool fountains, but she could not even get her head through the doorway: "and even if my head *would* go through," thought poor Alice, "it would be of very little use without my shoulders. Oh, how I wish I could shut up like a telescope! I think I could, if I only knew how to begin." For, you see, so many out-of-the-way things had happened lately, that Alice had begun to think that very few things indeed were really impossible.

There seemed to be no use in waiting by the little door, so she went back to the table, half hoping she might find another key on it, or at any rate a book of rules for shutting people up like telescopes: this time she found a little bottle on it ("which certainly was not here before," said Alice), and tied round the neck of the bottle was a paper label, with the words "DRINK ME" beautifully printed on it in large letters.

It was all very well to say "Drink me," but the wise little Alice was not going to do *that* in a hurry. "No, I'll look first," she said, "and see whether it's marked '*poison*' or not"; for she had read several nice little stories about children who had got burnt, and eaten up by wild beasts, and other unpleasant things, all because they *would* not remember the simple rules their friends had taught them: such as, that a red-hot poker will burn you if you hold it too long; and that, if you cut your finger *very* deeply with a knife, it usually bleeds; and she had never forgotten that, if you drink much from a bottle marked "poison," it is almost certain to disagree with you, sooner or later.

However, this bottle was *not* marked "poison," so Alice ventured to taste it, and finding it very nice (it had, in fact, a sort of mixed flavour of cherry-tart, custard, pineapple, roast turkey, toffy, and hot buttered toast), she very soon finished it off.

"What a curious feeling!" said Alice. "I must be shutting up like a telescope!"

And so it was indeed: she was now only ten inches high, and her face brightened up at the thought that she was now the right size for going through the little door into that lovely garden. First, however, she waited for a few minutes to see if she was going to shrink any further: she felt a little nervous about this; "for it might end, you know," said Alice to herself, "in my going out altogether, like a candle. I wonder what I should be like then?" And she tried to fancy what the flame of a candle looks like after the candle is blown out, for she could not remember ever having seen such a thing.

After a while, finding that nothing more happened, she decided on going into the garden at once; but, alas for poor Alice! when she got to the door, she found she had forgotten the little golden key, and when she went back to the table for it, she found she could not possibly reach it: she could see it quite plainly through the glass and she tried her best to climb up one of the legs of the table, but it was too slippery; and when she had tired herself out with trying, the poor little thing sat down and cried.

"Come, there's no use in crying like that!" said Alice to herself, rather sharply. "I advise you to leave off this minute!" She generally gave herself very good advice (though she very seldom followed it), and sometimes she scolded herself so severely as to bring tears into her eyes; and once she remembered trying to box her own ears for having cheated herself in a game of croquet she was playing against herself, for this curious child was very fond of pretending to be two people. "But it's no use now," thought poor Alice, "to pretend to be two people! Why, there's hardly enough of me left to make *one* respectable person!"

Soon her eye fell on a little glass box that was lying under the table: she opened it, and found in it a very small cake, on which the words "EAT ME" were beautifully marked in currants. "Well I'll eat it," said Alice, "and if it makes me grow larger, I can reach the key; and if it makes me grow smaller, I can creep under the door: so either way I'll get into the garden, and I don't care which happens!"

She ate a little bit, and said anxiously to herself, "Which way? Which way?", holding her hand on the top of her head to feel which way it was growing; and she was quite surprised to find that she remained the same size. To be sure, this is what generally happens when one eats cake; but Alice had got so much into the way of expecting nothing but out-of-the-way things to happen, that it seemed quite dull and stupid for life to go on in the common way.

So she set to work, and very soon finished off the cake.

The Pool of Tears

"Curiouser and curiouser!" cried Alice (she was so much surprised, that for the moment she quite forgot how to speak good English). "Now I'm opening out like the largest telescope that ever was! Good-bye, feet!" (for when she looked down at her feet, they seemed to be almost out of sight, they were getting so far off). "Oh, my poor little feet, I wonder who will put on your shoes and stockings for you now, dears? I'm sure *I* sha'n't be able! I shall be a great deal too far off to trouble myself about you: you must manage the best way you can—but I must be kind to them," thought Alice, "or perhaps they wo'n't walk the way I want to go! Let me see. I'll give them a new pair of boots every Christmas."

And she went on planning to herself how she would manage it. "They must go by the carrier," she thought; "and how funny it'll seem, sending presents to one's own feet! And how odd the directions will look!

> *Alice's Right Foot, Esq.*[2]
> *Hearthrug,*
> *near the Fender*[3]
> *(with Alice's love).*

Oh dear, what nonsense I'm talking!"

Just at this moment her head struck against the roof of the hall: in fact she was now rather more than nine feet high, and she at once took up the little golden key and hurried off to the garden door.

Poor Alice! It was as much as she could do, lying down on one side, to look through into the garden with one eye; but to get through was more hopeless than ever: she sat down and began to cry again.

"You ought to be ashamed of yourself," said Alice, "a great girl like you" (she might well say this), "to go on crying in this way! Stop this moment, I tell you!" But she went on all the same, shedding gallons of tears, until there was a large pool all round her, and four inches deep and reaching half down the hall.

---

2. Esq: Abbreviation for *Esquire.* A title of courtesy, corresponding to *Mr.*
3. Fender: A low metal frame or screen placed between the hearthrug and an open fireplace.

After a time she heard a little pattering of feet in the distance, and she hastily dried her eyes to see what was coming. It was the White Rabbit returning, splendidly dressed, with a pair of white kid-gloves in one hand and a large fan in the other: he came trotting along in a great hurry, muttering to himself as he came, "Oh! the Duchess, the Duchess! Oh! Wo'n't she be savage if I've kept her waiting!" Alice felt so desperate that she was ready to ask help of any one: so, when the Rabbit came near her, she began, in a low, timid voice, "If you please, Sir—" The Rabbit started violently, dropped the white kid-gloves and the fan, and skurried away into the darkness as hard as he could go.

Alice took up the fan and gloves, and, as the hall was very hot, she kept fanning herself all the time she went on talking. "Dear, dear! How queer everything is today! And yesterday things went on just as usual. I wonder if I've been changed in the night? Let me think: *was* I the same when I got up this morning? I almost think I can remember feeling a little different. But if I'm not the same, the next question is, 'Who in the world am I?' Ah, *that's* the great puzzle!" And she began thinking over all the children she knew that were of the same age as herself, to see if she could have been changed for any of them.

"I'm sure I'm not Ada," she said, "for her hair goes in such long ringlets, and mine doesn't go in ringlets at all; and I'm sure I ca'n't be Mabel, for I know all sorts of things, and she, oh! she knows such a very little! Besides, *she's* she, and *I'm* I, and—oh dear, how puzzling it all is! I'll try if I know all the things I used to know. Let me see: four times five is twelve, and four times six is thirteen, and four times seven is—oh dear! I shall never get to twenty at that rate! However, the Multiplication Table doesn't signify: let's try Geography. London is the capital of Paris, and Paris is the capital of Rome, and Rome—no, *that's* all wrong, I'm certain! I must have been changed for Mabel! I'll try and say '*How doth the little—*,'" and she crossed her hands on her lap as if she were saying lessons, and began to repeat it, but her voice sounded hoarse and strange, and the words did not come the same as they used to do:—

> *How doth the little crocodile*
> *Improve his shining tail,*
> *And pour the waters of the Nile*
> *On every golden scale!*

> *How cheerfully he seems to grin,*
> *And neatly spreads his claws,*
> *And welcomes little fishes in,*
> *With gently smiling jaws!*

"I'm sure those are not the right words," said poor Alice, and her eyes filled with tears again as she went on. "I must be Mabel, after all, and I shall have to go and live in that poky little house, and have next to no toys to play with, and oh, ever so many lessons to learn! No, I've made up my mind about it: if I'm Mabel, I'll stay down here! It'll be no use their putting their heads down and saying 'Come up again, dear!' I shall only look up and say 'Who am I then? Tell me that first, and then, if I like being that person, I'll come up: if not, I'll stay down here till I'm somebody else'—but, oh dear!" cried Alice, with a sudden burst of tears, "I do wish they *would* put their heads down! I am so *very* tired of being all alone here!"

As she said this she looked down at her hands, and was surprised to see that she had put on one of the Rabbit's little white kid-gloves while she was talking. "How *can* I have done that?" she thought. "I must be growing small again." She got up and went to the table to measure herself by it, and found that, as nearly as she could guess, she was now about two feet high, and was going on shrinking rapidly: she soon found out that the cause of this was the fan she was holding, and she dropped it hastily, just in time to save herself from shrinking away altogether.

"That *was* a narrow escape!" said Alice, a good deal frightened at the sudden change, but very glad to find herself still in existence. "And now for the garden!" And she ran with all speed back to the little door; but, alas! the little door was shut again, and the little golden key was lying on the glass table as before, "and things are worse than ever," thought the poor child, "for I never was so small as this before, never! And I declare it's too bad, that it is!"

As she said these words her foot slipped, and in another moment, splash! she was up to her chin in salt water. Her first idea was that she had somehow fallen into the sea, "and in that case I can go back by railway," she said to herself. (Alice had been to the seaside once in her life, and had come to the general conclusion, that wherever you go to on the English coast you find a number of bathing machines[4] in the sea, some children digging in the sand with wooden spades, then a row of lodging houses, and behind them a railway-station.) However, she soon made out that she was in the pool of tears which she had wept when she was nine feet high.

"I wish I hadn't cried so much!" said Alice, as she swam about, trying to find her way out. "I shall be punished for it now, I suppose, by being drowned in my own tears! That *will* be a queer thing, to be sure! However, everything is queer to-day.

---

4. **bathing machines:** Small bathhouses on wheels, to be driven into the water for bathers to undress, bathe, and dress in.

Just then she heard something splashing about in the pool a little way off, and she swam nearer to make out what it was: at first she thought it must be a walrus or hippopotamus, but then she remembered how small she was now, and she soon made out that it was only a mouse that had slipped in like herself.

"Would it be of any use now," thought Alice, "to speak to this mouse? Everything is so out-of-the-way down here, that I should think very likely it can talk: at any rate, there's no harm in trying." So she began: "O Mouse, do you know the way out of this pool? I am very tired of swimming about here, O Mouse!" (Alice thought this must be the right way of speaking to a mouse: she had never done such a thing before, but she remembered having seen in her brother's Latin Grammar, "A mouse—of a mouse—to a mouse—a mouse—O mouse.") The mouse looked at her rather inquisitively, and seemed to her to wink with one of its little eyes, but it said nothing.

"Perhaps it doesn't understand English," thought Alice. "I daresay it's a French mouse, come over with William the Conqueror." (For, with all her knowledge of history, Alice had no clear notion how long ago anything had happened.) So she began again: "Où est ma chatte?"[5] which was the first sentence in her French lessonbook. The Mouse gave a sudden leap out of the water, and seemed to quiver all over with fright, "Oh, I beg your pardon!" cried Alice hastily, afraid that she had hurt the poor animal's feelings. "I quite forgot you didn't like cats."

"Not like cats!" cried the Mouse, in a shrill, passionate voice. "Would *you* like cats, if you were me?"

"Well, perhaps not," said Alice in a soothing tone: "don't be angry about it. And yet I wish I could show you our cat Dinah. I think you'd take a fancy to cats if you could only see her. She is such a dear quiet thing," Alice went on half to herself, as she swam lazily about in the pool, "and she sits purring so nicely by the fire, licking her paws and washing her face—and she is such a nice soft thing to nurse—and she's such a capital one for catching mice—oh, I beg your pardon!" cried Alice again, for this time the Mouse was bristling[6] all over, and she felt certain it must be really offended. "We wo'n't talk about her any more if you'd rather not."

"We, indeed!" cried the Mouse, who was trembling down to the end of its tail. "As if *I* would talk on such a subject! Our family always *hated* cats: nasty, low, vulgar things! Don't let me hear the name again!"

"I won't indeed!" said Alice, in a great hurry to change the subject of conversation. "Are you—are you fond—of—of dogs?"

---

5. *"Où est ma chatte?"* (o͞o ä mä shät): Where is my cat?
6. **bristling:** Showing anger or annoyance.

The Mouse did not answer, so Alice went on eagerly: "There is such a nice little dog near our house I should like to show you! A little bright-eyed terrier, you know, with oh, such long curly brown hair! And it'll fetch things when you throw them, and it'll sit up and beg for its dinner, and all sorts of things—I ca'n't remember half of them—and it belongs to a farmer, you know, and he says it's so useful, it's worth a hundred pounds! He says it kills all the rats and—oh dear!" cried Alice in a sorrowful tone, "I'm afraid I've offended it again!" For the Mouse was swimming away from her as hard as it could go, and making quite a commotion in the pool as it went. So she called softly after it. "Mouse dear! Do come back again, and we wo'n't talk about cats or dogs either, if you don't like them!" When the Mouse heard this, it turned round and swam slowly back to her: its face was quite pale (with passion, Alice thought), and it said in a low trembling voice, "Let us get to the shore, and then I'll tell you my history, and you'll understand why it is I hate cats and dogs."

It was high time to go, for the pool was getting quite crowded with the birds and animals that had fallen into it: there was a Duck and a Dodo, a Lory and an Eaglet, and several other curious creatures. Alice led the way, and the whole party swam to the shore.

☑ Check Your Comprehension

1. What is Alice doing when she first sees the Rabbit?
2. Name three things about the Rabbit that are unusual.
3. Describe what happens as Alice falls down the rabbit-hole.
4. What happens to Alice after she drinks the contents of the bottle labeled "DRINK ME" and eats the cake labeled "EAT ME"?
5. Describe the sequence of events from the time Alice fans herself with the Rabbit's fan until she swims to the shore.

◆ Critical Thinking

INTERPRET

1. Based on Alice's words and actions, how would you describe her personality? [Analyze]

2. In chapter 2, Alice cries a pool of tears. Name two reasons that she is so sad. [Analyze]
3. Why do you think Alice talks so much about her cat and about the dog near her house? [Infer]

EVALUATE

4. Lewis Carroll wrote this story to entertain his young friend. Do you think a child would find this story entertaining? Explain your answer. [Evaluate]

COMPARE LITERARY WORKS

5. Name one way in which this book is similar to other children's books you remember reading. Name one way in which it is different. [Compare and Contrast]

Humpty Dumpty

from Through the Looking-Glass

However, the egg only got larger and larger, and more and more human: when she had come within a few yards of it, she saw that it had eyes and a nose and a mouth; and when she had come close to it, she saw clearly that it was HUMPTY DUMPTY himself. "It ca'n't be anybody else!" she said to herself. "I'm as certain of it, as if his name were written all over his face!"

It might have been written a hundred times, easily, on that enormous face. Humpty Dumpty was sitting, with his legs crossed like a Turk, on the top of a high wall—such a narrow one Alice quite wondered how he could keep his balance—and, as his eyes were steadily fixed in the opposite direction, and he didn't take the least notice of her, she thought he must be a stuffed figure, after all.

"And how exactly like an egg he is!" she said aloud, standing with her hands ready to catch him, for she was every moment expecting him to fall.

"It's *very* provoking," Humpty Dumpty said after a long silence, looking away from Alice as he spoke, "to be called an egg—*very*!"

"I said you *looked* like an egg, Sir," Alice gently explained. "And some eggs are very pretty, you know," she added, hoping to turn her remark into a sort of compliment.

"Some people," said Humpty, looking away from her as usual, "have no more sense than a baby!"

Alice didn't know what to say to this: it wasn't at all like conversation, she thought, as he never said anything to *her*; in fact, his last remark was evidently addressed to a tree—so she stood and softly repeated to herself:—

> *Humpty Dumpty sat on a wall:*
> *Humpty Dumpty had a great fall.*
> *All the king's horses and all the King's men*
> *Couldn't put Humpty Dumpty in his place again.*

"That last line is much too long for the poetry," she added, almost out loud, forgetting that Humpty Dumpty would hear her.

"Don't stand chattering to yourself like that," Humpty Dumpty said, looking at her for the first time, "but tell me your name and your business."

"My *name* is Alice, but—"

"It's a stupid name enough!" Humpty Dumpty interrupted impatiently. "What does it mean?"

"*Must* a name mean something?" Alice asked doubtfully.

"Of course it must," Humpty said with a short laugh: *my* name means the shape I am—and a good handsome shape it is, too. With a name like yours, you might be any shape, almost."

"Why do you sit out here all alone?" said Alice, not wishing to begin an argument.

"Why, because there's nobody with me!" cried Humpty Dumpty. "Did you think I didn't know the answer to *that*? Ask another."

"Don't you think you'd be safer down on the ground?" Alice went on, not with any idea of making another riddle, but simply in her good-natured anxiety for the queer creature. "That wall is so *very* narrow!"

"What tremendously easy riddles you ask!" Humpty Dumpty growled out. "Of course I don't think so! Why, if ever I *did* fall off, which there's no chance of—but *if* I did—" Here he pursed up his lips, and looked so solemn and grand that Alice could hardly help laughing.

"If I *did* fall," he went on, "*the King has promised me*—ah, you may turn pale, if you like! You didn't think I was going to say that, did you? *The King has promised me—with his very own mouth*—to—to—"

"To send all his horses and all his men," Alice interrupted, rather unwisely.

"Now I declare that's too bad!" Humpty Dumpty cried, breaking into a sudden passion. "You've been listening at doors—and behind trees—and down chimneys—or you couldn't have known it!"

"I haven't, indeed!" Alice said very gently. "It's in a book."

"Ah, well! They may write such things in a *book*," Humpty Dumpty said in a calmer tone. "That's what you call a History of England, that is. Now, take a good look at me! I'm one that has spoken to a King, *I* am: mayhap[1] you'll never see such another: and, to show you I'm not proud, you may shake hands with me!" And he grinned almost from ear to ear, as he leant forwards (and as nearly as possible fell off the wall in doing so) and offered Alice his hand. She watched him a little anxiously as she took it. "If he smiled much more the ends of his mouth might meet behind," she thought: "and then I don't know *what* would happen to his head! I'm afraid it would come off!"

"Yes, all his horses and all his men," Humpty Dumpty went on. "They'd pick me up again in a minute, *they* would! However, this conversation is going on a little too fast: let's go back to the last remark but one."

---

1. **mayhap:** Maybe, perhaps.

"I'm afraid I ca'n't quite remember it," Alice said, very politely.

"In that case we start afresh," said Humpty Dumpty, "and it's my turn to choose a subject—" ("He talks about it just as if it was a game!" thought Alice.) "So here's a question for you. How old did you say you were?"

Alice made a short calculation, and said "Seven years and six months."

"Wrong!" Humpty Dumpty exclaimed triumphantly. "You never said a word like it!"

"I thought you meant 'How old *are* you?'" Alice explained.

"If I'd meant that, I'd have said it," said Humpty Dumpty.

Alice didn't want to begin another argument, so she said nothing.

"Seven years and six months!" Humpty Dumpty repeated thoughtfully. "An uncomfortable sort of age. Now if you'd asked *my* advice. I'd have said 'Leave off at seven'—but it's too late now."

"I never ask advice about growing," Alice said indignantly.

"Too proud?" the other enquired.

Alice felt even more indignant at this suggestion. "I mean," she said, "that one ca'n't help growing older."

"*One* ca'n't, perhaps," said Humpty Dumpty; "but *two* can. With proper assistance, you might have left off at seven."

"What a beautiful belt you've got on!" Alice suddenly remarked. (They had had quite enough of the subject of age, she thought: and, if they really were to take turns in choosing subjects it was *her* turn now.) "At least," she corrected herself on second thoughts, "a beautiful cravat,[2] I should have said—no, a belt, I mean—I beg your pardon!" she added in dismay, for Humpty Dumpty looked thoroughly offended, and she began to wish she hadn't chosen that subject. "If only I knew," she thought to herself, "which was neck and which was waist!"

Evidently Humpty Dumpty was very angry, though he said nothing for a minute or two. When he *did* speak again, it was in a deep growl.

"It is a—*most—provoking—*thing," he said at last, "when a person doesn't know a cravat from a belt!"

"I know it's very ignorant of me," Alice said, in so humble a tone that Humpty Dumpty relented.

"It's a cravat, child, and a beautiful one, as you say. It's a present from the White King and Queen. There now!"

"Is it really?" said Alice, quite pleased to find that she *had* chosen a good subject, after all.

"They gave it me," Humpty Dumpty continued thoughtfully, as he crossed one knee over the other and clasped his hands round it, "they gave it me—for an un-birthday present."

---

2. **cravat** (krə vät´): A necktie.

"I beg your pardon?" Alice said with a puzzled air.

"I'm not offended," said Humpty Dumpty.

"I mean, what *is* an un-birthday present?"

"A present given when it isn't your birthday, of course."

Alice considered a little. "I like birthday presents best," she said at last.

"You don't know what you're talking about!" cried Humpty Dumpty. "How many days are there in a year?"

"Three hundred and sixty-five," said Alice.

"And how many birthdays have you?"

"One."

"And if you take one from three hundred and sixty-five, what remains?"

"Three hundred and sixty-four, of course."

Humpty Dumpty looked doubtful. "I'd rather see that done on paper," he said.

Alice couldn't help smiling as she took out her memorandum-book, and worked the sum for him:

$$\begin{array}{r} 365 \\ \underline{1} \\ 364 \end{array}$$

Humpty Dumpty took the book and looked at it carefully. "That seems to be done right—" he began.

"You're holding it upside down!" Alice interrupted.

"To be sure I was!" Humpty Dumpty said gaily, as she turned it round for him. "I thought it looked a little queer. As I was saying, that *seems* to be done right—though I haven't time to look it over thoroughly just now—and that shows that there are three hundred and sixty-four days when you might get un-birthday presents—"

"Certainly," said Alice.

"And only *one* for birthday presents, you know. There's glory for you!"

"I don't know what you mean by 'glory,'" Alice said.

Humpty Dumpty smiled contemptuously. "Of course you don't—till I tell you. I meant 'there's a nice knock-down argument for you!'"

"But 'glory' doesn't mean 'a nice knock-down argument,'" Alice objected.

"When *I* use a word," Humpty Dumpty said, in rather a scornful tone, "it means just what I choose it to mean—neither more nor less."

"The question is," said Alice, "whether you *can* make words mean so many different things."

"The question is," said Humpty Dumpty, "which is to be master—that's all."

Alice was too much puzzled to say anything; so after a minute Humpty Dumpty began again. "They've a temper, some of them—particularly verbs: they're the proudest—adjectives you can do anything with, but not verbs—however, *I* can manage the whole lot of them! Impenetrability![3] That's what *I* say!"

"Would you tell me, please," said Alice, "what that means?"

"Now you talk like a reasonable child," said Humpty Dumpty, looking very much pleased. "I meant by 'impenetrability' that we've had enough of that subject, and it would be just as well if you'd mention what you mean to do next, as I suppose you don't mean to stop here all the rest of your life."

"That's a great deal to make one word mean," Alice said in a thoughtful tone.

"When I make a word do a lot of work like that," said Humpty Dumpty, "I always pay it extra."

"Oh!" said Alice. She was too much puzzled to make any other remark.

"Ah, you should see 'em come round me of a Saturday night," Humpty Dumpty went on, wagging his head gravely from side to side, "for to get their wages, you know."

(Alice didn't venture to ask what he paid them with; so you see I can't tell *you*.)

"You seem very clever at explaining words, Sir," said Alice. "Would you kindly tell me the meaning of the poem called 'Jabberwocky'?"

"Let's hear it," said Humpty Dumpty. "I can explain all the poems that ever were invented—and a good many that haven't been invented just yet."

This sounded very hopeful, so Alice repeated the first verse:—

> 'Twas brillig, and the slithy toves
> Did gyre and gimble in the wabe:
> All mimsy were the borogoves,
> And the mome raths outgrabe.

"That's enough to begin with," Humpty Dumpty interrupted: "there are plenty of hard words there. '*Brillig*' means four o'clock in the afternoon—the time when you begin *broiling* things for dinner."

"That'll do very well," said Alice: "and '*slithy*'?"

"Well, '*slithy*' means 'lithe and slimy.' 'Lithe' is the same as 'active.' You see it's like a portmanteau[4]—there are two meanings packed up into one word."

---

3. **impenetrability:** The quality of being incapable of being entered or understood.
4. **portmanteau** (pôrt man′ tō): A traveling case or bag; a suitcase.

"I see it now," Alice remarked thoughtfully: "and what are '*toves*'?"

"Well, '*toves*' are something like badgers—they're something like lizards—and they're something like corkscrews."

"They must be very curious-looking creatures."

"They are that," said Humpty Dumpty: "also they make their nests under sun-dials—also they live on cheese."

"And what's to '*gyre*' and to '*gimble*'?"

"To '*gyre*' is to go round and round like a gyroscope.[5] To '*gimble*' is to make holes like a gimlet."

"And '*the wabe*' is the grass-plot round a sundial, I suppose?" said Alice, surprised at her own ingenuity.

"Of course it is. It's called '*wabe*,' you know, because it goes a long way before it, and a long way behind it—"

"And a long way beyond it on each side," Alice added.

"Exactly so. Well then, '*mimsy*' is 'flimsy and miserable' (there's another portmanteau for you). And a '*borogove*' is a thin shabby-looking bird with its feathers sticking out all round—something like a live mop."

"And then '*mome raths*'?" said Alice. "I'm afraid I'm giving you a great deal of trouble."

"Well, a '*rath*' is a sort of green pig: but '*mome*' I'm not certain about. I think it's short for 'from home'—meaning that they'd lost their way, you know."

"And what does '*outgrabe*' mean?"

"Well, '*outgribing*' is something between bellowing and whistling with a kind of sneeze in the middle; however you'll hear it done, maybe down in the wood yonder—and, when you've once heard it, you'll be quite content. Who's been repeating all that hard stuff to you?"

"I read it in a book," said Alice. "But I *had* some poetry repeated to me much easier than that, by—Tweedledee, I think it was."

"As to poetry, you know," said Humpty Dumpty, stretching out one of his great hands, "*I* can repeat poetry as well as other folk, if it comes to that—"

"Oh, it needn't come to that!" Alice hastily said, hoping to keep him from beginning.

"The piece I'm going to repeat," he went on without noticing her remark, "was written entirely for your amusement."

Alice felt that in that case she really *ought* to listen to it; so she sat down and said "Thank you" rather sadly.

> *In winter, when the fields are white,*
> *I sing this song for your delight—*

---

5. gyroscope (jī′ rə skōp): A device that is used to steady ships and aircraft and to indicate direction.

"Only I don't sing it," he added, as an explanation.

"I see you don't," said Alice.

"If you can *see* whether I'm singing or not you've sharper eyes than most," Humpty Dumpty remarked severely. Alice was silent.

> *In spring, when woods are getting green,*
> *I'll try and tell you what I mean:*

"Thank you very much," said Alice.

> *In summer, when the days are long,*
> *Perhaps you'll understand this song:*
>
> *In autumn, when the leaves are brown,*
> *Take pen and ink, and write it down.*

"I will, if I can remember it so long," said Alice.

"You needn't go on making remarks like that," Humpty Dumpty said, "they're not sensible, and they put me out."

> *I sent a message to the fish:*
> *I told them 'This is what I wish.'*
>
> *The little fishes of the sea,*
> *They sent an answer back to me.*
>
> *The little fishes' answer was*
> *'We cannot do it, Sir, because—'*

"I'm afraid I don't quite understand," said Alice.

"It gets easier further on," Humpty Dumpty replied.

> *I sent to them again to say*
> *'It will be better to obey.'*
>
> *The fishes answered, with a grin,*
> *'Why, what a temper you are in!'*
>
> *I told them once, I told them twice:*
> *They would not listen to advice.*
>
> *I took a kettle large and new,*
> *Fit for the deed I had to do.*
>
> *My heart went hop, my heart went thump:*
> *I filled the kettle at the pump.*

> Then some one came to me and said
> 'The little fishes are in bed.
>
> I said to him, I said it plain,
> 'Then you must wake them up again.'
>
> I said it very loud and clear:
> I went and shouted in his ear.

Humpty Dumpty raised his voice almost to a scream as he re-peated this verse, and Alice thought, with a shudder, "I wouldn't have been the messenger for *anything*!"

> But he was very stiff and proud:
> He said 'You needn't shout so loud!'
>
> And he was very proud and stiff:
> He said 'I'd go and wake them, if—'
>
> I took a corkscrew from the shelf:
> I went to wake them up myself.
>
> And when I found the door was locked,
> I pulled and pushed and kicked and knocked.
>
> And when I found the door was shut,
> I tried to turn the handle, but—'

There was a long pause.

"Is that all?" Alice timidly asked.

"That's all," said Humpty Dumpty. "Good-bye."

This was rather sudden, Alice thought: but, after such a *very* strong hint that she ought to be going, she felt that it would hard-ly be civil to stay. So she got up, and held out her hand. "Good-bye, till we meet again!" she said as cheerfully as she could.

"I shouldn't know you again if we *did* meet," Humpty Dumpty replied in a discontented tone, giving her one of his fingers to shake: "you're so exactly like other people."

"The face is what one goes by, generally," Alice remarked in a thoughtful tone.

"That's just what I complain of," said Humpty Dumpty. "Your face is the same as everybody has—the two eyes, so—" (marking their places in the air with his thumb) "nose in the middle, mouth under. It's always the same. Now if you had the two eyes on the same side of the nose, for instance—or the mouth at the top—that would be *some* help."

"It wouldn't look nice," Alice objected. But Humpty Dumpty only shut his eyes, and said "Wait till you've tried."

Alice waited a minute to see if he would speak again, but, as he never opened his eyes or took any further notice of her, she said "Good-bye!" once more, and, getting no answer to this, she quietly walked away: but she couldn't help saying to herself, as she went, "Of all the unsatisfactory—" (she repeated this aloud, as it was a great comfort to have such a long word to say) "of all the unsatisfactory people I *ever* met—" She never finished the sentence, for at this moment a heavy crash shook the forest from end to end.

☑ Check Your Comprehension

1. What does Alice know about the king's horses and the king's men that Humpty Dumpty does not know?

2. (a) What is an "un-birthday"? (b) How many un-birthdays can a person have in a year?

3. (a) What is a portmanteau word? (b) Give an example of such a word, and explain what it means.

4. What does Humpty Dumpty think about people's faces?

◆ Critical Thinking

INTERPRET

1. Do you think that Humpty Dumpty has good manners? Find two examples in the story to support your answer. **[Analyze]**

2. Would you consider Humpty Dumpty to be smart? Support your answer with two examples. **[Analyze]**

3. Shortly after Alice leaves Humpty Dumpty, a heavy crash shakes the forest. What do you think happened? **[Speculate]**

APPLY

4. (a) What does Humpty Dumpty mean when he tells Alice, "If you can see whether I'm singing or not, you've sharper eyes than most"? (b) What word might he suggest that Alice use instead of *see*? **[Infer]**

5. The quotation above is an example of word play, or using words in a clever or funny way. Find two other examples of word play in the story, and explain what they mean. **[Connect]**

Lewis Carroll
Comparing and Connecting the Author's Works

◆ Literary Focus: Nonsense Literature

Carroll's work is full of puns, word play, double meanings, and made-up words. **Nonsense literature** is entertaining and often whimsical. It frequently turns logic upside down and can be either delightful or maddening (or both) in its silliness. A writer may use many devices—irony, parody, or ambiguity, for instance—in nonsense literature. Limericks and tongue twisters are examples of nonsense literature.

Main Features of Nonsense Literature

- Lacks logical development
- Often poses its own trivial problems
- Uses made-up and newly coined words
- Poetry has a strong, rhythmic quality

1. Reread the conversation between Alice and Humpty Dumpty. Name at least one trivial problem that they discuss.
2. Find two other details in the conversation between Alice and Humpty Dumpty that classify it as nonsense literature.

◆ Drawing Conclusions About Carroll's Work

One way to better understand a story is to respond to a critical opinion of it. In *Argument of Laughter,* D. H. Munro writes that the way Carroll uses language is to "take some well-worn, trite form of words and explore it for unexpected and impossible meanings."

Below is an example of two ordinary, familiar words that Carroll uses in an unexpected way by combining them to make a new word.

lithe	**+**	**slimy**	**=**	**slithy**

These words are called *portmanteau words* because they stuff two words into one package, like a portmanteau, or a suitcase.

Create a similar equation for at least two other portmanteau words in *Through the Looking-Glass.* Do the same with at least one word that is commonly used today. Then, write one paragraph in which you explain the effect that portmanteau words and other forms of word play have on Carroll's work.

◆ Idea Bank

Writing

1. **Letter** Lewis Carroll often made games of the letters he wrote to his young friends. Instead of left to right and top to bottom, he used different methods, such as writing in a spiral, in a mirror image, or backward. Write a letter in one of these unusual styles. In your letter, tell Carroll why you do or do not enjoy his tales about Alice. **[Art Link]**

2. **Nonsense Poem** In *Through the Looking-Glass,* Alice and Humpty Dumpty discuss the first four lines of the poem "Jabberwocky." With a partner, discuss the stanza from "Jabberwocky" below. Try to decipher the meanings of the nonsense words.

   "'And has thou slain the Jabberwock?
   Come to my arms, my beamish boy!
   O frabjous day! Callooh! Callay!'
   He chortled in his joy.'"

3. **Compare and Contrast** Alice talks to a mouse and to Humpty Dumpty. In both conversations, she has a disagreement with the other character. Write a paragraph that compares and

contrasts Alice's opinion on a certain topic, such as cats, with those of either the mouse or Humpty Dumpty. Make an analysis chart like the one below to help you organize your thoughts.

CATS	
Alice	**Mouse**
Says Dinah is a "dear, quiet thing"	Calls cats "nasty, low, vulgar things"

Speaking and Listening

4. **Dramatic Presentation** Working with a small group, choose a scene from the *Alice* books to present as a play. Assign group members to the following roles: actor, director, or maker of sets, props, or costumes. Present the scene to the class. **[Performing Arts Link; Group Activity]**

5. **Meaningful Names** According to Humpty Dumpty, names must mean something. In a dictionary or a book of names, look up your own name. Write a paragraph that explains what it means, and whether you think it fits your personality. Present your findings to the class.

Researching and Representing

6. **Book Illustrations** Read another chapter of one of the *Alice* books. Choose two of the scenes that are not illustrated by Sir John Tenniel, and make your own illustrations. **[Art Link]**

7. **Children's Book** Make up a story you might tell a young friend to entertain him or her on a long trip. Write it down and illustrate it. If possible, share it with a young friend and take note of his or her reaction. **[Art Link; Media Link]**

◆ Further Reading, Listening, and Viewing

- Lewis Carroll and Martin Gardner: *The Annotated Alice: The Definitive Edition*

(1999). This edition reprints both *Alice* books with notes and explanations, including the previously deleted "Wasp in a Wig" section.

- Anne Clark Amor: *Lewis Carroll, A Biography* (1979).

- Jackie Wullschlager: *Inventing Wonderland* (1995). This volume introduces five children's authors of the Victorian period, including Carroll.

- Lewis Carroll: *Alice in Wonderland* (1995). This audio cassette features Michael Page reading the unabridged edition.

- *It's Storytelling Time: Alice in Wonderland, Nightingale Collection, . . .* (1999). This audio cassette offers a collection of classic tales narrated by Catherine O'Hara, Tom Bosley, and Margot Kidder.

- Lewis Carroll: *Alice in Wonderland* (1985). This VHS recording is directed by Harry Harris.

- *Alice in Wonderland—A Dance Fantasy* (1993). This VHS recording presents a fanciful performance by the Prague Chamber Ballet and the Czech Philharmonic Orchestra.

- *Alice in Wonderland* (1951). This Walt Disney animated film, seventy-five minutes long, features the voices of Kathryn Beaumont, Ed Wynn, Richard Haydn, Sterling Holloway, Jerry Colonna, and others. The film includes such songs as "I'm Late" and "The Unbirthday Song."

On the Web:

http://www.phschool.com/atschool/literature
Go to the student edition *Copper*. Proceed to Unit 9. Then, click Hot Links to find Web sites featuring Lewis Carroll.

Virginia Hamilton In Depth

> "I call myself a wordkeeper, or a keeper of words. I enjoy words and looking at them on all sides. . . . Words are magnificent. . . . They form rhythms of living in meaningful prose. . . . It is the force of my desire, my wish to make myself understood, that powers these words."

—Virginia Hamilton

VIRGINIA HAMILTON has written many award-winning books for young people. Her books often combine elements of history and fantasy. Some of Hamilton's many topics include contemporary novels about young adults, stories about slavery, and collections of African American folktales.

A Story-Telling Tradition Virginia Hamilton was born in 1936 in Yellow Springs, Ohio, where her grandfather settled after escaping from slavery on the Underground Railroad. Though daily life on the Hamilton's farm was difficult, Virginia, who was the youngest child in her family, remembers a happy childhood. She has fond memories of playing with her siblings and of listening with great interest to the stories her relatives told. She describes her family members as "reluctant farmers but great storytellers."

Hamilton left home to attend college and stayed away for more than ten years, but she returned to Yellow Springs in her early thirties and remains there to this day. Comfortable in the land of her ancestors and surrounded by family members, Hamilton explores in her writing the experiences of African Americans of the past and of today.

Finding Success Hamilton never had any doubts about her career goals. "I started writing as a kid," she says. "It was always something I was going to do." After earning scholarships and studying at Antioch College and Ohio State University, Hamilton moved to New York to become part of the art world.

While studying in New York, Virginia met and fell in love with Arnold Adoff, a young poet. They got married in March 1960 and continued to live in New York while they started their family.

In 1967, Hamilton published *Zeely*, her first novel. It was an unusually successful first novel, in part because of its realistic portrayal of African American characters.

Hamilton's second novel, *The House of Dies Drear* (1968), is a mystery set in modern times about a house that was once a stop on the Underground Railroad. In it, Hamilton blends information and stories about slavery into an intriguing, suspenseful tale.

Hamilton continued to write novels that combine genres and explore elements of African American history. She also began to collect and retell the tales she heard as a child. She selected her favorites and published them in collections such as *The People Could Fly: American Black Folktales* (1985) and *In the Beginning: Creation Stories From Around the World*.

A reviewer once asked Hamilton what she was trying to accomplish with each book. Her reply was quick and to the point: "You're not trying to 'accomplish' anything but tell a good story, and my books are full of good stories."

Recognition and Awards Hamilton has received almost every major award in the field of children's literature, including the Hans Christian Anderson Medal, the Laura Ingalls Wilder Medal, and an NAACP Image Award.

She is also a four-time winner of the Coretta Scott King Award, which honors authors and illustrators of African descent. The award commemorates Dr.

Martin Luther King, Jr., and his widow, Coretta Scott King, for their determination in working for peace and world brotherhood. It recognizes writers who do the same though their work.

◆ The Underground Railroad

Virginia Hamilton has written many stories about slavery and about the daring escapes of slaves, such as her grandfather, who used the Underground Railroad as a way out of the South.

The Underground Railroad was a loosely organized system that helped slaves escape to freedom. Though it was neither underground nor a railroad, its activities had to be carried out in secret, and the fugitive slaves often traveled by night to avoid detection. Railway terms were used to refer to parts of the system. For example, the various routes were called lines, stopping places were called stations, and those who helped the slaves along the way were called conductors.

Most active in helping slaves escape were former slaves such as Harriet Tubman, Northern abolitionists (people who opposed slavery), and church leaders, such as Levi Coffin, a Cincinnati Quaker. Professional slave catchers, who were paid to seize fugitive slaves, made the work dangerous.

The exact number of slaves who escaped by using the Underground Railroad is not known, though estimates range from 40,000 to 100,000. Harriet Tubman alone is believed to have led more than 300 slaves to freedom.

◆ Literary Works

Novels
- Zeely (1967)
- The House of Dies Drear (1968)
- The Planet of Junior Brown (1971)
- M. C. Higgins, the Great (1974)

- Arilla Sun Down (1976)
- The Justice Trilogy (1978–1981)
- Sweet Whispers, Brother Rush (1982)
- Willie Bea and the Time the Martians Landed (1983)
- The Magical Adventures of Pretty Pearl (1983)
- A Little Love (1984)
- Junius Over Far (1985)
- The Mystery of Drear House: The Conclusion of the Dies Drear Chronicle (1987)
- Cousins (1990)
- Plain City (1993)
- Second Cousins (1998)
- Bluish (1999)

Biography and Nonfiction
- W.E.B. DuBois (1972)
- Paul Robeson (1974)
- Anthony Burns: The Defeat and Triumph of a Fugitive Slave (1988)
- Many Thousand Gone: African Americans From Slavery to Freedom (1992)

Story Collections
- The People Could Fly: American Black Folktales (1985)
- In the Beginning: Creation Stories From Around the World (1988)
- The Dark Way: Stories From the Spirit World (1990)
- The All Jahdu Story Book (1991)
- Her Stories: African American Folk Tales, Fairy Tales, and True Tales (1995)
- Jaguarundi (1995)
- When Birds Could Talk and Bats Could Sing: The Adventures of Bruh Sparrow, Sis Wren, and Their Friends (1995)
- A Ring of Tricksters: Animal Tales From America, the West Indes, and Africa (1997)

Doc Rabbit, Bruh Fox, and Tar Baby

Heard tell about Doctor Rabbit and Brother Fox. They were buildin a house. And they kept a crock of cream in the bubbly brook down below the house they were buildin. Every once in a while, Doc Rabbit got thirsty. And he hollered aside so Bruh Fox wouldn't know who it was, "Whooo-hooo, whooo-hooo, whooo-hooo," like that. Scared Bruh Fox to death.

"Who is it there?" Bruh Fox say.

"Sounds like somebody callin bad," said Doc Rabbit.

"Well, can you tell what they want?" Bruh Fox say.

"Can't tell nothin and I'm not lookin to see," said Doc.

"Oh, but yer the doctor. Yer the doctor, you'd better go see," says Bruh Fox.

So Doc Rabbit went off down to the bubbly brook where the water ribbled,[1] keepin the cream cold. He drank a long drink of sweet cream. Then he went back to help Bruh Fox with the house.

"Who was it callin?" asks Bruh Fox.

"Just started callin me, was all it was," said Doc Rabbit.

So Doc Rabbit got down to work. But the sun was hot and he came thirsty again. He went about callin out the side of his mouth:

"Whoo-ahhh, whooo-ahhh, whoo-ahhh!"

"Who is callin so scared?" says Bruh Fox, trembly all over.

"Somebody callin me for help, I expect," Doc Rabbit said. "But I am sure not goin this time, me."

"You have to go. You have to, yer the only doctor. Go ahead on, you," Bruh Fox say.

Big Doc Rabbit went down to the brook again. The water was so cool and ribbly and it kept the crock of cream so fresh and cold. Doc Rabbit drank about half of the cream this time. Then he went back up to help Brother Fox with the hard labor of raisin the roof.

Bruh Fox says, "What was the name of the one callin you this time?"

"Name of about half done callin," mumbled Doc Rabbit. "Whew! This work is a hard labor."

The rabbit toiled and sweated until his fur was wringin wet. He took off his fur coat, too. He wrung it dry and put it back on. But that didn't even cool him any. He says over his shoulder, says, "Whooo-wheee, whooo-wheee!" like that.

---

1. **ribbled:** A made-up word that combines the words *rippled* and *bubbled* and means a combination of the two.

The fox says, lookin all around, "Somebody else callin you, Rabbit."

"I sure am not goin this time," Doc Rabbit said. "I'll just stay right here this time."

"You go on," says Bruh Fox. "Go ahead on, folks needin you today."

So Doc Rabbit scurried down to the ribblin brook. It was nice by the water. He sat himself down, took up the crock of cream. He drank it all down. Then he ran off.

Fox feel a suspicion. He went down there, saw the cream was all gone. He filled up the crock with some lemon and sugar water he had. He knew Rabbit was after anything cold and sweet.

"Think I'll catch me a doctor and a hare together," Fox says to himself.

Next, he made a little baby out of the tar there. The baby lookin just like a baby rabbit. He named it Tar Baby and sat it right there on the waterside. Bruh Fox went back up the hill and he worked on his house. He thought he might keep the house to himself. Doc Rabbit was bein bad so and not workin atall.

Doc Rabbit came back for a drink. He spied the new crock full. And he spied Tar Baby just sittin, gazin out on the water.

"What you doin here, baby rabbit?" Rabbit asked Tar Baby.

Tar Baby wouldn't say. Too stuck up.

"You better speak to me," Doc Rabbit said, "or I'll have to hurt you."

But the Tar Baby wasn't gone speak to a stranger.

So Doc Rabbit kicked Tar Baby with his left hind foot. Foot got stuck, it did. "Whoa, turn me loose!" the rabbit cried. "Turn me loose!"

Tar Baby stayed still. Gazin at the water. Lookin out over the ribbly water.

So Doc Rabbit kicked hard with his right hind foot. "Oh, oh, I'm stuck again. You'd better let me loose, baby," Doc Rabbit said. "I got another good foot to hit you with."

Tar Baby said nothin. Gazin at the water. Lookin far on by the waterside.

Doc Rabbit kicked Tar Baby with another foot, and that foot got stuck way deep. "Better turn me loose," Rabbit hollered, gettin scared now. Shakin now. Says, "I got one foot left and here it comes!"

He kicked that tar baby with the one foot left, and that got stuck just like the other three.

"Well, well, well," said Doc Rabbit, shakin his head and lookin at Tar Baby.

Tar Baby gazin on the water. Watchin out for the pretty birds.

"Well, I still got my head," Doc Rabbit said. "I'm mad, now! I'm agone use my head, too."

He used his head on the little tar baby. Butted his head in the tar baby's stomach as hard as he could. Doc Rabbit's head got stuck clear up to his eyes. His big rabbit ears went whole in the tar of Tar Baby.

That was the way Bruh Fox found him. Doc Rabbit was stuck in Tar Baby. Bruh Fox got him loose.

"What must I do with you?" Bruh Fox said. He led Rabbit along to the house they were buildin. "You the one drank up my crock of cream. I didn't get one taste. Have a mind to burn you in a fire, too."

"Oh, I like fires," Doc Rabbit said. "Do go on burn me up, Bruh Fox, for it's my pleasure to have my coat on fire."

"Well, then, I won't burn you," said the fox. "Burnin up is too good for you."

"Huh," grunted Doc Rabbit. He said no more. Bruh Fox had him in his mouth, a-danglin down his back. Then he laid the rabbit under his paws so he could speak.

"Well, think I'll throw you in that thorny briar patch," Bruh Fox said. "How you like that?"

"Oh, mercy, don't do that!" cried Doc Rabbit. "Whatever you do with me, don't dare throw me in those thorny briars!"

"That's what I'll do, then," Bruh Fox said.

And that's what Brother Fox did. He sure did. Took Doc Rabbit by the short hair and threw him—*Whippit! Whappit!*—right in the briar patch.

"Hot lettuce pie! This is where I want to be," Doc Rabbit hollered for happiness. He was square in the middle of the briar patch. "Here is where my mama and papa had me born and raised. Safe at last!"

"Didn't know rabbits have they homes in the briars," Bruh Fox said, scratching his tail.

He knows it now.

There are some three hundred versions of the Tar Baby tale. Variants of the tale appear in many countries. In the Bahamas the elephant creates the tar baby; in Brazil an old woman or man traps a monkey in a sticky wax baby. There is a version from India, and there are African versions among the Ewes and Yorubas, all showing the great antiquity and universality of this tale.

Long ago, in certain localities of Georgia, the tar baby was considered an actual, living, monstrous creature. The monster was composed of tar and haunted isolated places on the plantation. It would insult people to the point at which they would strike out at it and thus become trapped in its sticky substance.

☑ Check Your Comprehension

1. Why does Doc Rabbit keep making trips to the brook?
2. Describe the way Bruh Fox uses Tar Baby to trap Doc Rabbit.
3. (a) In the end, where does Bruh Fox throw Doc Rabbit? (b) How does Doc Rabbit react to this?

◆ Critical Thinking

INTERPRET

1. Why does Doc Rabbit feel he has to lie to Bruh Fox when he wants to get a drink? **[Infer]**
2. Why is Bruh Fox so angry when he learns that Doc Rabbit has been lying? **[Analyze]**

3. Is Bruh Fox's punishment of Doc Rabbit justified? Explain your answer. **[Draw Conclusions]**

EVALUATE

4. Which character do you think is smarter, Doc Rabbit or Bruh Fox? Support your answer with at least two details from the story. **[Make a Judgment]**

APPLY

5. Doc Rabbit gets himself into trouble when he loses his temper with Tar Baby. (a) What lesson do you think this teaches him? (b) How might you apply this lesson to your own life? **[Relate]**

Virginia Hamilton

Carrying the Running-Aways

Never had any idea of carryin the runnin-away slaves over the river. Even though I was right there on the plantation, right by that big river, it never got in my mind to do somethin like that. But one night the woman whose house I had gone courtin to said she knew a pretty girl wanted to cross the river and would I take her. Well, I met the girl and she was awful pretty. And soon the woman was tellin me how to get across, how to go, and when to leave.

Well, I have to think about it. But each day, that girl or the woman would come around, ask me would I row the girl across the river to a place called Ripley. Well, I finally said I would. And one night I went over to the woman's house. My owner trusted me and let me come and go as I pleased, long as I didn't try to read or write anythin. For writin and readin was forbidden to slaves.

Now, I had heard about the other side of the river from the other slaves. But I thought it was just like the side where we lived on the plantation. I thought there were slaves and masters over there, too, and overseers[1] and rawhide whips they used on us. That's why I was so scared. I thought I'd land the girl over there and some overseer didn't know us would beat us for bein out at night. They could do that, you know.

Well, I did it. Oh, it was a long rowin time in the cold, with me worryin. But pretty soon I see a light way up high. Then I remembered the woman told me to watch for a light. Told me to row to the light, which is what I did. And when I got to it, there were two men. They reached down and grabbed the girl. Then one of the men took me by the arm. Said, "You about hungry?" And if he hadn't been holdin me, I would of fell out of that rowboat.

Well, that was my first trip. I was scared for a long time after that. But pretty soon I got over it, as other folks asked me to take them across the river. Two and three at a time, I'd take them. I got used to makin three or four trips every month.

Now it was funny. I never saw my passengers after that first girl. Because I took them on the nights when the moon was not showin, it was cloudy. And I always met them in the open or in a house with no light. So I never saw them, couldn't recognize them, and couldn't describe them. But I would say to them, "What you say?" And they would say the password. Sounded like "Menare." Seemed the word came from the Bible somewhere, but

---

1. **overseers:** The people who supervised the work of the slaves.

I don't know. And they would have to say that word before I took them across.

Well, there in Ripley was a man named Mr. Rankins, the rest was John, I think. He had a "station" there for escaping slaves. Ohio was a free state, I found out, so once they got across, Mr. Rankins would see to them. We went at night so we could continue back for more and to be sure no slave catchers would follow us there.

Mr. Rankins had a big light about thirty feet high up and it burned all night. It meant freedom for slaves if they could get to that bright flame.

I worked hard and almost got caught. I'd been rowin fugitives for almost four years. It was in 1863 and it was a night I carried twelve runnin-aways across the river to Mr. Rankins'. I stepped out of the boat back in Kentucky and they were after me. Don't know how they found out. But the slave catchers, didn't know them, were on my trail. I ran away from the plantation and all who I knew there. I lived in the fields and in the woods. Even in caves. Sometimes I slept up in the tree branches. Or in a hay pile. I couldn't get across the river now, it was watched so closely.

Finally, I did get across. Late one night me and my wife went. I had gone back to the plantation to get her. Mr. Rankins had him a bell by this time, along with the light. We were rowin and rowin. We could see the light and hear that bell, but it seemed we weren't gettin any closer. It took forever, it seemed. That was because we were so scared and it was so dark and we knew we could get caught and never get gone.

Well, we did get there. We pulled up there and went on to freedom. It was only a few months before all the slaves was freed.

We didn't stay on at Ripley. We went on to Detroit because I wasn't taken any chances. I have children and grandchildren now. Well, you know, the bigger ones don't care so much to hear about those times. But the little ones, well, they never get tired of hearin how their grandpa brought emancipation to loads of slaves he could touch and feel in the dark but never ever see.

"Carrying the Running-Aways" is a reality tale of freedom, a true slave narrative. The former slave who first told the tale was an actual person, Arnold Gragston, a slave in Kentucky. His story of rowing runaways across the Ohio River represents thousands of such stories of escape to freedom.

The abolitionist who helped the runaways once they were across the river was John Rankin, a Presbyterian minister and a southerner who lived in Ripley, Ohio. The town is still there, situated on the great river. A rickety wood staircase leads up Liberty Hill from Ohio River bottom lands to the Underground "station" house of the Rankin family. From 1825 to 1865, more than two thousand slaves were sheltered at the house and guided on by the family. Today, the Rankin house is a State Memorial open to the public from April though October.

Another fugitive, Levi Perry, born a slave, crossed the Ohio River into freedom with his mother about 1854. They were rescued by John Rankin and were taken in and taken care of at the house with the light. Years later, every six months or so, Levi Perry would settle his ten children around him and he would begin: "Now listen, children. I want to tell you about slavery and how my mother and I ran away from it. So you'll know and never let it happen to you." This tale was told to me recently by my mother, Etta Belle Perry Hamilton, who is 92 years old and Levi Perry's oldest daughter.

☑ **Check Your Comprehension**

1. Why does the speaker start rowing runaway slaves across the river?
2. Why does the speaker have enough freedom to be able to row across the river?
3. After the first girl, why doesn't the speaker see any of his passengers?
4. Describe the way Mr. Rankin helps slaves escape.
5. Describe the time the speaker almost gets caught.
6. When the speaker and his wife finally escape, where do they go, and why?

◆ **Critical Thinking**

INTERPRET

1. The speaker's owner forbids him to read and write. Why do you think these activities were forbidden to slaves? **[Analyze]**

2. What keeps the speaker from making his own escape during the four years he rows others across the river? **[Infer]**
3. Why do you think the speaker finally decides to escape with his wife? **[Draw Conclusions]**

EVALUATE

4. In your opinion, which of the speaker's qualities make him a good candidate to row slaves across the river ? **[Assess]**
5. Why do you think the speaker and Mr. Rankin help slaves escape even though it is very dangerous? **[Relate]**

APPLY

6. What do you think Hamilton's grandfather means when he says "I want to tell you about slavery…so you'll know and never let it happen to you"? **[Interpret]**

Virginia Hamilton

Anthony Burns

Anthony Burns was born a slave in 1834. He grew up as a favored slave child of his owner, John Suttle of Virginia. When Suttle died, his son Charles took over the maintenance of his father's slaves. Charles sold some slaves away in order to pay debts and began hiring Anthony Burns out.

Anthony was clever and brought in good money for his owner, so Charles Suttle also favored him. He even let Anthony arrange where he would work and what would be paid by the white men who hired him. Anthony often worked away from home and didn't see Suttle for weeks at a time.

As luck would have it, Anthony got a job near the Richmond docks in 1854. And it was here that he planned his escape. With the aid of a sailor friend, he hid aboard a ship bound for Boston, Massachusetts.

The hiding space was damp and dark, no better than a hole. It allowed Anthony to lie on one side, but it was so narrow that he could not turn. It was early spring, and Anthony had never known such cold weather. His feet half froze in his boots, and he became deathly ill from seasickness. The trip, which usually took ten days to two weeks, took almost three weeks.

"At the next port, put me off, please," Anthony begged his friend. "I cannot stand it any longer. Put me off the ship!"

But what about freedom? the sailor asked Anthony.

"It dies, because surely I am dying!" Anthony answered.

His friend assured Anthony that he would not die. He supplied Anthony with fresh water and bread and, once in a while, meat. When they docked in Boston, Anthony walked away limping, muscles aching, but a free man at last.

His freedom was short-lived. Charles Suttle, informed of Anthony's disappearance, had quickly discovered his whereabouts. He slipped into Boston and made arrangements for Anthony's capture.

One evening, as Anthony came home from work, he was set upon by a group of men, who arrested him and led him to the courthouse jail. There, Anthony was met by his owner.

Suttle bowed before Anthony. "How do you do, *Mistah* Burns!" he said with heavy sarcasm.

Later tried under the Fugitive Slave Act of 1850,[1] Anthony

---

1. Fugitive Slave Act of 1850: A law that mandated the return of runaway slaves, regardless of where in the Union they might be at the time of their discovery or capture.

Burns was defended by the leading abolitionist lawyers of the day. His capture in the North and his trial at the moment of the passage of the Kansas-Nebraska Bill[2] were the last straw for anti-slavery people, who poured into Boston by the thousands to give Anthony Burns their support. Overzealous[3] abolitionists even stormed the courthouse, but that failed to free Burns.

Despite the sympathy he aroused, Anthony Burns lost his case. He had recognized Suttle that fateful evening of his capture and had addressed Suttle as his owner. These facts were used against Anthony by the prosecution, which was intent on upholding the Fugitive Slave Act.

Through streets thronged with thousands of citizens crying, "Shame! Shame!" and with hundreds of troops guarding him, Anthony Burns was marched to the docks and returned south by ship.

Again a slave, he was imprisoned and severely punished for a year. Each day, he was taken to the prison courtyard and exhibited like an animal. Indeed, he was called the Boston Lion by Southerners.

Eventually, his friends in Boston, led by the Reverend Leonard Grimes (himself a former slave), discovered Anthony's whereabouts and bought his liberty. Anthony Burns returned to Boston a hero and lectured widely on his treatment as a slave prisoner.

He moved to St. Catharines, Canada, and became the much-beloved minister of a congregation there. Yet the hardships he had suffered shortened his life. He died in July 1862.

Anthony Burns lived twenty-eight years, only nine of them as a free man. The life he lived would have defeated most men. Yet his was an important life. His case spurred the passage of the Massachusetts Personal Liberty Law on May 21, 1855. The law guaranteed that no individual could be arrested and jailed without first going before a judge or a court to decide whether the arrest had been justified.

After Anthony Burns, no fugitive from slavery was ever again taken back into bondage from the state of Massachusetts.

---

2. Kansas-Nebraska Bill: A law that allowed the people in the territories of Kansas and Nebraska to decide for themselves whether or not to allow slavery within their borders. This act repealed the Missouri Compromise of 1820, which prohibited slavery north of latitude 36°30'.
3.Overzealous (o´ vər zel´ əs): Extremely enthusiastic.

Virginia Hamilton

Alexander Ross, Down From Canada

Alexander Ross was a Canadian, a physician and a naturalist who wrote frequently about birds and insects. He knew the effects of slavery from seeing with his own eyes what it had done to fugitives in Canada, but reading *Uncle Tom's Cabin*[1] spurred him to action. He came to the United States and sought out abolitionist Gerrit Smith. Smith in turn introduced him to distinguished radicals[2] of the day. They all agreed that with his scientific knowledge, Ross might very well "invade" the South posing as a "muddled"[3] professor. Under that cover, he could help the cause of freedom of slaves. And that is exactly what Alexander Ross did.

Because he was white and a gentleman, Ross could travel the South freely. He first went to Richmond, Virginia, to watch people and to learn. Before long, he talked to forty slaves at a preacher's house, telling them about routes north. These routes, he told the slaves, would take them along the Underground Railroad to safety. Ross gave the slaves names of people who would help them and directions to their towns. He also asked the slaves to pass the information on to other slaves who might want to run.

Word got around that a Northerner was in the area giving slaves directions for escape. Alexander Ross did even more than that. He provided another fugitive group with money, weapons, food, and a compass.

He quickly left the South for Pennsylvania before he could be captured. It was there that he developed a code for leading fugitives from one station on the Underground to the next.

In Ross's code, the number 29 was the town of Seville, Ohio. Medina, Ohio, was number 27. *Hope* was Cleveland and *sunrise* was Sandusky. *Midnight* was Detroit, Michigan. One can imagine one of Ross's messages: "We *hope* to rise at *sunrise*; then we will rest by *midnight*." The message marked the path of travel and the main towns where slaves would be helped on the Railroad.

Going to Canada, a fugitive might enter the country from *Glory to God*, Ross's code for Windsor, Ontario, or *God be Praised*, Port Stanley.

---

1. Uncle Tom's Cabin: An 1852 novel by Harriet Beecher Stowe that stirred up great opposition to slavery in the North and in Canada. Southerners claimed that the picture it painted of slavery was inaccurate.
2. radicals: People who favor extreme change.
3. muddled: Mixed up; confused.

After a time Alexander Ross returned to the South. Under cover of his scientific field work, he moved from place to place, contacting slaves. No one ever realized that when slaves disappeared from one plantation, "Professor" Ross was likely to be hunting rare insects in a field nearby!

Ross continued his secret work from the last years of the 1850's until the first guns sounded the beginning of the Civil War.

☑ Check Your Comprehension

1. In "Anthony Burns," how does Anthony Burns finally become free from slavery?
2. What law was inspired by the case of Anthony Burns? What does this law guarantee?
3. In "Alexander Ross, Down From Canada," how does Alexander Ross help the slaves?
4. Why is Alexander Ross able to travel the South freely?

◆ Critical Thinking

INTERPRET

1. Why were abolitionists so upset about the case of Anthony Burns? **[Infer]**
2. How might the Massachusetts Personal Liberty Law have helped Anthony Burns? **[Hypothesize]**

3. (a) Describe the code that Ross develops in "Alexander Ross, Down From Canada." (b) Why does he feel that a code is necessary? **[Infer]**

APPLY

4. Alexander Ross is inspired to help free the slaves after he reads Uncle Tom's Cabin. Tell about a time a book or story inspired you to do something. **[Relate]**

COMPARE LITERARY WORKS

5. Both Alexander Ross and the speaker in "Carrying the Running-Aways" help slaves find freedom. In what ways are their experiences similar? In what ways are they different?

Virginia Hamilton

Comparing and Connecting the Author's Works

◆ Literary Focus: Folk Tales

Folk tales, also called **folk literature, folklore,** and **traditional literature**, are stories that communicate the important values or ideas of a culture. Folk tales are composed orally and then passed from person to person by word of mouth. Most folk tales are anonymous: No one knows who first composed them. When modern writers such as Virginia Hamilton retell a folk tale, they try to capture the feeling and spirit of the tale as it has been told for hundreds of years.

In general, the characters in folk tales are simple and have only one major trait, such as honesty, cleverness, or deceitfulness. They are often animals. The characters are usually flat, rather than round. This means that they don't change during the course of the story.

The conflicts in folk tales are often simple and straightforward. For example, in "Doc Rabbit, Bruh Fox, and Tar Baby," Bruh Fox must stop Doc Rabbit from lying and stealing his cream. Once the goal is achieved, the story ends quickly. Good usually triumphs over evil.

Folk tales tend to have a lot of repetition. Words, phrases, and events occur more than once, making the key parts easy to remember. In addition, folk tales often contain elements of fantasy or magic.

1. In "Doc Rabbit, Bruh Fox, and Tar Baby," what are the main character traits of Doc Rabbit and Bruh Fox?
2. Are Doc Rabbit and Bruh Fox flat or round characters? Use details from the story to support your answer.
3. Name three characteristics of "Doc Rabbit, Bruh Fox, and Tar Baby" that make it a folk tale.
4. What value do you think "Doc Rabbit,

Bruh Fox, and Tar Baby" teaches readers? Explain your answer.

◆ Drawing Conclusions About Hamilton's Work

Virginia Hamilton has always been fascinated by the tales told by African Americans during the period of slavery in the United States. These tales include first-hand accounts of slave life, folk tales told among slaves, and tales of escape from slavery.

Choose one of Hamilton's stories about slavery, and explain why you think it was told during the time of slavery. Then, explain why you think it's important to tell today.

Before you begin to write, organize your thoughts in a chart like the one below. Make sure to use details from the story to support your answers.

Importance Then	Importance Now

◆ Idea Bank

Writing

1. **News Article** Imagine that you are a reporter at the trial of Anthony Burns, and write a news article about the trial. Remember that a news article gives facts, not opinions. Use a chart like this one to gather the facts. You may invent details that are not in the story, such as witnesses, spectators, and speeches. **[Media Link]**

Who?	Burns is a twenty-year-old runaway slave captured in Boston shortly after his escape.
What?	
When?	
Where?	
Why?	

2. **Journal Entry** Choose one of the characters who helps slaves escape the South, such as Alexander Ross or Mr. Rankin. In that character's voice, write a journal entry that describes an attempted escape. Make sure that the character explains why he chose to participate in this risky work.

3. **Monologue** Choose one of the animal characters from Hamilton's tales, and write another folk tale about it. For example, you might write about another time Bruh Fox tries to trick someone with Tar Baby. Use Hamilton's stories as models for style.

Speaking and Listening

4. **Performance** With a partner or a small group, perform a scene from one of the stories. Create a script that includes both dialogue and stage directions. Use props that you think will make the performance more exciting. [**Performing Arts Link; Group Activity**]

Researching and Representing

5. **Further Reading** In the library, find another story by Virginia Hamilton.

After reading the story, design a book jacket for it. The front should contain the title and an illustration. The back should contain a plot summary and your critical evaluation of it. Use a paperback book from the library or from your classroom as a model. [**Art Link**]

6. **Historical Research** Form a group and research the history of the Underground Railroad. Make a poster that includes written and visual information about it, and share your findings with your class. [**Social Studies Link; Group Activity**]

◆ Further Reading, Listening, and Viewing

Books
- Houston, Gloria. *Bright Freedom's Song: A Story of the Underground Railroad* (1998).
- Woodruff, Elvira. *Dear Austin: Letters from the Underground Railroad* (1998).

Collections of Folk Tales
- *African Folktales: Traditional Stories of the Black World.* Roger D. Abrahams, editor (1983).
- Arnott, Kathleen. *African Myths and Legends* (1990).
- Lester, Julius. *Black Folktales* (1991).

On the Web:

http://www.phschool.com/atschool/literature
Go to the student edition *Copper*. Proceed to Unit 10. Then, click Hot Links to find Web sites featuring Virginia Hamilton.

Alfred A. Knopf Inc.
"Carrying the Running-Aways," "Doc Rabbit, Bruh Fox, and Tar Baby," and "Papa John's Tall Tale" by Virginia Hamilton from *THE PEOPLE COULD FLY*. Text copyright © 1985 by Virginia Hamilton. "Alexander Ross, Down From Canada," "'All Right, Sir!,'" and "Anthony Burns" by Virginia Hamilton from *MANY THOUSAND GONE*. Copyright © 1993 by Virginia Hamilton.

Wendy Lipkind Agency
"Alberic the Wise" by Norton Juster from *ALBERIC THE WISE*. Copyright © 1965 by Norton Juster.

Random House, Inc.
"It's All in How You Look at Things" by Norton Juster from *THE PHANTOM TOLL-BOOTH*. Text copyright © 1961 by Norton Juster.

Scholastic Inc.
From *THE GLORY FIELD* by Walter Dean Myers. Copyright © 1994 by Walter Dean Myers.

Gary Soto
"Where We Could Go" by Gary Soto from *A FIRE IN MY HANDS: A BOOK OF POEMS*. Copyright © 1990 by Scholastic, Inc. All rights reserved.

Note: Every effort has been made to locate the copyright owner of material reprinted in this book. Omissions brought to our attention will be corrected in subsequent printings.

Photo Credits

• • • •